Alfred Hitchcock

The Legacy of Victorianism

Alfred Hitchcock

The Legacy of Victorianism

Paula Marantz Cohen

THE UNIVERSITY PRESS OF KENTUCKY

Scholarly publisher for the Commonwealth,
serving Bellarmine College, Berea College, Centre
College of Kentucky, Eastern Kentucky University,
The Filson Club, Georgetown College, Kentucky
Historical Society, Kentucky State University,
Morehead State University, Murray State University,
Northern Kentucky University, Transylvania University,
University of Kentucky, University of Louisville,
and Western Kentucky University.

Editorial and Sales Offices: Lexington, Kentucky 40508-4008

Library of Congress Cataloging-in-Publication Data

Cohen, Paula Marantz 1953–
Alfred Hitchcock : the legacy of Victorianism / Paula Marantz Cohen.
p. cm.
Includes bibliographical references and index.
ISBN 0–8131–1930–8 (alk. paper)—ISBN 0-8131-0850-0 (pbk.: alk. paper)
1. Hitchcock, Alfred, 1899–1980—Criticism and interpretation.
I Title.
PN1998.3.H58M27 1995
791.43′0233′092—dc20 95-2325

This book is printed on acid-free recycled paper meeting
the requirements of the American National Standard
for Permanence of Paper for Printed Library Materials.

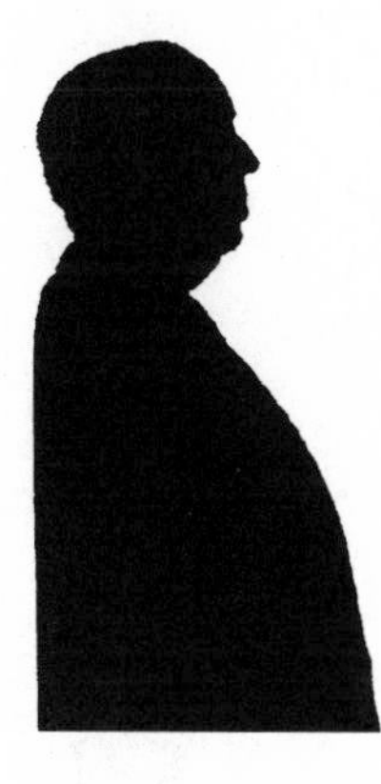

Contents

Acknowledgments

The first and most fundamental influence on this book comes from my parents, Murray and Ruth Marantz Cohen. Their talk, sometimes at cross-purposes, always invigorating, lies at the heart of my method. I would also like to thank my sister, Rosetta Marantz Cohen, whose critical spirit and humor have kept me honest; my husband, Alan S. Penziner, who acted as a trusted reader and beloved movie companion; and my colleague, D.B. Jones, with whom I taught the Hitchcock course that served as the inspiration for this book. I would also like to thank a number of colleagues and friends whose insights on Hitchcock and related matters have helped me generate new ideas and revise old ones: Rosemary and Fred Abbate, David Plaut, Mark Greenberg, Beth Kowaleski-Wallace, Frank Nesko, Gertrude Penziner, and Samuel Scheer. This book was written during a sabbatical leave granted by Drexel University.

Photo stills were provided by the Museum of Modern Art in New York City.

An earlier version of chapter 2 appeared under the title "The Ideological Transformation of Conrad's *The Secret Agent* into Hitchcock's *Sabotage*" in *Literature/Film Quarterly* 22, 3(1994), and is reprinted by permission.

Introduction

Alfred Hitchcock's career spans the greater part of the twentieth century. He made his directorial debut in 1922, his last film in 1975, and he was still trying to shape a new project at his death in 1980. His work is a mirror of cinematic development: from silent to sound, from black and white to color, from the shoestring productions of his early London years to the expensive vehicles of his Hollywood period. In the process, he dabbled in technical innovations such as 3-D and VistaVision, experimented in special effects and editing techniques, and developed an extensive repertoire of original camera setups and shots. He evolved with the times in other respects as well. He treated sex and violence first indirectly, then in stylized representation, and finally with graphic directness. He employed actors who epitomized the taste of each period in which he worked: Robert Donat and Madeleine Carroll during his British period, and Ingrid Bergman, James Stewart, Grace Kelly, and Cary Grant during his most successful Hollywood years. In his last films—*Frenzy* and *Family Plot*—he chose to employ British repertory performers in one case and Hollywood newcomers in the other, reflecting the emerging public taste for the quirky, nonstellar cast.

Yet for all his uncanny ability to reflect evolving fads and trends, Hitchcock was also doggedly unstylish. He presented himself as a bourgeois family man, seemingly indifferent to the glamorous hedonism of Hollywood. His highly mannered, uninflected speech and his bulky, inert figure suggested the Victorian gentleman stranded in a more frivolous age. Indeed, he seemed to relish the image of himself as a physical anachronism, and he capitalized upon the marketability of this image, even to the point of appearing as a corporeal signature in most of his films.

Hitchcock's choice of the formal Victorian persona on the one hand and his drive to satirize and commercialize that persona on the other describe the underlying dynamic of his career. He was the son of small London tradespeople—uneducated, modest in their means, churchgoing, and scrupulously conventional. His parents were Victorians, citizens of a still complacent Britain, in whom attitudes regarding the individual, the family, and the moral life were deeply inculcated. Hitchcock did not repudiate the Victorian world into which he was born. Instead, he carried the values of his childhood into cinema, transformed them in the process, and then proceeded to transform cinema through the continued infusion of these values.

Critical approaches to Hitchcock have occupied two extremes. One, associated with the auteur theory of the 1960s and early 1970s, has tended to ignore context and examine the films as the unique expression of a gifted personality. The other, more recently promulgated by feminist and deconstructionist critics, has "read" Hitchcock's films as social texts—powerful reflectors and enforcers of ideology. My approach bridges these two extremes or, rather, finds them not to be mutually exclusive. Hitchcock's films are certainly ideological artifacts and not without their propagandistic function, yet they also exhibit a distinctiveness and a developmental continuity that demonstrate their passage through a singular, if ever-changing, filter. This filter is the person of the filmmaker.[1]

I conceive of Hitchcock's career as falling into three phases, each of which reflects the convergence of his personal experience with trends in cinematic development and more general trends in culture.

The first phase marks Hitchcock's initiation into the technical and thematic conventions of his craft and spans the more than fifteen years in which he directed films in Britain. While his technical acumen and stylistic originality became apparent very early, these films nonetheless conform to a general tendency within the nascent genre of narrative film to oppose the kind of complex characterizations associated with nineteenth-century novels. These films also encode conventional gender and familial relationships that correspond to the form of Hitchcock's own newly created family during this period.

The second phase of Hitchcock's career extends from 1939, when he came to America to work for David O. Selznick, to the early 1960s, when he had reached the end of his most commercially successful period. The films of this phase are characterized by a drive to reclaim, for cinematic use, the novelistic concept of character that narrative film—and his own British films—had initially sought to suppress. This drive is informed not only by the influences and opportunities offered by Hollywood but also by changes in the structure of his own family—in particular, his more evolved relationship with his daughter, Patricia, who would appear in three films of this period.

The last phase of Hitchcock's career overlaps with the second and can be described as a gradual process of detachment from former influences. This phase begins as a shift in emphasis in his films of the late 1950s and 1960s and reaches its apotheosis in his last three films, made between 1968 and 1975. These last films cease to refer to a novelistic tradition or a family nexus. They no longer support consistent norms or encourage emotional investment but operate, rather, as exercises in design and purveyors of sensation. The films of Hitchcock's old age coincide with the old age of Western culture and express what has come to be referred to as a "postmodern condition."

Let me use this introduction to sketch in some of the issues and assumptions that inform this developmental perspective on Hitchcock.

As I discuss more fully in chapter 1, entertainment film developed as it did in part as a reaction to the influence novels had come to exert in Western culture. By the end of the nineteenth century, novels had become an important means of relaying affective and expressive values associated with women. As a result, they posed a threat to the more codified, literalistic values associated with men. Early feature films, with their simplicity of theme and image, were able to recapture the cultural outposts that had come under the sway of the female sensibility and to reassert a hierarchy in which plot and action took precedence over feeling and relationship.

Growing up at the turn of the century, an overweight boy from a lower middle-class home, Hitchcock can be said to have experienced on a personal level the sense of vulnerability and defensiveness that characterized patriarchical culture more generally during this period. As one former classmate recalls, Hitchcock was the boy always standing alone in the schoolyard, watching the others play ball.[2] Filmmaking would provide this ungainly boy on the sidelines with mastery both of a new technical apparatus and of a new means of representation capable of ordering and defining the world to his specifications: of recreating and thereby controlling the schoolyard from which he had been excluded. Yet once Hitchcock had mastered the technical rudiments of the new medium, he also began to incorporate the more introspective values that were the hallmark of the outsider's role. One might say that he spent his career juggling the two faces of Victorianism: the feminine legacy of feeling and imagination associated with the domestic novel and the masculine legacy of law and hierarchy—the world of the schoolyard—associated with dominant institutions and values.

Hitchcock's paradoxical relationship to his Victorian heritage is at least partially explained when we examine his concept of "the cinematic." Film, he would maintain throughout his career, was primarily a visual and dynamic medium: "When we tell a story in cinema, we should resort to dialogue only when it's impossible to do otherwise. I always try first to tell a story in the cinematic way, through a succession of shots and bits of film in between."[3] Yet, as I discuss in chapter 2, Hitchcock's concept of the cinematic had literary underpinnings. His films almost invariably had their source in a work of prose fiction that was discarded once the idea had taken root: "What I do is read a story only once, and if I like the basic idea I forget all about the book and start to create cinema."[4] His method encourages a comparison to that of the late nineteenth-century novelist Henry James. James often described how he got ideas for his stories from newspaper articles and personal anecdotes but quickly removed them from their factual context.[5] Thus, whereas Hitchcock's cinematic narrative derived from novelistic narrative, James's novelistic narrative derived from factual anecdote. In a film like *The Wrong Man,* where Hitchcock took a Jamesian approach and based the screenplay on a news account of a true story, the result is hard to watch. It suffers in skipping the intermediary step—the detour through prose fiction.

What literature, and novels in particular, appear to have offered Hitchcock was a unique conception of *character*. Nineteenth-century novels pioneered the representation of human psychology; they employed descriptive language to depict an internal life of imagination and emotion for their characters. Since the cinematic, according to Hitchcock's definition, works to reduce a dependence on language, it becomes possible to understand his experiments in technique as efforts to find nonlinguistic expression for the kind of psychological character central to late nineteenth-century novels. The confined shooting space in *Lifeboat,* the special effects in *Spellbound,* the long takes in *Rope,* and the carefully designed set in *Rear Window* can all be understood as attempts to render psychological character cinematically. As I discuss in chapter 3, *Spellbound* defines the parameters of the problem in a highly schematic way. The film relies on surrealist visuals (non-narratized images of the psyche: dreams and symptoms) on the one hand and wordy explanation of these images on the other. It maps out the challenge—of how to narratize the psyche in a visual medium—that Hitchcock would struggle to meet for the greater part of his career.

Ultimately, of course, this effort to represent psychological character cinematically would alter the very conception of character being represented. This becomes apparent when we consider the effects Hitchcock derived from his actors. "I suppose the best casting man is the novelist," he once asserted; "he describes his character minutely and it's always what he intended."[6] Lacking the linguistic tools that made it possible for the novelist to describe the inner workings of character, Hitchcock had to rely on the signifying potential of his performers. Yet he did not call for his actors to emote ("In real life," he explained, "people's faces don't reveal what they think or feel"[7]). Rather, he manipulated the physical variables associated with performance: he became intimately involved in the casting, the choice of clothing and accessories, the choreography of movement, and the use of lighting, close-ups, camera angles, and so forth. Siegfried Kracauer's observation that in cinema the actors' "appearance is in a measure symptomatic of their nature" finds reinforcement in Hitchcock's celebrated statement that "actors should be treated like cattle."[8] For if the goal is to produce character as a novelist does, then the choice to use actors as one would sets, props, or, indeed, cattle—to favor "negative acting" (and, specifically, to oppose the emotional exercises of the Method School)—allows the filmmaker more control over meaning than were he to rely on his actors' facial expressions. The paradox of this approach is that in finding cinematic substitutions for literary expression, Hitchcock could not help but radically alter the way character came to be understood. Thus, in his 1936 British film *Sabotage*, he insisted that the heroine's face remain blank as she holds the knife before stabbing her husband. The rationale appears to derive from Eisenstein's experiments with montage: a blank expression can be "filled in" by the spectator given the appropriate context (in this case, we have already been informed of the heroine's extraordinary grief and turmoil at the death of her brother). But the blank face also has an important structural importance in the film. It works to promote an indeterminacy that will support the plot. By denying us access to what she feels, the heroine's blank face makes it possible for us to acquit her of responsibility for the act of murder (see chap. 2 for further discussion of this scene). Later films would exploit the indeterminate image more extensively, using the character's blank face less to suggest hidden depths of emotion or to resolve a plot impasse than to offer multiple possibilities for meaning. In *Rear Window,* the protagonist's face registers predictable frustration and horror when he sees his girlfriend in danger across the courtyard, but it is his sleeping face set beside that same girlfriend that is used to designate the union of the two characters at the end of the movie—a union whose undefined quality is precisely the point. The heroine's blank stare at the end of *The Birds* is another such expression of open-endedness; it throws the resolution of the film back upon the spectator. In *Family Plot,* Hitchcock's last film, the heroine's exaggerated wink directly at the camera in the final shot is a variation on blankness in that it denotes pure ambiguity. Is she a psychic or a sham? The question is left open, not to arouse the audience to probe the heroine's deeper motives, but to tantalize and tease. Reality here is like the throw of a coin: one guess is as good as another.

The characters in Hitchcock's last films are, in the terms outlined above, supremely cinematic. Although built on a conception of the self that was developed in novels and psychoanalytic case histories, in which talk and behavior pointed to some larger, explanatory narrative, these later characters exist only as shifting pieces in a kaleidoscopic design. While this insistence upon the surface as a limit to the meaning of character in Hitchcock's last films has, in one sense, worked an apparent reversal on the idea of character put forward in novels, it resembles the other medium insofar as it renders a concept of identity that is consistent with the conventions that define it. The idea of an internal life is what literary prose is able to deliver; it can depict a place hidden within the self that connects to a world of action and things. Deep selves grow out of the conventions of textuality: the unconscious is structured like a language when we are dealing with a world of texts. Hitchcock's films begin by accepting a textual notion of character, then gradually discard the textual supports, real or implied, on which that notion was built. If filmic conventions concentrate on rendering surfaces, then the cinematic drive becomes an effort to represent and, in so doing, to construct a new concept of identity that corresponds only to surfaces.

It is not sufficient, however, to understand Hitchcock's development of the cinematic in purely formal terms. Although he was influenced by the conventions of the medium to the extent that these were already shaped by past usage and the constraints of ideology, he was also operating very near to the origin of narrative cinema and hence he was in a position to define many of its formative conventions himself. His own position in ideology as it dovetailed with and fed into the development of narrative cinema must therefore be examined. Here, I turn to Hitchcock's family life as a central shaping force behind his work.

What we know of his family of origin springs from a handful of anecdotes, the most celebrated being the story of a childhood punishment. Having committed some misdemeanor (the nature of which he claims to have forgotten), he was sent by his father to the local police station with a note that instructed the officer on duty to lock him up.[9] Whether true or apocryphal, the anecdote describes a strict patriarchal family and, perhaps more telling, a legal system willing and able to act as surrogate and tool of the family patriarch. The experience is one likely to engender in its subject both a fear of authority and a curiosity about its mechanisms—a combination that finds expression in Hitchcock's thrillers, where conformity to convention exists alongside a drive to uncover and understand.

Hitchcock's family of origin laid the foundation for his identity. Yet, in the context of his career, of more interest than that childhood family was the family he "made": his wife, Alma (née Reville), and his daughter, Patricia. This family was an evolving system, keeping pace, as it were, with his development as a filmmaker. I should note at once that the power of Hitchcock's family to inform his films seems related to its paradigmatic nature—the extent to which it conformed to the stereotypical nuclear family that achieved its apotheosis in England under Queen Victoria. To concentrate on the representative aspect of Hitchcock's family experience makes it possible to assimilate biographical facts to the collective nature of cinematic production. It also helps account for the sustained popular appeal of his films.

We can understand the paradigmatic nature of Hitchcock's family experience by reviewing the evolution of the nuclear family as a cultural institution. According to most historians of the family, a traditional, "open-lineage" family structure began to give way by the end of the seventeenth century to a more compact, "nuclear" model. What helped precipitate this shift was a democratizing impulse that favored the companionate marriage (the marriage for love) over the marriage of convenience (the arranged marriage).[10] Instead of finding its anchorage in blood ties, property, or title, the new couple found its anchorage in a complementarity of sexual roles: the female partner was expected to be docile, loving, and understanding; the male to be strong, ambitious, and discerning. Romantic love thus offered a means of bringing people together based on values that were, if more associated with the individual than in the past, nonetheless gender specific and highly conventionalized. And it was the very conventionality of these gender-specific ideals that posed a problem for the long-term stability of the couple. For how was the marriage to survive once the romantic illusion of complementarity had dissipated? As I have argued at length in a previous book, the reproductive capacity of the couple would make possible a structural solution to this problem.[11] The child's role, and the female child's in particular, was to provide the father (by convention, the founder and head of the family) with those qualities that his wife had only appeared to possess—to provide, in short, a real structure of complementarity upon which the family could depend for its stability. The father-daughter dyad thus became the means of stabilizing the nuclear family as an institution while also humanizing the father and empowering the daughter in a mutually evolving interaction.

We arrive finally at the long-term effects of this model as they support my earlier remarks about the feminization of culture toward the end of the nineteenth century. The daughter's complementary position with respect to her father was to make her potentially more powerful than her male peers of brother and husband—a threat, in short, to patriarchy in the next generation. No wonder, then, that late nineteenth-century society perceived itself as feminized. The effects of this feminization get translated into novels through an increasing focus on introspection and imagination—what, in chapter 1, I will argue both reflects and intensifies a female subjectivity with which the culture was obliged to reckon. And it is a short step from the cultivation of a female point of view to the articulation of a political feminism. Unsurprisingly, by the end of the nineteenth century, some novelists had begun to espouse radical changes in gender roles and to be linked to a growing feminist movement.

Narrative film evolved in part as a reaction to these trends. Film reinstituted simple plot lines and enforced social norms by abolishing the internal life of character that novels had pioneered. Thus courtship was returned to the realm of plot complication and the heroine's family became flattened to serve as backdrop. But the more complicated, mutually revising effects of the father-daughter dynamic could not help but find their way back into movies when the technical and conceptual framework was sophisticated enough to allow it. This was the case with Hitchcock, whose relationship to his own daughter supported this revisionary impulse. His career recapitulates the process that had produced the very feminization that film had emerged to suppress. As I discuss in chapter 4, a majority of Hitchcock's films produced between 1940 and 1950 contain a father-daughter relationship, and two of the films feature his own daughter in a supporting role. In his 1950s films, the father-daughter theme ceases to be explicit, but the "daughter's effect"—a tendency to represent women as pressures on the plot, symbols of a subjectivity that both entices and threatens men—remains.

Finally, in Hitchcock's last films, this "daughter's effect" disappears, and character itself takes on a new meaning. I have already discussed the last films as consistent with a cinematic drive to validate surfaces over depths. This shift in perspective can also be understood in terms of an unraveling family ideology. The severing of the father-daughter bond is reflected in a reduction of emotional investment in character and in a setting loose of effects formerly contained within the closed system of gender complementarity modeled by the nuclear family. The last films feature open spaces traversed by cars and planes with no sense that there will be a final dwelling place, site of closure, or romantic union. The characters in these films are not repressed psychopaths but freewheeling sociopaths: good businessmen who also happen to swindle, rape, and kill as part of their extensive array of communication techniques. The unevenness of the late films has been explained as a symptom of Hitchcock's failing health and spirits, but this ignores the logic of these films' more diffuse structures, the way in which they build on tendencies discernible in the earlier films (which is not to say that old age and emotional exhaustion don't contribute to that logic). The shift from presenting complementary values (where one value is balanced against and at the expense of another) to emphasizing passages between values accounts for why these last films seem disappointing. After all, Hitchcock promoted himself as a master of suspense, and suspense requires the gradual coming to the surface of what has been unknown or hidden—in psychosocial terms, of what has been "repressed." This is a *quid pro quo;* something lost for something gained: knowledge paid for by disillusionment, security paid for by the drabness of routine. Sexual role complementarity is itself the expression of such a *quid pro quo*—one gains qualities in one's partner by banishing them in oneself. The impossibility of sustaining such an exchange for Hitchcock, and arguably for culture at large, spells the demise of a genre capable of linking suspense to character and relationship. One could argue that in his last films Hitchcock transcended the conventions he was capable of manipulating, overshooting his own ideological horizon. He developed entertainment film to the point where it would leave him behind, charting a course that creative mass-market filmmakers such as Robert Altman and Martin Scorsese, less conditioned within a tradition of gender complementarity, would be able to pursue more effectively.

In this respect, another comparison can be drawn between Hitchcock and Henry James, the great practitioner of the novel at the very point at which it was superseded by the new medium of film (and an interesting counterpoint to Hitchcock in being an expatriate in the opposite direction). James developed from a fairly standard action-oriented storyteller, to a psychological novelist, to a novelist for whom the literariness of his medium came to take on a life of its own. In the late work of Henry James, every phrase, every word even, became "overdetermined"—packed with an unfixable, always permutating meaning, subverting all pretense to linear plot or realistic character. James's late work has its enthusiasts, but the general consensus is that this work struggles to burst the constraints of its ideological moment and perhaps of the genre as well, although it is unable to surmount those limits fully. Indeed, the last work is about exhaustion as much as it is about innovation. The same charge can be leveled against late Hitchcock.

Entering upon his career as a filmmaker coincident with the birth of narrative film, Hitchcock developed with his medium and helped to revise it. His films trace a journey from relatively primitive vehicles for plot and spectacle to an intricate weave of these elements. Just as Henry James can be said to have anticipated the new medium of film even as his work appears to represent the antithesis of the values associated with that medium, so Hitchcock, despite his reputation as a master of classical narrative film, can be said to have anticipated the very unclassical trends in representaton with which our culture is presently engaged.

1 The Rise of Narrative Film

In 1975 Laura Mulvey's "Visual Pleasure and Narrative Cinema" helped launch a new direction for film studies.[1] Mulvey argued that all classical narrative films (generally speaking, feature films of the Hollywood era) are tailored to the male point of view (in cinematic terms, the male "gaze"). Women, she maintained, are represented in these films either as passive appendages of men or as ideally desirable bodies (larger-than-life cultural icons, i.e., "stars"). In this dual function, they serve both as an image of the castration which the male viewer fears for himself and as a fetish to allay this same castration anxiety. Mulvey then went on to consider the difficulty facing the female spectator at the movies, who has no choice but either to assume the male point of view, thereby denying her point of view as a woman, or to submit to a masochistic identification with the female victim/object. In elaborating her argument, Mulvey cited two Hitchcock films from the 1950s—*Rear Window* and *Vertigo*—as prime examples of the sexist dynamic inherent in the genre.

Mulvey's essay was part of a general trend among film theorists writing for scholarly journals such as *Screen* and *Camera Obscura* during the 1970s to see entertainment cinema (with Hitchcock's films as its archetypal representative) as the product and purveyor of an oppressive patriarchal culture. However, this argument has undergone moderate revision over the past decade. Feminist film theorists such as Robin Wood and Tania Modleski have since maintained that there are important calls to female identification in Hitchcock's films, basing their arguments on Freud's postulate about human bisexuality. Other recent critics have argued that classical narrative cinema may not be the monolithic instrument of patriarchal oppression that has been suggested.[2]

Yet even these emendations seem to suffer from some of the normative smugness that characterized Mulvey's original piece. "Saving Hitchcock for feminism"[3] or measuring his resistance to a dominant ideology assumes that the critic stands in the enlightened position and that dominant ideology is without redeeming character or the capacity for self-revision. Even a theorist such as Teresa de Lauretis, who acknowledges her implication in the system she describes, cannot also grant that her ability to so thoroughly critique the system may be a point in its favor.[4] No recent theorist seems prepared to take a more forgiving view of history, seeing it less as benighted than as recursive—the source and inspiration for the present.

This historical long view is what I would like to offer here. For me, Hitchcock is a well-paved bridge between the past and the present. Then, subjectivity was constructed in the form of a gender hierarchy: male subjectivity counted more and to a large extent obliterated female subjectivity. Now, such a hierarchy is breaking down and subjectivity is being reconstructed along new lines in which gender may not be the central organizing principle. Yet we could not have arrived here without first having been there, a fact that Hitchcock's films, viewed as a historical continuum, powerfully demonstrate.

Such a historical perspective, however, requires its own frame of reference, which is why, in this chapter, I examine the representation of subjectivity in the novel—the narrative form that served as popular (albeit not mass) entertainment before the advent of film. The novel was a literary genre that helped shape the female point of view and made possible its infiltration into certain realms of experience in Western culture. An examination of how a female subjectivity was cultivated in the novel can help clarify the notion of subjectivity itself and its relationship to representation. It can then offer a richer base from which to explore the male gaze associated with classical narrative film and the kinds of changes that Hitchcock worked within the genre.

It is hard for us today to imagine the significant entertainment role performed by novels in the nineteenth century. Novel-reading had begun to be popular with the middle class in the eighteenth century with the rise of literacy and with the greater availability of books due to technical advances in printing and publishing. Novels, though not inexpensive, became increasingly affordable and were readily available from the circulating libraries by the mid-1700s. In the nineteenth century, with increased literacy and the popularity of magazine serialization, novels had acquired a wide, if not a mass, readership among the middle class. This readership, significantly, consisted primarily of women.[5]

Women read novels in such great numbers because, unlike men, they had the leisure to do so. Even the gentleman landowner with ties to a once-leisured aristocracy was, by the turn of the eighteenth century, less able to indulge literary tastes. He was burdened with substantial administrative and financial responsibilities, experimenting with "improvements" to bolster the often meager income that his land now afforded him. Jane Austen and Fanny Burney both show their wealthy protagonists as busy men, perennially traveling to town on business. The wives of these men, by contrast, possessed what Thorstein Veblen termed the "vicarious leisure" of their hard-working husbands. Even women of the lower orders who were consigned to serve wealthy families (depending upon the type of occupation allotted to them) often had time to read (assuming, of course, that they were literate). Hence, Samuel Richardson's heroine Pamela, a waiting-maid in the home of Mr. B., is represented as both a novel reader and a prolific "scribbler" in her own right (her letters to her parents consistitute the greater part of the novel). As Ian Watt explains of Pamela: "She stormed the barriers of society and of literature alike by her skillful employment of what may be called conspicuous literacy, itself an eloquent tribute to the extent of her leisure."[6] One might well argue that the length of novels (which often filled three volumes—hence the term *triple decker*) was directly related to the need to fill the leisure time that the culture had bequeathed to middle-class women.

If novels gave these women something to do, they also reminded them that their destiny was to do nothing. They reinforced the doctrine of "separate spheres" as it had evolved in the wake of industrialization. This doctrine connected men with action and women with feeling—feeling apparently rendered more acute, if not actually engendered, by the absence or neglect of men. As Ann Elliot explains in Jane Austen's last novel, *Persuasion*: "We [women] live at home, quiet, confined and our feelings prey upon us; you [men] are pushed on to exertion."[7] George Eliot draws a similar distinction in *The Mill on the Floss*. She connects women's emotional nature to their position as anxious onlookers to a world of action that tends to dull feeling in its participants: "So it has been since the days of Hecuba and Hector, tamer of horses: inside the gates, the women with streaming hair and uplifted hands offering prayers watching the world's combat from afar, filling their long, empty days with memories and fears; outside, the men, in fierce struggle with things divine and human, quenching memory in the stronger light of purpose, losing the sense of dread or even of wounds in the hurrying ardour of action."[8] Novels like those of Austen and Eliot delineated a female sphere of vulnerability and longing and, at the same time (by engrossing their readers' attention and expressing sympathy for their plight), served as distraction and palliation.

Although novels were a means of conventionalizing the female role and of reconciling women to that role, the genre was not static and its function was not single or predictable. For one thing, the solidification of a female reading public entailed the development of a system of exchange between that public and the novels' authors. Women who were possessed of the time and education needed to indulge literary tastes wished to read about what they deemed important: the life of home and community, and the feelings this life engendered. Writers, eager to be successful, wished to give readers what they wanted. Unsurprisingly, there was a surge of female authorship, beginning in the eighteenth century, as women found it possible to make a living by capitalizing upon subject matter they knew well. Here was a vocation in which they could turn the physical restriction of their lives to profit. By the same token, the existence of a female market encouraged male novelists to dig deeper into what might otherwise have seemed trivial or pedestrian and to cultivate the dramatic potential of the domestic sphere. Samuel Richardson carried on a copious correspondence with his female readers, adding footnotes to later editions of his novels in response to their queries. Charles Dickens amended endings and developed or dropped characters according to the way his readers responded to the serialized installments of his novels.

Even though novelists were in commercial thrall to a mostly female reading public, they nonetheless enjoyed certain unique creative opportunities in ministering to this public. They were in a position to explore new styles of writing and new themes within the domestic context. And they could delve into the minds of their characters, probing the mechanisms of instinct and emotion and taking tendencies associated with the female role to their logical extreme.

In his social history of the English novel, Ian Watt argues that the genre was built out of a concern for domestic detail that appealed especially to women and that resulted in "a more complete separation of the male and female roles than had previously existed."[9] However, he does not address the underlying questions: how much did a preexisting female "nature" influence the subject matter of novels, and how much did the novels themselves shape the development of such a nature? Both Gustave Flaubert and Henry James clearly identified with their female protagonists; their own "feminized" positions (in sedentary life-styles, unconstrained by a professional routine, and unconnected with a conventional masculine role within a family) no doubt made them more attuned to the female point of view than many men would have been. Yet they also possessed the privileges of their sex, and they exhibited confidence, even bravura, in approaching their craft. As men, they could establish a norm for female thinking and feeling that was perhaps more of their own invention than of their readers' experience. In analyzing

Flaubert's famous words, "Emma Bovary, c'est moi!" it is hard to say whether the author was declaring the existence of the woman in himself or simply claiming her as his complete creation. In similar fashion, Henry James would justify his use of a female "central intelligence" in *Portrait of a Lady* by arguing "how absolutely, how inordinately, the Isabel Archers, and even much smaller female fry, insist on mattering," only to confide, in the next breath, how his own "due ingenuity" has made Isabel matter so much.[10] That women also wrote novels in great numbers (and many were enormously gifted at it) would seem to suggest that novelists were drawn to the female point of view because it was more attuned to the life of imagination and emotion. Yet female novelists, even the greatest among them, tended to work within existing conventions of plot and character. The innovators in the genre tended to be men. Thus we can trace the origins of the domestic novel to Samuel Richardson, a successful printer, who began writing at the age of fifty, well apprised of the interests and tastes of a female market. He was a businessman-moralist, eager to speak to this market in a voice it could understand, but who also self-consciously sought to "cultivate," as he put it, certain kinds of feelings in his readers. By the same token, it was a group of male novelists toward the end of the nineteenth century that began to question the conventional marriage plot that had been the established formula for domestic novels for over a century, and to move the genre in a new direction. Elaine Showalter, in her account of the female novelistic tradition, has explained the dearth of female innovators in terms of the rise of a domestically oriented ideological program over the course of the nineteenth century. This program, she says, "diverted attention from female experience to a cultist celebration of womanhood and motherhood."[11] But what she views as an unfortunate case of an ideology of domesticity quelling female literary innovation becomes, according to another logic, a case of such an ideology as the product of the literary tradition itself. In other words, the fact that novelists had for over a century focused obsessively on the domestic sphere helped to breed in female readers and writers an increasingly self-aware, even "cultist," celebration of the female condition.

To what extent, then, did novels help to shape the female point of view they professed to describe? It seems logical to conclude that they both described and shaped. On the one hand, novels were powerful tools for maintaining the status quo; on the other hand, the complexity of their form—their ability to encompass varied and sometimes contradictory subject matter—was such as to work unpredictable changes on established ideas.

And indeed, even from the beginning of the genre, novels were problematic forms of propaganda. Richardson's Clarissa was praised as a paragon by some; to others, she was an appalling example of female self-assertion. By the nineteenth century, there appeared to be a recognition that novels could have an unsettling effect on female readers, leading them down forbidden paths.[12] Thus, even as novels proliferated, forms of censorship and surveillance—anti-novel propaganda—also grew apace. A genre designed for and marketed to women, novels were often seen as dangerous to young girls. Henry James depicts this paradox in a satirical scene in *The Awkward Age,* where the appearance of a French novel on a table produces the scandalous suspicion that the heroine, an unmarried girl, has read it. Emma Bovary is a dramatic case of a woman whose imaginative life was shaped by what she read: the results prove disasterous for her married life. Female novelists in particular were often seen as frivolous and corrupting if they were not professional examples of piety such as Hannah Moore and Maria Edgeworth. George Eliot, herself immune in being considered one of the most serious novelists of her day, would refer scornfully to the damage done by "silly novels by lady novelists," and George Henry Lewes, despite his devotion to Eliot's career, would complain that novel-writing was being taken over by "women, children and ill-trained troops."[13] Even Jane Austen early in the century would include warnings in several of her novels against an overindulgence in the gothic, a genre associated almost exclusively with women.

What precisely was the danger that novels were seen to pose to an unsophisticated female readership? Ostensibly, the threat was sexual knowledge (terms such as "sensual," "animal," "gross," or—the most favored term—"coarse" abounded in contemporary reviews). But, in fact, very few novels tackled the subject of sex directly, tending to be as circumlocutionary in this area as was the society of the period. The danger that novels posed lay not in what they said but in what they encouraged their readers to feel. While novel-reading filled the gap of inactivity that was left to middle-class women, it also fed imaginative and emotional yearnings: it excited and incited, and it did so in a style that was realistic and familiar. In its most developed form, it could, as one critic has aptly put it, "include any element of [a human being's] life experience, even the most unforeseen."[14]

Market demand for long novels and payment to novelists by the page were arguably the crux of the problem. Although the basic plot line might be formulaic, complicated and potentially subversive things could happen in the process of getting from beginning to end if the space between were protacted enough and the individual wielding the pen had a gift for character development or extended reasoning. In short, the combination of lengthy narrative with female characters confined to a domestic space was logically prone to produce complex and unpredictable "subjectivities"—characters likely to exceed the exigencies of plot or the constraints of appearance. No novelist reflected the complicating potential of literary narrative more strikingly than

Dickens, whose late novels, if only by their sheer heft, signal an obsessive drive on the part of their author to write against the grain of his conventional plots. *Dombey and Son* is a good example. The book presents us with the case of Edith Dombey, the protagonist's wife, who commits adultery (or appears to) and suffers social ostracism as a result—a proper Victorian conclusion. But Dickens spends so much time filling in the details of Edith's upbringing and the influences that surround her in her daily life that he ends by producing a figure with whom we sympathize despite her calculated breach of society's moral code. We are thus made uneasy with the conventional ending, especially as her husband, far more the sinner than she, is less severely punished.

Even the virtuous woman in the domestic novel, though she might never deviate from a prescribed social role, often asserts a personality at odds with that role. Charlotte Brontë's *Jane Eyre,* to take a well-known example, seems superficially to follow a conventional formula: a poor girl achieves a successful marriage by dint of her patient, scrupulously moral, and self-effacing behavior. But a closer look shows how fully Brontë has permeated the conventional plot with a feminist critique. Jane is an orphan, but she fails to prosper at the Reeds, her adoptive home, less because of their native cruelty than because she is not pretty and doesn't fit the model of the charming little girl. Later she must work as a governess, despite her energy and intelligence, because no other avenue is open to her. Ultimately, the best she can do is marry her employer and gain an extra modicum of freedom by the fact that he is crippled and blind. No wonder that many readers were scandalized by the book when it first appeared, and that even a female novelist of stature such as Mrs. Oliphant saw it as threatening the established hierarchy of the sexes.[15] Jane Eyre voices her feelings only to herself and never mounts a soapbox, but her internal dialogue, more than any soapbox speech, gives women implicit permission to be discontented, to question, and to imagine alternatives.

Toward the end of the century, there emerged a cluster of novelists whose perspective on their culture was openly critical. George Gissing, George Meredith, Thomas Hardy, and Henry James addressed the sexual double standard, the stifling circumscription of domestic life, the frustration of being yoked within a loveless marriage, and the financial distress and social neglect suffered by unmarried women. They made their points not by declaiming against sexual exploitation but by showing the feelings that such exploitation engendered in highly individualized female characters. Clara Middleton in Meredith's *Egoist,* Isabel Archer in James's *Portrait of a Lady,* and Sue Brideshead in Hardy's *Jude the Obscure* are very different in social background and personality, and yet all make us feel the oppressiveness of a society that equates a woman's destiny with marriage. By critiquing women's position in society from the point of view of their female characters, these novelists influenced how women saw themselves and their roles.

The literary historian Ann Douglas has depicted the feminization of culture, fueled by domestic novels in the late nineteenth century, as a trivializing, intellectually enfeebling impulse.[16] But a female orientation is bound to seem trivial within a society in which it has not yet achieved an established, institutionalized form and where it is still hampered in its own self-conception by the limitations attached to the female role. Feminist historians and literary critics have attempted to reframe how we look at things like popular literature, social etiquette, religious observance, and so forth, to see the feminization of this period as progressive. My aim, however, is different. I am less interested in the excavation and revaluation of what has been denigrated for its feminine associations than in understanding why this denigration occurred and in tracing the short-term and long-term implications of this selective process.

In the realm of elite culture, the denigration of the female point of view assisted in the development of a "serious" literary tradition and a scholarly apparatus to support it. By designating female subjects and styles as inferior, scholars found a convenient, "natural" starting point by which to assess literary merit.[17] In the realm of popular culture, an emerging entertainment cinema performed the same function. It became the means of promoting male values and putting women in their place.

If novels reflected and helped to shape a tendency to imagine and feel, films address a tendency to see and act. The distinction is one upon which the separate spheres ideology of the nineteenth century was based. This is less important in demonstrating certain intrinsic qualities of either medium than in clarifying the ideological function of each. Domestic novels developed as a kind of sop to the woman at home (much the way television soap operas—the subgenre that most replicates the original ideological function of novels—operate today). However, they had come, through an unforeseen but retrospectively logical evolution, to foster disruptive and subversive tendencies in that arena. Narrative film seems to have developed to oppose and redirect these tendencies in women while also offering men a means of bolstering an identity that had been eroded by the pressures of both a workaday life and a feminized cultural climate that had evolved in their absence.[18]

It is within the context of such factors, then, that film's gender-recouping function can now be analyzed. In dispensing with the requirement that its audience be literate, film effectively neutralized female literacy. (Indeed, up until the advent of sound in 1927, a point of artistic pride among filmmakers was to dispense as far as possible with intertitles.[19]) Women's novel-reading must have seemed threatening to men not only because it consumed large quantities of time that might otherwise have been spent on domestic duties but also because it quietly raised their literacy level above that of men, their supposed mental superiors. The brevity of films, designed to be seen in one sitting, also contrasted with the length of novels, which took weeks or, when serialized, months to read. Thus film substituted a male time frame and attention span (given the mental habits fostered by a hectic work routine) for the more leisurely pace associated with a middle-class female life-style. Film also permitted a more extensive exclusion of women from the arena of production, since an elaborate financial and bureaucratic structure made it easy to discriminate against them. (Pencil, paper, and, occasionally, a male pseudonym were all that had been needed for a woman to launch a literary career.) Thematically, films also opposed the subjective values that novels had cultivated: they offered simple plot lines that gained interest through the representation of dramatic spectacle or action. This was especially true in the early years of the medium. Primitive silent films were designed around protonarrative elements: slapstick or chase. Character was represented in caricatured form through so-called libretto acting: facial grimaces, uplifted eyes, and flailing arms.[20]

Finally, narrative film defined and elevated male subjectivity over female subjectivity on a more basic psychological level, as film theorists have pointed out. This was through the mechanism by which the camera eye, the locus of control (being the position from which the film's representation of reality springs) was made to correspond with the male spectator's gaze. The female position, by extension, was made the object of that gaze—when it did not serve as a spectacle for male desire, it constituted a symbolic obstacle to that desire.

The rise of entertainment film cannot, of course, be reduced to the one ideological goal of recouping a gender hierarchy.[21] Moviegoing was a new leisure activity that the family could experience together without recourse to time-consuming or expensive travel arrangements. It also offered cheap diversion and appeasement to a large immigrant population, providing a rapid means of assimilating them to the images and norms of their new society. It even provided women with a respite from the domestic sphere, giving them a place to go and an excuse for getting out of the house. Yet these benefits, though they may seem unrelated and even opposed to the gender-recouping function of film, were also hidden supports for that function. Only through a confluence of factors does a medium take the direction it does, and without these subsidiary inducements narrative film might well have failed to prosper as mass entertainment.

What was the role that film played for women, and how did it both take over and change female subjectivity as it had been represented in the novel? The so-called woman's picture that studios began producing in the 1920s and early 1930s offers a good place to begin, because this kind of film borrowed heavily from the novelistic tradition that it superseded and because these films appear to contradict the assumption that the woman in classical cinema is, in Mulvey's terms, a fetish constructed to accommodate male desire.

The spate of sensationalistic Cecil B. DeMille films about infidelity in the early 1920s and the so-called confession films that also dealt with adultery and romantic betrayal in the early 1930s succeeded in luring women into movie-houses in large numbers on a regular basis. These films told stories of women led astray, then restored to their domestic role, usually by dint of their own determination to get their man. In confession films, the plot was especially formulaic: a low-born heroine, her trust betrayed by an irresponsible but attractive and wealthy man, discovers ingenious ways of luring back the man who seduced her. In the end, she achieves respectability through marriage. Constance Bennett was featured in many of these films; her refined manner, at odds with the lower-class roles, enhanced the films' fairy-tale quality. In a group of related films, more exotic types such as Marlene Dietrich and Joan Crawford were cast in the leading roles. Although they lacked the refinement of Bennett, their tough flamboyance functioned in the same way: it gave them a cinematic invulnerability and lent to their suffering an appearance of unreality and glamour.

The theme of the erring woman either brought back to the fold or punished according to the nature of her sin had, of course, been central to novel plots from Samuel Richardson through Thomas Hardy. Like the films, the novels had offered women the opportunity to participate vicariously in a moral lapse but then have their conventional beliefs confirmed by the imposition of punishment or the embrace of an established norm at the end. But the fantasy structures supplied by the films need to be distinguished from the imaginative structures fostered by the novels. Fantasy, as I am using it here, is essentially featureless and unspecific; it is a skeleton upon which one can dress up personal daydreams. Imagination, by contrast, involves acts of discrimination: to imagine a relationship is to imagine its difficulties as well as its pleasures, to see the loss as well as the gain, and to see who else might be affected in possibly long-term and peripheral ways. In novels, especially those being written toward the end of the nineteenth century, the imagination of loss had become so acute that the conventional rewards and punishments rang false. I have already discussed this effect in Dickens's *Dombey and Son.* Thomas Hardy's *Tess of the D'Ubervilles* dramatizes the point even more compellingly. The image of Tess at the end of her story is the image not of proper punishment but of a human sacrifice that shakes the very foundations of our belief in social justice and personal relationship.

Women's films, while they were popular as fantasies, did not offer this kind of psychological insight into character and motivation or, by extension, delve into the inequities of experience as novels could. In a 1931 film with Joan Crawford, *Dance, Fools, Dance*, produced by MGM, the limitations of the genre in this respect are especially evident. The heroine is a society girl who rejects her original suitor when she concludes that he feels duty-bound to marry her after her father loses his fortune. In the end, after she suffers a series of ordeals at the hands of gamblers and gangsters, the original suitor returns and she agrees to marry him. What makes this so strikingly unlike a superficially similar plot line in a domestic novel is that the film suggests no reason why the heroine has changed her mind. The earlier decision isn't discredited, but neither is the suitor shown to have undergone a transformation (in fact, he barely appears in the body of the film). Whereas the novels provide evidence of male transformation in the process of courtship (such as Darcy's transformation in Austen's *Pride and Prejudice,* Eugene Wrayburn's in Dickens's *Our Mutual Friend,* or the Prince's in James's *The Golden Bowl*), the films are not dependent upon such material. The wealth of visual detail—in this case, colorful gangster meetings and nightclub acts—eclipse a concern for character transformation.

It could be argued that women found pleasure watching these films by adding their own explanations to the skeletal plot lines and providing complex motives for the heroines' actions. At their best, the actresses in these roles exuded qualities of personal charisma and strength of character that were truly admirable and worth fantasizing about.[22] Part of the pleasure that female audiences found in these films might also be said to involve a tendency that feminist critics have diagnosed as "masochistic": viewers took solace not so much in the promise that the heroine would be rewarded for her suffering as in knowing that, with a reward, the value of the heroine's suffering (and by extension theirs) had been confirmed. Indeed, film theorist Teresa de Lauretis has argued that women's pictures maintain the same overall structure as male-oriented action films: the woman is positioned as the waiting object, her fate determined by the eventual arrival or nonarrival of the man whom she loves (the classic example of this thematic structure is *Back Street*). The woman, according to de Lauretis, is central to the film only insofar as she serves as "a memory spectacle" for what needs to be continually reaffirmed for men and reconditioned in women.[23]

Admittedly, the theme of the waiting woman was also central to the domestic novel, where the trials and tribulations of courtship constituted the principal subject matter. The difference is that "waiting" in the novel, in which an effort was made to fill in an internal life for the heroine, became a source of personal self-realization, indeed, of self-creation (an end rather than a means), despite the conventions of plot and the drive for closure. This is particularly evident in Henry James's novels that take waiting women and then quite purposefully dismantle or discredit the conventional objects for which they wait. James provides highly self-conscious examples within the genre, but even the "sensation" novels of the 1860s present heroines whose energy seems at odds with their prescribed destinies.[24] This is what accounts, I would argue, for the extraordinary investment that readers came to have in the characters in novels. (Such investment, termed *Bovaryism* after Emma Bovary's novel-driven desires, was viewed as something of a disease in the late nineteenth century.) The identification that novels fostered in their female readers may help clarify what Mary Ann Doane refers to as women's tendency to "overidentify with the image" (which she contrasts with men's ability to maintain a psychological distance from what they see).[25] By offering formidable characters for identification, novels can be said to have encouraged a habit of investment that was transferred to film with less-satisfying results. In her study of women's response to Hollywood films, Jeanine Basinger poses the problem implicitly when she notes that while film is like literature in tapping into "a desire to know what you didn't know, have what you didn't have, and feel what you were afraid to feel," we accept these desires as noble in literature but condemn them as foolish in film.[26] The difference in the public perception of the two genres can be explained if we consider that novels are more likely than films to require a fuller context and rationale for the desires they enact.

The recent deluge of highly theoretical feminist criticism with its refusal to invest in character except on its own terms suggests that film has not maintained its hold on women in the way novels did.[27] Indeed, it may be the very failure of movies to nurture the affective lives of women (the absence, that is, of characters who encourage emotional investment from the spectator) that has produced the angry self-consciousness of female theorists and pushed women generally into demanding more rights and roles in a larger arena. What has also been ignored is the potentially positive role played by the double identification that many films require of the female spectator. As theorists have pointed out, classical narrative film demands that women identify both with the female image as passive spectacle and with the position of the camera which finds a correlative in the usually male figure of action inside the film. While the former may well be masochistic, the latter seems potentially empowering by providing subjective access to a position that was not available in the domestic novel (where the hero appeared only in a domestic guise, his worldly life located outside the novel frame). Although this double identification has generally been seen as a double bind, this may underestimate the creative ways in which image identification can be employed in the construction of subjectivity. Given the tendency on the part of women to identify with subjects on the screen, female access to images of enterprise and action and to a position that offers training in identification with them may be the great hidden gain for feminism in the rise of film as popular entertainment.

Yet this takes us into the present and future prematurely. However one assesses film's long-term value for women, it must be acknowledged that the medium worked to suppress a female subjectivity that had been nurtured by novels, circulating in its stead a simpler, more controllable image of woman. As for men, who were largely ignorant of the style and sensibility of domestic novels, film seems to have performed another function. Ostensibly, of course, it catered to what was already defined stereotypically as a male style of cognition: it served to recoup and anchor a patriarchal culture in distress. But I also contend that the influence of narrative film was more complicated than this—that it also, paradoxically, assisted in the revision of the male subject along more feminine lines. In short, I want to suggest that the male orientation of narrative cinema served a progressive function for men: it gave them access, albeit in a highly simplified form, to a subjective identity that had been available to women for over a century.

The notion of separate spheres had widened over the course of the nineteenth century with respect not only to the kind of work middle-class men and women did but also to the kind of entertainment they enjoyed.[28] While women found their principal entertainment reading novels, men found diversion in nonnarrative pastimes such as sports and music-hall entertainment. This separation reflected a difference in the notion of identity. Novels conceived of identity as a narrative and, hence, as capable of growth and change; sports and burlesque conceived of identity as fixed. Although film initially centered on protonarrative elements that correlated with dominant forms of male entertainment (indeed, the earliest films were shown in music halls and vaudeville houses), only with the addition of narrative did film become a medium of mass entertainment. Christian Metz writes that film took "the narrative road" where other roads might have been possible, and that this direction was the result of a "demand" on the part of the spectator.[29] This demand would seem to follow logically from the threat that novels posed to patriarchal culture. Film, in other words, not only had to bolster patriarchy but also to retrofit it, to bring it, as it were, up to par with the female subject and, relatedly, to make it competitive within a modern context.

I have already explained that novels, given their association with a female sphere of leisure, were able to develop a complex subjectivity, if only by default. I would now like to extend this argument to include a position that a number of recent critics of the novel have suggested, namely that the female subjectivity forged in novels was a paradigm for modern subjectivity itself.[30] The idea of the self as a psychological entity, as possessed of an "unconscious" or, in the terminology of Jacques Lacan, as predicated upon a lack of knowledge and a misrecognition of the self, can be said to have been born with the novel, just as the novel can be said to have been born out of a democratic, industrialized social context. Freud's notion of the psyche is, after all, a version of novelistic identity. His patients, predominantly women, were the point of departure for his theories, and his case histories resemble novelistic narratives.[31] Freud's method was the logical extrapolation of a novelistic tradition; he solidified a concept of character that the domestic novelist Samuel Richardson had pioneered in the eighteenth century. His approach testifies to the fact that there were advantages to conceiving of identity in narrative terms.

We now begin to see why the female association with novels eventually became a source of ideological difficulty. For how was the new idea of subjectivity that had been forged through novels and in which women, as devoted novel-readers, had been conditioned, to become accessible to men? Instead of focusing on where film diverges from the novel, it becomes helpful, in light of this question, to focus on where it conjoins. For narrative film was unique in being a truly mass medium that relied on a fictional narrative to relay not only plot but also character, albeit in a far less complex form than novels did. This recipe was precisely what was needed to lead men to embrace a narrative identity and to handicap women in a process where they had taken the lead. This also provides one way of interpreting film's positioning of women in the role of the object to be looked at. For the assignment of the woman to the position of stasis and spectacle reverses the way that male and female subjectivity actually existed at the turn of the twentieth century. The male, conditioned as an observer to entertainment spectacle, was more likely to conceive of himself as a fixed subject, a cultural given. The female, conditioned by novel-reading, was more likely to conceive of herself as a temporal, mutable subjectivity.

To understand the cultural implications of these differing self-conceptions requires a brief detour into narrative theory. The literary critic Robert Scholes has associated fictional narrative with a masculine drive to know and possess (analogizing the fictional trajectory with the trajectory of the male sexual act). This view has been elaborated upon with respect to cinema by Stephen Heath, who draws on the vocabularly of Lacanian psychoanalysis. Heath sees cinematic narrative as an ongoing drive to gain mastery over a "lack"—a sense of incompleteness and misapprehension in the subject—which is "perpetually remade with safe fictions"(much as Scholes's sexualized narrative drive can be said to find temporary appeasement through narrative closure).[32] Thus Heath describes the subject's drive for a unified identity while also pointing out its illusory nature: although narrative continuity may serve to temporarily obscure a lack of wholeness, it is also built on and fueled by this lack. It must forever invoke it—hence, the male dependence, as feminist theorists have argued, on the woman as the image of castration (lack) and of wholeness (fetish to compensate for that lack).

What is missing from this kind of analysis is a realistic sense of the viewer's awareness. Theorists tend to assume that the audience is either totally benighted or, like themselves presumably, fully aware. They ignore the sense in which the awareness on which their critical insights are predicated has evolved and is itself a function of modern subjectivity. For the modern subject is not a decentered subject or subject in process so much as it is a subject *aware* of being decentered and in process. Freud's controversial discovery of the unconscious was not a discovery about subjectivity but a way of thinking about the self that produced a new kind of subjectivity. Novels, with their relentless probing of their heroines' contradictory motives and desires, had pioneered this new self-conception (despite the formal drive for closure that Scholes equates with the masculine drive). Film would continue to sow this awareness even as it sought to suppress it. In other words, when narrative focuses on character, it in some sense disrupts or undercuts any static, unified self-conception, creating a sense of "lack." The linkage of character to narrative thus introduces the notion of identity changing in time and helps produce, in the spectator, a new kind of self-awareness that is the basis for a new kind of subjectivity. Sergei Eisenstein's remarks on the kinship of novels and films take on fuller meaning in this context. Eisenstein maintained that novels bore the same relationship to their readers that films bear to their audiences: "They compelled the reader to live with the same passions."[33] What differed was the gender being targeted and the historical relationship between the two genres, film emerging in the wake of the novel.

Once cinematic narrative is understood as a drive for totalization that, at the same time, educates its viewers in the nontotalized temporality of character, it becomes possible to read narrative film as a kind of compromise between these two conceptions of character—one fixed (allied to a traditional male identity), the other in process (allied to a female novelistic identity)—and to see the balance as capable of shifting.[34]

Alfred Hitchcock's films, spanning a long career and paralleling the development of entertainment film, are a fertile ground for the study of how this balance of two conceptions of character worked—and, eventually, failed to work. While Hitchcock made no attempt to delineate an internal life of the kind that prose fiction could describe, he increasingly employed cinematic effects to produce a sense of character that could be equated with, if it could not be said to correspond to, the subjectivity produced by novels. Part of this process involved the use of female characters to physically embody an *idea* of subjectivity. Women in Hitchcock's films—particularly, as I shall argue, at the high point of his Hollywood period in the 1940s and 1950s—served as iconic subjects, signposts of that complicated psychological and emotional responsiveness that had been at the center of nineteenth-century novels. This is the theme of *Rear Window,* whose protagonist undergoes an experience that includes a deeper understanding of the female position—an experience that parallels that of the generic male spectator watching the movie (see chap. 6).

The brutalization of women in Hitchcock's films can be understood in this context as an effort to make the male spectator feel something about women's exploitation by representing it in the most extreme form. "If he victimizes women," one especially acute critic has noted, "he does so in order to make us come to their defense."[35] Yet because the brutality is represented from the outside (from the male point of view and oriented to the male gaze), the film sometimes appears to be complicitous with the brutalizer. In other words, if one is to jolt the male viewer into feeling sympathy, one also risks activitating the sadism that that sympathy is meant to counter. This would explain some of the controversy that surrounds Hitchcock's films whenever the issue of his treatment of women is raised. The best feminist critics seem forced to admit that there is no simple misogyny at work in Hitchcock; they generally resort to referring to his "ambivalence." In my view, the confusing effect of the films with regard to their representation of women resides in the way they try to bring a Victorian concept of subjectivity, associated with the female point of view of novels, into the realm of cinema, where that point of view has been formally suppressed. It is the substitution, then, of one kind of subjectivity by another that is nonetheless seeking to comprehend what it has replaced. The result is an apparent distortion on both sides, a kind of cancelling out of subjectivity altogether. In the end, Hitchcock's focus on surface appearance and action to produce characterizations that have their origin in textual, "deep" notions of character works to recast the idea of character into something altogether different from the novelistic conception.

A shift to another vocabulary may help to clarify my argument. If the pictorial image can be seen as an essential element in film (still photography being conceived of as the technical precursor), then narrative film must be understood as combining elements of realistic narrative, inherited from a novelistic tradition, with nonnarrative elements from a pictorial tradition. We know that the exclusion of narrative elements in painting dates from the

Renaissance and arose out of deference to a concept of truth based on a desire to represent what reality looked like.[36] By the same token, literature traditionally emphasized plotted elements in keeping with the conventions of narrative realism. As soon as literature began to focus on character, however, that which had formerly been the precinct of pictorial representation fell within the jurisdiction of narrative and hence was revised to include a temporal dimension. Character came to involve not just an inherent moral or behavioral "nature" but a potential for growth and change—a mix of pictorial and narrative elements. Film would emerge as the apotheosis of this amalgamation: of narrative on the one hand, as this reflects the unfolding story of character in time, and of picture on the other, with its associations with a frozen reality and a transcendent truth. The combination was ideal to make realistic representation more powerful than it had ever been in structuring the observer's experience. But what this combination of narrative and picture also meant was that film could potentially shift the weight of these elements to create some new "take" on experience. Hence, picture (or spectacle) and narrative, which theorists have tended to find mutually supporting of the male gaze in classical narrative cinema, are also elements capable of existing in tension, of subverting each other, or of being configured in a new balance. Does the holding pattern produced in a musical comedy by the spectacle of a song-and-dance number have a self-reflexive effect? Does the prolonged delay of the appearance of a female character (a delay central to the power of films such as *Rebecca* and *Laura* but also part of what makes Marlene Dietrich's performances so enticing: one is forced to wait for them) have a similar effect, forcing the viewer to recognize the mechanism by which the film depends upon the woman *as* spectacle? Critics of classical narrative film have tended to think otherwise and to read all elements in a production as reinforcing a dominant ideology.[37] But we need to relate such thematic and structural effects to present avant-garde experiments, and to recognize the historical continuity between the two. There is a direct line of descent, in other words, between narratized character and Brechtian distanciation that more explicitly decenters our view of character. Narrative when applied to character does not simply contain and diffuse ideological contradiction, it also produces it and, hence, fuels the development into new forms of any medium that depends upon narratized character for the articulation of ideology.

And again, Hitchcock offers a convenient and fruitful means of exploring this historical continuity. As a master of suspense, he was devoted to the unfolding of narrative, but he was also a devotee of the shot or shot sequence, those technical and visual set pieces that often served as his films' impetus and center. Given this dual loyalty, Hitchcock's career can be read as a series of shifts in the balance of narrative and pictorial values. In his earliest films he did not concern himself much with the development of identity over time, but the suspense elements of the narrative compensated for this, subordinating visual gimmickry to plot revelation and supplying a structure within which we might fill in an identity for the hero or heroine. This formula holds especially for his most successful early action-suspense films, *The 39 Steps, Secret Agent, Young and Innocent,* and *The Lady Vanishes.* In later films he altered the rules of suspense, or rather made new rules (Hitchcock came to define suspense as the art of letting the audience know what the character didn't), so that the focus fell on character rather than on plot revelation, thus turning the mechanism of plot into something closer to literary narrative.[38] Now elaborate shots and set pieces became codes for character and relationship (at their best, as in the Mount Rushmore scene in *North by Northwest* or the opening shot of the apartment building in *Rear Window*, they seem to operate as a kind of blueprint for the film's larger narrative). But in Hitchcock's last films he enacted yet another shift in the balance of narrative and pictorial values. In their concentration on ingenious effects, these films abandon concern for character, thereby severing the Victorian novelistic legacy that had informed Hitchcock's work for so long. What is left is visual pattern, drained of context, offering no point for identification by the spectator.

Wendy Steiner, in her study of the exchange between narrative and pictorial traditions, notes that "if narrative is a realistic repetition of identity across time, repetition not modified by time becomes design." She sees this excision of identity from narrative as central to the work of postmodern artists such as Andy Warhol ("repeating identical instances of a crucial scene") and Roy Lichtenstein ("isolating parts of narrative sequences").[39] But she might also have looked to the medium of film in its more contemporary manifestation, where the complementary tendencies she identifies with these two artists get combined. In late Hitchcock, as I demonstrate in chapter 9, we no longer find ourselves drawn to know and identify with characters, only to trace and interpret the patterns—pieces of old setups and old stories—that characters leave in their wake.

There is a parallel that can be drawn here to the genre of contemporary cultural criticism and to more radical forays into technological creativity in which author and critic, performer and spectator, exchange places or merge. Indeed, I wish to suggest that the transformation effected by film and epitomized by Hitchcock's last films is the source of yet another cultural transformation—a transformation into critical discourse and cultural free play. In this quintessentially contemporary mode of dealing with experience, matters of subjectivity and representation that had taken on a different meaning in the shift from novel to film are again radically revised. What Hitchcock's last films reflect is another level of abstraction, what has been termed *pure cinema,* but which I would define more broadly, borrowing terms from different theoretical vocabularies, terms such as *third-order learning, ecological thinking,* or *language games.* It is the metaperspective that coincides with the contemporary deconstructionist point of view and that places itself outside the traditional dualities by which culture has supported such distinctions as self and other, art and reality, imaginative representation and critical interpretation. This conceptual long shot, analogous to the camera eye at the beginnings of *Psycho* and *Frenzy,* sees in the particulars of the world the fragments of a design that find their meaning only in the viewer's mind. It substitutes interpretations for the truths that were the hallmarks of an earlier tradition of the self. Thus the trajectory from novel to film to contemporary "virtual reality" is a journey from a deep sense of self to a surface sense of self to a sense of self discarded in favor of ever-permutating patterns and sources of interpretive energy.

Novel into Film: *Sabotage*

Hitchcock's British period dates from the mid-1920s when he made his directorial debut, until 1939 when, as England's most acclaimed director, he left London for Hollywood. Serious critics initially saw his move to America as a sellout and insisted that his subsequent films were not up to the level of his best British pictures. This perspective began to change in the 1950s and 1960s, when Charles Rohmer, Claude Chabrol, and other auteur critics championed the Hollywood films as the fullest expression of Hitchcock's mature style. Yet even as the focus has shifted to the Hollywood period, the British films have continued to draw attention. Many are good by any standard and are still supremely watchable. They are also of special interest to the film theorist and historian as the formative work of a gifted director within a developing medium.

In this chapter, I focus on *Sabotage,* made and released in 1936 for Gaumont-British Pictures. This film demonstrates, more vividly than any other from this early period, how Hitchcock's concept of the cinematic derived in opposition to trends in literary representation. By the same token, insofar as the film failed to digest and reconstitute its literary source fully, it laid the groundwork for Hitchcock's films of the 1940s and 1950s, in which he would attempt to reclaim for cinema a novelistic (which is to say, a psychological) conception of character.

During the years he directed films in Britain, Hitchcock's choice of material for adaptation to the screen ranged more widely than it would later.

He tried his hand at a drama of manners (*Easy Virtue*), a picaresque comedy (*Rich and Strange*), an urbane who-dun-it (*Murder!*), a romantic musical (*Waltzes from Vienna*), and a historical action romance (*Jamaica Inn*)—to name a few deviations from the more familiar adventure thrillers by which he made his reputation during this period. Quite a number of his early films were based on plays, and a smattering were based on original scenarios by Hitchcock, his wife, and the writer Charles Bennett. The majority, however, were based on stories by minor contemporary novelists, the kind of work he would rely on throughout his career as germs for his movies. His rationale for choosing this kind of property, he later explained to François Truffaut, was that it offered no artistic competition and could be altered and bowdlerized with impunity: "*Crime and Punishment* is somebody else's achievement. . . . An author takes three or four years to write a fine novel; it's his whole life. Then other people take it over completely [in making it into a movie]. . . . I simply can't see that."[1] But he deviated from this rule in one important instance, when he chose to make an adaptation of Joseph Conrad's 1907 novel, *The Secret Agent.* It is the one movie of his career that is based on an irrefutably great work, a work that not coincidentally stands at the end of the tradition associated with the nineteenth-century British novel.

Hitchcock adapted Conrad's novel to the screen under the title *Sabotage* (by a coincidence, he had just completed a film entitled *Secret Agent,* based on a Somerset Maugham story). *Sabotage* followed *The 39 Steps* by only a year, and it was *The 39 Steps* that made his reputation and earned him a free hand in choosing properties and exerting control over production. The choice of the Conrad novel was thus his and not the studio's, and he brought in Charles Bennett to write the scenario. He was also intimately involved in the casting, selecting the American star Sylvia Sidney for the female lead and the acclaimed German actor Oscar Homolka for the villain. His only disappointment was the male lead: Robert Donat, his first choice, was unavailable, and he had to settle for John Loder.

Despite the extensive control Hitchcock wielded over the production, *Sabotage* was not a box-office success. This may be why Hitchcock never again attempted an adaptation of such an important literary work. Nonetheless, the movie seems to me to be Hitchcock's most interesting British film precisely because it is an adaptation of this novel. Conrad's *Secret Agent* encapsulates the challenges to representation that a literary tradition posed for Hitchcock and for cinema more generally as it adjusted to the demands of a mass market.

Conrad's novel is set in London in the 1880s, a period in which the anarchist movement had precipitated a series of terrorist incidents, or "dynamite outrages," as Conrad refers to them in his author's note.[2] The central character, Adophe Verloc, is a spy for a foreign government, pretending to be part of London's anarchist community in order to further his employer's political goals. In everyday life he maintains the cover of running a pornographic book shop (the effect is thus of levels of secrecy and illicit behavior). The reasons for Verloc's involvement in clandestine activity are vague and entirely unheroic. He is a security-loving, rather cowardly man, complacently fond of his domestic comforts and of his wife Winnie. His work allows him a stipend without requiring a great expediture of time or energy. Winnie Verloc, for her part, is no more of a romantic character than her husband. Incurious and unexpressive, she moves somnolently through the motions of her life, maintaining a true attachment to only one person, her retarded brother Stevie, whom she has seen mistreated by their father throughout their childhood. We learn early on that she married Verloc largely to provide a home for Stevie.

The drama of the novel is launched when Verloc is ordered to commit an act of sabotage to prove himself to a new official at the embassy. Frightened by the prospect of losing his salary and his cover, he exploits his retarded brother-in-law's gullibility and naive idealism by enlisting him to carry the bomb. The plot proceeds according to plan, but Stevie trips on the way to his destination, the bomb explodes, and he is killed. When Winnie finds out about her brother's death and realizes her husband's involvement in it, she stabs Verloc with a kitchen knife, then runs off in a daze with one of his anarchist colleagues. When he deserts her, she commits suicide.

What drew Hitchcock to Conrad's novel? In its surface plot line, *The Secret Agent* resembles the kinds of stories that appealed to Hitchcock during this period. Between 1934 and 1938, he made six consecutive thrillers (often referred to as his classic thriller sextet), five of which also involved political intrigue. *Sabotage* was the fourth in this series. What may have further recommended the novel was its setting. Up until *Sabotage,* Hitchcock had set his thrillers in foreign locales, but the novel deviated from Conrad's own general penchant for exotica in taking place in London in the kind of seedy blue-collar neighborhood that would have been familiar to the filmmaker. It thus subscribed to the principle that Hitchcock had already begun to appreciate but had not yet fully implemented—namely, that a prosaic setting can harbor enormous possibilities for suspense. This principle had informed the conclusion of *The 39 Steps,* where the hero unmasks an elaborate espionage plot during a London music-hall performance. In *Sabotage,* Hitchcock heightened the sense of familiarity by updating the story and capitalizing on the prevailing fear of German sabotage.

Finally, Hitchcock must have been drawn to the Conrad novel because it featured a favorite thematic motif: the structural and moral kinship of the policeman and the criminal. This theme is explicitly stated in the novel by the

Chief Inspector of Special Crimes when he muses on the nature of his work: "He could understand the mind of a burglar, because, as a matter of fact, the mind and the instincts of a burglar are the same kind as the mind and the instincts of a police officer. Both recognize the same conventions, and have a working knowledge of each other's methods and of the routine of their respective trades."[3] The theme linking policeman and criminal had appealed to Hitchcock from the beginning of his career (and had drawn him to the thrillers of Fritz Lang). It had already been operative in *The Lodger* and *Blackmail,* in which police are shown to act according to vested interests and to manipulate justice. Later, in *Notorious* and *North by Northwest,* the observations of Conrad's Chief Inspector were given wider application as criminal and police organizations are shown to mirror each other in their more general structure and function.

But Conrad was ultimately less interested in the way social institutions and roles can be corrupted or compromised than in a deeper kind of confusion at the heart of all human action. This is where Hitchcock, in making the adaptation, parted ways with his source. The movie, unlike the novel, makes no attempt to explore the complex motives that drive the characters. Indeed, with the exception of the character of Verloc, who remains a resonant enigma from beginning to end (a tribute both to the nuanced performance of Oscar Homolka and, as Hitchcock would later attest, to the limitations of the script), the other characters in the film are depicted as conventionalized versions of their novelistic counterparts. The most notable example is the character of Mrs. Verloc (her first name is never given in the film), who has been recast as the story's heroine. In contrast to the emotional and physical heaviness attributed to the character in the novel, Mrs. Verloc in the film is appealingly tremulous and fragile, the embodiment of femininity in distress (Sylvia Sidney's waiflike figure and face contribute substantially to this effect). The film studiously revises or ignores all elements in the character that might tend to arouse moral suspicion: we never learn precisely why she left America or married Verloc, and the business that she runs with her husband is changed from a pornographic book shop into a movie-house. Her affections continue to center around her brother Stevie (Desmond Tester), but he is portrayed as a normal preadolescent boy rather than a retarded adult. She is also provided with a love interest in the film in the character of Sergeant Ted Spenser (John Loder), a young detective who is a wholesome composite of a number of far less savory characters from the novel (in the film, only when the heroine has been properly widowed—albeit by stabbing her husband to death—is the suitor permitted to fully proclaim himself). At the end of the film, a bomb conveniently destroys the evidence that might have implicated Mrs. Verloc in her husband's death. She is thus free to go off with the detective, and the last scene shows the couple escaping into the crowd, presumably to start a new life together on the Continent.

The changes that Hitchcock worked on the novel initially seem to support his later declaration about how he adapted literary works to the screen: "If I like the basic idea, I just forget all about the book and start to create cinema."[4] However, while *Sabotage* may seem like the mere skeleton of the novel, the boast about "forgetting all about the book" does not stand up to scrutiny. The more one studies the novel and the film together, the more one begins to see how extensively Hitchcock borrowed material from Conrad's novel and found new applications for it. Indeed, given the extent to which Hitchcock's vision opposed Conrad's, one might say he "sabotaged" the novel for cinematic ends. The novel, for its part, took its revenge: it refused to be domesticated, and the film failed to make money. Even so, Hitchcock must be said to have gained from wrestling with Conrad. As I argue later in this chapter, the adjustments he was obliged to make in adapting this complex work to the screen provided him with clues for expanding his notion of the cinematic later in his career.

As evidence that Hitchcock used the novel for more than a plot and character outline, we need to look for more creative kinds of borrowing. Thus, for example, Conrad's description of London as a "cruel devourer of the world's light" seems the hint for the film's highly dramatic and original opening scene of a citywide power outage, Verloc's first act of sabotage (there is no counterpart to it in the novel). In another example, Hitchcock literalizes Conrad's description of the streets of London as a "slimy aquarium from which the water had been run off,"[5] making London's zoo aquarium the actual site of Verloc's fateful meeting with his employer (in the novel, that meeting happens in a room in the foreign embassy). There is also Stevie's trip across London with the package containing the bomb—a scene that seems to have been adapted from an episode in the novel in which Stevie and his sister travel across the city to take their mother to a charity home. Although the tenor of the two scenes is entirely different (the novel's is Dostoyevskian tragedy; the film's, Chaplinesque comedy), both serve as precursors to death. In the novel, the trip creates the mood that will make Stevie susceptible to Verloc's scheme; in the film, the trip literally culimates in the explosion of the bomb that kills Stevie (and all the occupants of the bus in which he is riding). Earlier in this episode, Hitchcock had shown Stevie on foot, dawdling on his way to his destination and collared by a sidewalk peddlar who uses him to demonstrate toothpaste and hair tonic to the amusement of bystanders. Such a scene has no place in the novel, but Conrad does describe Verloc as possessing "the air of moral nihilism common to . . . the sellers of invigorating electric belts and inventors of patent medicines."[6] The salesman who exploits Stevie for his demonstration and indirectly contributes to his death by delaying him is clearly in this category, a seemingly comic and trivial version of the darker Verloc. Hitchcock drives home the callousness of the man by having him push the boy on his way at the end of the demonstration with a curt: "Go on, bugger off, you little bastard." His words echo Verloc's earlier, snappish impatience with Stevie in the film ("Go on already!"), as he hurries him off on his fatal errand.

Perhaps the most amusing and evocative example of the way Hitchcock took cues from the Conrad novel involves the representation of the Professor, a pivotal character in the book who occupies a more peripheral role in the film. Conrad's Professor is a frightening embodiment of modern alienation. A specialist in explosives, he devotes his life to the creation of a bomb detonator "that would adjust itself to all conditions, and even to unexpected changes of conditions . . . a really intelligent detonator."[7] The police cannot touch him because he carries on his body just such a device, one that, at the slightest provocation, could destroy not only himself but anyone within his vicinity. This device operates, he explains to an anarchist colleague, according to "the principle of the pneumatic shutter for a camera lens."[8] Obviously intrigued by the metaphorical correspondences between the bomb expert and the filmmaker suggested by this metaphor, Hitchcock changed the Professor from a lean and solitary monomaniac into a rotund, fumbling eccentric who produces his bombs within an amusingly disreputable family setting. (In the movie, the Professor's "cover" is a bird shop in Islington, the site of the Gaumont-British studio where Hitchcock made the film.) As if he needed to drive home the point, he cast an actor in the role who bore a striking resemblance to himself.

Each of these examples (and more could be enumerated[9]) tells us something about Hitchcock's emerging notion of the cinematic. Each is a concrete rendering of what in the novel exists as metaphor. Even the characterization of the Professor falls into this category insofar as it literalizes the comparison of a bomb to a camera by making the character resemble the filmmaker. I have already given some reasons why Hitchcock may have been drawn to direct a film based on *The Secret Agent.* But the appeal of theme and setting alluded to above hardly seems sufficient to explain why he might have literalized the novel's metaphors as extensively as he did. This requires a broader explanation that takes into account the personal histories of Conrad and Hitchcock and the cultural history of their respective genres.

Born in the Ukraine in 1857 to an aristocratic Polish family involved in revolutionary efforts to free Poland from the czar, Joseph Conrad grew up in exile and lost both his parents before the age of twelve. He spent his youth first in Marseilles, sailing on various ships (he claimed to have been involved in gunrunning), and then in England, where he enlisted in the British merchant service and rapidly rose to the rank of captain. He entered the more staid and domestic portion of his life in his thirties when he married, had children, and began a career as a writer.[10]

It is hard to think of a background more in contrast to Alfred Hitchcock's. Son of uneducated London merchants, Hitchcock grew up in an atmosphere of extreme provincialism and conventionality. He embarked upon a career as a filmmaker in his early twenties, with nothing in the way of life experience behind him (his weight kept him out of the military in World War I). Conrad began to write, one might surmise, to do justice to what he had lived; Hitchcock began to direct films as compensation for not having done much of anything at all. His career in the movies would provide the vehicle by which his life could take its shape and by which experience could be had, if vicariously, through the fantasies he projected on the screen.

The differences between these two men correspond to differences in their respective genres. When Conrad took to writing, the realistic novel had already reached its apex in the work of great Victorian novelists such as Eliot and Dickens. It was a weary, well-traveled genre. It was also being attacked from two opposing cultural fronts. Literary modernism took issue with the idea of realistic representation and turned to stylistic and formal experimentation as a means of revitalizing art. A strong strain of misogyny also fueled the movement and made it antagonistic to the feminized sensibility of the Victorian novel.[11] By the same token, in the realm of popular culture, narrative film had begun to eclipse novelistic fiction. This new form of mass entertainment was tailored to the male gaze, in counterpoint to the female point of view favored by novels. Unlike modernist art, however, entertainment film sought to bolster rather than erode realistic representation (positioning the spectator to identify with the detached, controlling eye of the camera). Within this context, Conrad's novels can be understood as transitional works. Their subjects are adventure, political intrigue, and war, and their protagonists tend to be male—an orientation that would seem to anticipate entertainment cinema (and which, as I have already suggested, might well have been the initial appeal of *The Secret Agent* for Hitchcock). But Conrad's novels are also psychological works. They take that concern for the inner life of the individual that nineteenth-century novelists had evolved through their focus on the female role and bring these insights to bear on a wider world of male action and adventure. Such an expansion of the psychological perspective might theoretically be viewed as a means of revitalizing the novel, opening it to a wider audience and affording male readers access to a richer and more flexible subjectivity. But even a cursory familiarity with Conrad's work contradicts such a notion. His novels are not expanded versions of domestic novels. The process of extending psychological analysis beyond the domestic sphere served not to invigorate but to compromise the validity of a life of action. This is the central theme of *The Heart of Darkness* and *Lord Jim,* Conrad's most acclaimed novels. *The Secret Agent* and its direct predecessor, *Nostromo,* simply take the theme further. Indeed, these "first political-detective novels," as they have been called, combine an analysis of the corrupting effects of individual action with an indictment of the political machinations that frame this action (*Under Western Eyes,* written later, continued this analysis of the far-reaching and systematic effects of corruption). In Conrad, it was as though the fine moral distinctions that domestic heroines were able to support within their circumscribed space lost their anchorage when brought up against the facts of the "real" male-inhabited world outside that space. Conrad's novels both lament the failure of a moral vision to operate in the larger world and record the inevitability of that failure. They are in a line with their nineteenth-century predecessors (and F.R. Leavis significantly includes Conrad as the final figure in his *Great Tradition*), but they can also be placed with modernist fiction as they seem to lose faith in traditional values and institutions and, by way of compensation, engage in experiments in narrative sequence and style. And while they anticipate cinema in their often obsessive concern with visual and material imagery, they are unlike cinema in seeking to show the disparity between the surface of things and their internal mechanisms. The scene in the novel in which Winnie Verloc murders her husband, for example, is cinematic in the way in which "things"—the carving knife, the roast beef, the dripping blood, the dead man's hat—are positioned and rendered as concrete images. But the scene is also profoundly literary in the way that the sordid human emotions that lie behind these objects are relentlessly plumbed.

If Hitchcock's adaptation of Conrad's novel seems a form of "treason," as has been suggested in some quarters,[12] it is treason insofar as it represents the transformation of his story for a mass market—that repository of modern, materialistic values the novel decries. However, by adapting Conrad's cynical vision of the modern to a truly modern medium, Hitchcock also activates a sense of moral idealism that seems to hearken back to Conrad's predecessors, the Victorians.

The transformation of values to which I refer is evident in Hitchcock's decision to change the pornography shop, which serves as the cover for Verloc's activities in the novel, into a movie-house in the film. *The Secret Agent,* like all of Conrad's novels, is about the disparity between surfaces and depths, between appearances of propriety and routine and the hidden motives and desires that can fuel unexpected action. Pornography suggests individual desire reduced to its most squalid and unsavory—the unfettered id transferred to the page. Conrad's novel, in its relentless exposure of its characters, operates like pornography in stripping the veil that might support sentimentality or moral idealism. Yet even as he lays bare this corrosive vision, Conrad is terrified of an alternative that he perceives as the future—an approaching apocalypse of the masses that will obliterate all possibility of individual will and desire. The Professor seems to be voicing the horror of his creator when he describes the London crowds as "swarm[ing] numerous like locusts, industrious like ants, thoughtless like a natural force, pushing on blind and orderly and absorbed, impervious to sentiment, to logic, to terror, too, perhaps."[13] While the client of pornography has humanly comprehensible, if unseemly, motives, the masses, as depicted here, are forces that do not conform to the rules of individual motivation. The novel connects the masses with modern science: both are subject to a mechanical, generalized belief system destined to prevail once the individual has been debased and devalued.

Hitchcock realizes this prophecy literally in turning Conrad's novel into a film (the product of modern technology directed at a mass audience) and by transforming the protagonist's "cover" from a pornographic book shop into a movie-house. Whereas pornography is the debasement of the personal, film is the triumph of the communal. The Verlocs carry on their family life behind the screen of the movie theater, but the implication is not, as it is in Conrad, that the private life is somehow proceeding undercover of a public spectacle that bears no relation to it. Instead, private life is a version of that spectacle, penetrated by its images and conventions. When a scream from the movie is heard in the Verloc home, the detective, Ted, exclaims that he thought someone was being murdered. "Someone probably is," Verloc says, "up on the screen there." But the distinction he draws will soon prove illusory; the scenario will be played out at home, and he will be the victim. If Verloc's domestic life is one side of the screen, we the audience are the other. Our private fantasies, our sense of self, and our values and goals as citizens of society are shaped by what we see. Where the novel plumbs hidden motives and discredits all individual pretension to idealism, thereby discrediting idealism itself, film works in the opposite direction to build a consensus of agreed-upon values that can stand despite the fact that an individual may, on occasion, stray from them.

The difference between the structure of Conrad's novel and the structure of Hitchcock's film can be understood in this context. The novel has proceeded to tell its story by repeatedly circling back to explore the viewpoint of each character as it relates to a central event. The result is a relentless dismantling of appearances. No sooner do we see the Verloc family than we come to understand in detail the motives behind Winnie's marriage and the little lies and mercenary acts that brought the marriage to fruition and now sustain it. No sooner do we see Verloc and Stevie going off together "as though they were father and son" than we sense the irony in that comparison, for we already know that Verloc is a desperate man, anxious at all costs to come up with a plan to protect himself and please his employer. Nowhere does the novel assume that conventional relationships are anything but superficial or corrupt.

Hitchcock's film, by contrast, progresses with painstaking linearity and relies for its effect on visual set pieces that, far from dismantling conventional values, lend them support. The paradigmatic instance of this occurs early in the film when Verloc and Stevie are shown quietly seated at the dinner table as Mrs. Verloc begins carving the roast. As the meal begins, Verloc voices dissatisfaction with the cabbage—an expression of pique that is not out of keeping with the image of routinized patriarchal authority (though it also hints that this patriarch is autocratic, taking unreasonable advantage of his authority). Stevie is then sent out for some lettuce, and the grocer next door (really the detective, Ted, in disguise) returns with him, offering Verloc a choice of greens in a cheerfully insolent way. What distinguishes Hitchcock's family scene from any depiction of family life in the novel is the fact that we are not moved to repudiate it. Although Verloc's fitness as patriarch is being subtly undercut, the idea of his authority is not. Ted's insolence is amusing, but we cannot as yet condone it.[14] Midway through the movie, Hitchcock shows another meal, this one involving Ted, Mrs. Verloc, and Stevie in a restaurant, as a means of suggesting a replacement for the family at the dinner table. The restaurant family has the same configuration as the original but more warmth and humor. But, because the scene takes place in a restaurant, the makeshift character of this family is also emphasized. Though it is an appealing play, it cannot be taken seriously. (The contrast between "real" and "play" family is given a different spin in *Shadow of a Doubt*, a film that also relies on the family dinner as an organizing structure. Differences between the two films are discussed in chapter 4.) Only at the end of *Sabotage,* when the scene at the dinner table is restaged with Stevie's place empty, are we finally in a position to give up the image of the Verlocs as a legitimate family. In this later scene, Verloc is again seated and waiting to be served while his wife mechanically prepares to carve the roast. Once again, he makes his routine complaint about the greens. This time, however, he is brought up short as he realizes that the usual pattern of dialogue and action cannot be maintained (Stevie is dead, the grocer next door has been exposed as a detective). As he sits waiting, his wife holds the knife indecisively above the meat, drops it, stares blankly, begins carving again, puts it down—actions that make Verloc gradually aware of what she may be thinking. When he rises and attempts to take the knife from her, she stabs him. The scene progresses rapidly and without dialogue, communicating an extraordinary emotional intensity. Yet had the earlier dinner scene not held a solid, conventional attraction—if, in other words, we did not continue to hold to an *idea* of patriarchal family—this scene would lose much of its power. Indeed, the stabbing that culminates the scene seems to come less from the human agent, Mrs. Verloc, than from the scene itself—to be the product of its shattered symmetry. As the stabbing approaches, Hitchcock focuses the camera on hands and torsos represented in rapid cuts; he avoids full-face shots (an approach also employed for the struggle on the train in *Shadow of a Doubt,* a scene that is similarly ambiguous in relaying the heroine's intentions). When we do see Mrs. Verloc's face, it is expressionless—a cue that Hitchcock took from the novel, which refers to the "unreadable stillness" of Winnie Verloc's face in her grief. The difference is that Conrad keeps up a running commentary, telling us what Winnie really feels, while Hitchcock uses the indeterminacy of the heroine's blank expression to acquit her of responsibility for a crime. After the stabbing, he simply has her intone her brother's name.

Far from discrediting the original image of the family at the dinner table, the stabbing scene serves to reinforce that image as a generic symbol. Patriarchal authority, domestic security, the duty to care for children, and for children to obey and trust in parents are all given support, even though the particular family in question has been betrayed on all these counts. It is the film's support of these values that makes Verloc's death appear an act of divine justice—of justice without a human agent—so that the detective gains our moral as well as our sentimental support in his decision not to turn Mrs. Verloc in. Unlike *The Lodger,* in which a policeman appears to be led by personal interests to contravene the law, this film asserts a higher law that it assumes its audience shares (or, rather, that it brings its audience to share).[15] Those who would discredit or damage certain sacred institutions are shown to be not only worthy of being murdered but fated to die.

The essential difference between the Conrad novel and the Hitchcock film may now be encapsulated as follows: where one is a social critique that sees no limits to what it can unearth and expose, the other is a form of social control, a simplification not only of character but of values—an attempt to repress the excess meanings that literature has set in motion. The traditional locus of control and value (the male position) had first undergone eclipse by a female "central intelligence" in the course of the nineteenth century, fueled by an evolving novelistic tradition. Finally, in the work of novelists such as Henry James, George Meredith, Thomas Hardy, Joseph Conrad, and other protomodernists, the male position—and the life of action along with it—had been more directly and profoundly critiqued. The very foundation of social institutions and values came under attack by the penetrating power of words to seek out and describe ulterior motives and feelings.[16] Film, while it could in some sense be viewed as the fullest realization of a loss of value, was also the potential source of a revitalization, a return through images to the representation of simple roles and pure motives for relationship. In place of psychological desire, Hitchcock substitutes the possibility of controlled feeling—salvation from the outside rather than the inside. The mass audience, in this context, is the human embodiment of the outside. It serves both as the rationale for a simplication of meaning and as the raw material from which a new view of character as the lever for an emotional response can be carved. So conceived, the mass audience may be understood as a composite of the two most vulnerable characters in the Conrad novel: Winnie Verloc, whom Conrad describes as "think[ing] in images," and Stevie, who "though apt to forget mere facts . . . had a faithful memory for sensations."[17] In other words, Hitchcock takes what in Conrad are the crippled products of a blighted modernity—of that crowd, "numerous like locusts"—and creates a cinema for and through them.

To explain how Hitchcock does this, it is helpful to look at his use of crowd imagery in the film. He had used crowds before, most notably in *The Lodger* and in *The 39 Steps.* In *Sabotage,* however, he extends the role of the crowd so that it runs parallel to the film's plot and directs an evolution in the self-perception and response of his audience.

The first of the crowd scenes depicts a crush of laughing subway passengers reacting to the blackout that begins the film. The crowd imagery here is purely descriptive of the unruliness and unpredictability of public reaction. Soon after, however, we see another crowd, this time an angry one, demanding its money back from Mrs. Verloc because the power outage has cut short its entertainment. Ted, the detective, comes to the rescue and placates the group by preaching demagogic nonsense (a scene reminiscent of the political rally in *The 39 Steps,* where the hero extemporizes a rousing speech to an increasingly appreciative audience). Now we see unruliness channeled and controlled, though with no coherent aim (Mrs. Verloc has already been instructed by her husband to refund the money and, when the power returns, the issue is dropped as the audience files back into the theater). Still later, we are presented with another crowd—a group of amused bystanders who watch the sidewalk demonstration involving the unwilling Stevie. This crowd differs from the earlier ones in that it is focused on a spectacle; this is also the first time that a response is elicited from us as a group similarly focused. The scene operates to establish our likeness to the crowd in the scene but, at the same time, to separate us from that crowd by infusing us with a sense of moral awareness. Knowing that Stevie is being fatally delayed, we cannot lose ourselves in the slapstick of the scene. We judge what we see, and that judgment includes not only the toothpaste salesman but also the crowd of bystanders for its callous disregard of the boy's feelings.

Finally, toward the end of the film, Hitchcock stages a scene that mirrors most closely our own position as audience to the film. The sequence begins as the distraught heroine, after learning of her brother's death, wanders into the movie theater attached to her home. The movie on the screen is Walt Disney's *Who Killed Cock Robin?* and the audience is responding with boisterous appreciation. The pranks and pratfalls of the animated characters and the delighted reactions they elicit remind us of Stevie's comically inept behavior, inserted throughout the film for our amusement. (The episode leading up to Stevie's death, in which he is sidetracked and taken advantage of on his way to Picadilly Station, is particularly evocative of a cartoon sequence, with the boy cast in the role of the good-natured, ill-fated cartoon character.) But at the very point at which Mrs. Verloc is caught up in the film and actually begins to laugh—a fleeting recreation of the joy she took in Stevie when he was alive—we are shown the screen and the image of Cock Robin, shot by an arrow and falling to earth. The cartoon bursts out in the raucous refrain of "Who killed Cock Robin?" and the audience explodes into laughter. The camera returns to Mrs. Verloc's face, which has collapsed into shocked recognition, then grief, as she recalls herself to the present. The child is dead, and the amusement of the crowd now seems brutally callous. The cartoon, instead of distracting the heroine, now directs her to recognize her brother's murderer ("Who killed Cock Robin?") and to suggest that she avenge herself. The next scene is the dinner, and her obsessive focus on the carving knife becomes utterly comprehensible.

Yet Mrs. Verloc's precise thoughts and feelings as she holds that carving knife remain unknown to us. Indeed, the scene at the dinner table depends on our *not* knowing whether she intends to kill Verloc (an ambiguity reinforced by our uncertainty as to whether the cartoon image of Cock Robin pierced by an arrow refers to Stevie, killed by Verloc, or to Verloc, to be killed by her). What is required is that we feel *for* her. Unlike Conrad's description, which places us inside his character's head, Hitchcock's approach places us outside, as onlookers to her emotion. Our position is like that of the audience laughing at Cock Robin, but we are an audience directed at a different spectacle—an audience schooled in a proper reaction, whereas the audience within the movie, through no fault of its own, is shown to be reacting improperly. Thus we are being called upon to identify not with a character but with a communal reaction (the emotionalized version of what theorists have referred to as a "gaze")—a *corrected* version of the crowd's reaction inside the film. In the climactic scene in which Mrs. Verloc stabs her husband, this communal reaction has become so focused and powerful that it now seems to participate in the making of the scene. The death of Verloc, as I have already discussed, appears to have no agent inside the film. Instead, it seems to be willed by us. (The same effect occurs in Hitchcock's next film, *Young and Innocent,* where the camera's insistent gaze on the face of the guilty drummer produces the impression that we are willing him to twitch and give himself away.) The filmmaker has transformed us from an unfocused reactive group (the correlative of the unruly crowd at the beginning of the film) into a coordinated group sharing a "proper" reaction. And that reaction seems not only to be produced by the film but also to double back to produce the film. We not only feel justly, we feel as though we enact justice.[18] (This feeling is further discussed in chapter 6 on *Rear Window*, in which in which the protagonist becomes the individual embodiment of our morally empowered position as spectators.) In its ability to incorporate the viewer into its mechanism, Hitchcock's film metaphorically corresponds to that "perfect . . . really intelligent detonator" to which Conrad's Professor devotes his life.

One gains a better understanding of Hitchcock's relationship to a mass audience at this point in his career when one considers the extent to which he must have conceived of himself as being like that audience. The son of lower middle-class Cockney-Catholics, he came, quite literally, from those crowds "numerous like locusts" that Conrad depicts with fear and contempt in his novel. Physically ungainly and socially inept, he often sought to place himself in the background—to disappear into the anonymity of the crowd (a placement that is ironically transformed into the self-promoting gimmick of the cameo appearances he makes in the background of his films).[19] This sense of kinship and familiarity with crowds accounts for the way he depicted them in his films. They are not represented as incompehensible forces of the kind common to Fritz Lang films, but as conglomerates of ordinary souls—sometimes unruly and misdirected, but generally amusing and capable of being controlled given the proper intervention. Even in *The Lodger* when the crowd almost kills the hero, the people appear more benighted—spurred on by misinformation from the police—than terrifying. At the end of *Sabotage,* Hitchcock has his hero and heroine disappear into the crowd, testifying to their affinity with ordinary people and their eagerness to return to an anonymous existence. Something of the same sense of shared humanity characterizes the great Victorian novels. At the end of Dickens' *Little Dorrit,* for example, the hero and heroine are described as going "quietly down into the roaring streets" to meet their future together.[20] However, Dickens and other Victorian novelists had insisted upon the uniqueness of each of their most ordinary characters, setting the stage for the comprehensive unmasking of individual motives that would characterize later novels like Conrad's. Hitchcock, one might say, was trying to effect a return from a new place—to reproduce those universal values that psychological novels had picked apart, and to reweave those values with images rather than words. The indulgences associated with the Conrad novel—indulgences in stylistic innovation and cynical perception—had to be leashed if the filmmaker was to reach and shape a mass audience.

Despite Hitchcock's attempt to make Conrad's novel serve his cinematic ends, *Sabotage* was not a box-office success. Audiences were apparently put off by the treatment of Stevie's death. As I have already noted, Hitchcock worked many changes on this event as it was originally written. In the novel, Stevie's naive idealism has been enlisted by his brother-in-law, and he carries the bomb knowingly in what he thinks is a noble cause. In the film, Stevie is ignorant of any plot; he is simply a convenient errand boy, and he carries the bomb in a package without knowledge of its contents. In the book, the explosion occurs in an isolated suburb, demonstrating its peripheral importance to the public at large and bringing into relief the total isolation of the boy's sister. In the movie, the death occurs in a crowded urban bus and has important public effects: it links the heroine to a larger community of sufferers, just as the film connects our response to a communal response. But perhaps the most important difference between the book and the film is that in the book the event is mediated. We learn of the boy's death from a newspaper account read by a series of characters: the Professor, the police investigator, and, finally, Winnie Verloc. In the film, the event is unmediated. We watch as the boy, seated in the crowded bus holding the package containing the bomb, amuses himself with a little dog on the next seat. The next moment, we hear the explosion. While Conrad wants us to find power in the boy's death as it affects his sister and produces a series of publicly invisible ripples in the legal and political system, Hitchcock is intent on producing an emotional effect—on making us feel the horror of the death and see its dramatic physical result in the charred rubble in the middle of London.

The scene is an important harbinger of later Hitchcockian effects. It corresponds to what the filmmaker was beginning to evolve into his "rules of suspense": we know something that the character inside the scene does not. (This is the key to the emotional effectiveness of the episode in *Notorious* in which we know that Alicia is being poisoned but Devlin thinks she is simply drunk.) The scene in *Sabotage* is also an elaborate symbolic set piece of the kind Hitchcock employed throughout his career to code for a moral narrative—in this case, humor and pathos are exploited to dramatize the idea of innocence betrayed (in *North by Northwest,* to take another example, the chase on Mount Rushmore dramatizes the puny but heroic efforts of individuals to stand up against institutional pressures). The scene leading to Stevie's death is also an early example of Hitchcock's technical aptitude for using episodic subject matter to build a mood of increasing tension. The final shots on the bus that crosscut between the boy playing with the dog and the clock faces that are being passed as the hour of the explosion draws near anticipate the adept use of crosscutting in *Strangers on a Train,* when Guy rushes through his tennis match while Bruno struggles to reach the incriminating cigarette lighter that has fallen through a sewer grate.

In all these respects, the scene is highly cinematic, and yet it is not cinematic in the more comprehensive, conceptual sense in which Hitchcock used the term. For the whole thrust of the film has been to prove that control *can* be effected—that virtuous characters and moral plots are possible—and that, unlike the disgruntled audience at the beginning of the film, we have no reason to demand our money back. The boy's death reverses these expectations, puts a new spin on things, and creates a wave of disorder that cannot be checked. Despite the differences in detail and in focus, the novel episode and the film scene resemble each other in stressing the quasi-accidental nature of the explosion and hence the gratuitousness of the boy's death. For the death serves no purpose, not even the ends of the villain. In the film, Verloc is shown to give the package to the boy out of desperation. He needs to get rid of the bomb, and police surveillance makes it impossible for him to transport it himself. He carefully instructs Stevie on the need to deliver the package to the cloakroom in Picadilly Circus by 1:30. It should be noted that the decision to plant the bomb in crowded Picadilly Station already compromises the movie protagonist more than the novel protagonist, who has chosen a remote observatory as his target. Even so, in a film where situations have been defined in more clear-cut ways, Verloc's ambiguous relationship to the boy's death strikes a jarring note. And this is precisely where Hitchcock centers his analysis of what he should have done: "The way to handle it would have been for Homolka to kill the boy deliberately, but without showing that on the screen, and then for the wife to avenge her young brother by killing Homolka."[21] Thus he traces the problem back to one of characterization: Verloc (Homolka) has not been adequately defined as a villain, and hence the need for the boy's death must be ascribed, not to an evil human agent, but to an accident. It then becomes all the more necessary to render the heroine's murder of her husband as ambiguous. What we have is a chain of adjustments that would not have been necessary had the script been "properly" (i.e., cinematically) conceived.

That said, however, it is precisely those elements in the film that jar with its overall conception and point back to the complexity of a literary tradition that can be said to operate as determining factors in Hitchcock's future development. The control through which he set about defining the cinematic in counterpoint to the literary would ultimately be loosened, allowing some of the contradictory and overdetermined effects associated with a literary tradition to find cinematic expression. Although this change in Hitchcock's relationship to the medium is explored more fully in subsequent chapters, I should like to discuss briefly how problem elements from *Sabotage* were incorporated more successfully in his later films.

Let me begin with the lack of calculation in the villain's actions, what Hitchcock retrospectively saw to be a problem: "The way to handle it would have been for Homolka to kill the boy deliberately." This criticism recognizes that by representing the boy's death as partially accidental, Verloc cannot be unequivocally condemned. For the film to work in the cinematic terms it has delineated for itself, Verloc must be reduced to a simple villain or acquitted entirely. Such a simplification would not have precluded a concentration on hidden, emotionally fraught aspects of the character, but it would have made these serve an overarching moral and thematic purpose. It should be noted that Hitchcock's films had already featured psychologically resonant characters. Robin Wood rightly refers to an Expressionist tendency in his earliest films—the result of the influence of Fritz Lang and other early German filmmakers.[22] In *The Lodger,* the1926 silent film about a mysterious man (Ivor Novello) who comes under suspicion as a serial killer, Hitchcock focuses intensively on the brooding, enigmatic face and figure of the protagonist and on strange details of his behavior, the cause of which we do not learn until the end. Likewise, *Blackmail,* Hitchcock's first sound film, made in 1929, and *Murder!,* made a year later, both use innovative effects to render psychological turmoil. In *Blackmail,* the protagonist, Alice (Anny Ondra), kills a man who tries to rape her and is haunted by visual and aural reminders of the crime. In *Murder!,* a famous actor, Sir John Menier (Herbert Marshall), finds himself guilt-ridden after sitting on a jury that has condemned to death a woman whom he really believes to be innocent; to relay his guilt, Hitchcock has Sir John engage in a dialogue with himself in front of his shaving mirror. What distinguishes the representation of these characters from that of Verloc in *Sabotage* is that their ambivalence seems a function of their situations. They are conventional people who have been acutely traumatized by external events, and their actions can be explained and their psyches appeased to produce a sense of eventual closure and conformity. In *The Lodger,* the protagonist's strange behavior is resolved when we learn that the real murderer had killed his sister and that he is seeking revenge. In *Blackmail,* Alice ceases to be the focus of interest once her policeman boyfriend discovers a way to shield her. In *Murder!,* Sir John's guilt disappears when he manages to catch the real murderer and not only clear the woman he had helped to indict but assist her in her acting career. These films are technically innovative in their rendering of emotional turmoil, but they are conventional in their concept of character. *Sabotage,* by contrast, represents a character who seems independent of external events. As Verloc sits at the dinner table waiting to be served following Stevie's death, it is not villainy that he projects but emotional egotism—a psychological malady that reflects no simple cause and carries no simple cure. He is out of joint with the rest of the film and with the cinematic characterizations of the period.

During his Hollywood period, Hitchcock mobilized cinematic effects and thematic motifs to represent character as a condition of being and not just as a response to experience. He effected this by assigning the role of subjectivity to the woman. As a result, the balance between plot and character in his films shifted and so did the relative priority of the male and female role. His relationship to his audience also underwent revision. The earlier conception of character corresponds to a view of the audience as clay to be emotionally and morally shaped; the later, to a more intimate and reciprocal view of the audience (a topic discussed in chapter 4).

With regard to the second element of *Sabatoge* that Hitchcock criticizes himself for—that it was a mistake to show the boy's death on screen—we can chart a more extended evolution in the development of his films whereby this kind of scene eventually becomes possible, that is, gets effectively integrated into the whole and becomes acceptable to a mass audience. The scene of Stevie's death dramatically demonstrates how the engine of plot—in this case the anarchist plot of Verloc—can impinge upon and destroy innocent lives. The general rule of Hitchcock's British films is that exploitation and meanness can hold only temporary sway. For example, the jury's faulty verdict in *Murder!* and the indifference of the passengers in *The Lady Vanishes* are eventually corrected and avenged. A more complicated example of how an exploitative event can be cancelled occurs in *Secret Agent,* the film Hitchcock made directly before *Sabotage.* The hero Ashenden (John Gielgud) is recruited as a British agent and sent to Switzerland to track down a German spy and kill him. He is given as contact and assistant an unsavory little character nicknamed the General (Peter Lorre). At the Swiss resort where the two men are staying, they think they find their man: an Englishman married to a German. They convince him to accompany them on a mountain-climbing expedition, and in the course of their climb, the General maneuvers their suspect to the edge of a cliff and pushes him off (Ashenden, upset by the prospect of the murder, stays behind in the ski lodge and watches through a telescope). While the murder is transpiring, Hitchcock introduces a parallel action scene. The suspect's wife is shown sitting at home as their little dog begins scratching furiously at the door of the room. The scratching escalates in intensity until, suddenly, the dog stops scratching and gives out a plaintive howl, meant to coincide with the moment of his master's death. In a subsequent scene, we discover that the spy is still at large and that the murdered man was innocent. The scene has many points in common with the boy's death in *Sabotage,* and yet it does not arouse the same kind of negative audience reaction. For one thing, when the murder takes place, the audience believes, as the hero does, that the victim is the spy. Hitchcock has not yet perfected his rules of suspense by which he would have let us know that the man was innocent in advance of the murder. For another thing, the victim is not a boy but a grown man and, hence, less prone to evoke a sentimental response (although the scene with the dog certainly adds pathos).[23] In moving from *Secret Agent* to *Sabotage,* Hitchcock pushed further his rendering of the fatal implications of narrative action on innocent lives, pushed so far, in fact, that he overreached what the film and its audience could support. In the 1940s and 1950s, when the cinematic representation of psychological character became Hitchcock's central concern, death became a means of illuminating character—or character "lack," as I suggest in chapter 5 on *Rope*—and not just the character of the killer, but the character of the bystander as well. Miriam's death in *Strangers on a Train* not only helps us to know Bruno, her killer, but also Guy, the man falsely accused, and even more obliquely, Barbara, who just happens to comprehend what has happened (see my discussion in chapter 4). Although something of this tendency to use murder to illuminate character still operates in *Psycho,* that film represents a departure in that it also forces an awareness of the gratuitousness of death that had been relegated to the background since *Sabotage.*

The death of Marian Crane (Janet Leigh) in *Psycho* is a highly gratuitous act, occurring, against all expectation, in the middle of the film after we have been allowed to develop some degree of sympathy for the victim. Unlike *Sabotage,* however, where the boy's death seems a scene out of joint with the spirit of the rest of the picture, Marion's death is clearly structured into the film with great deliberation. The shower scene in which she is stabbed combines horror with a certain aesthetic formality: we are emotionally involved but we are also distanced; the death is horrible but fascinating; we are upset but not outraged. Some feminist critics may differ with me here, but I am speaking of the emotional reaction of audiences to the film at the time it was shown. (To be sure, some contemporary viewers condemned the film, but such reactions served more to heighten than to diminish its popular appeal.)[24] Audiences were not outraged by Marion's death as they were by the boy's death in *Sabotage* because the film was able to stem that outrage and yet still achieve a powerful effect. I attribute this to three things. First is a matter simply of changing social codes and expectations. The 1960 audience was more inured to violence than the 1936 audience and hence more willing to accept a scene involving violent death. Second is the fact that Marion Crane's death fits within the film's overall design (see chap. 8 for further discussion of *Psycho*'s design). The scene serves both as an example of a fractured landscape (present from the opening tracking shot, which seems to zero in arbitrarily on the hotel room window where Marion and her lover are engaged in an illicit tryst) and as a dramatic metaphor for that landscape, in which people and things are no longer bound in any natural or necessary relationship to each other. Even the filming of the death supports this disjunction as the camera cuts from knife to body part without ever connecting the two.

The third reason I believe the death of Marion Crane was accepted by audiences where the death of the boy was not hinges on the fact that the death of a woman appears less gratuitous than the death of a boy, however gratuitous either death may be. Let me fill in the logic of this statement. Marion's death has been anticipated in the sense that she is an adult—a fact emphasized by her hotel tryst and brought home to the audience even before they enter the theater through publicity posters that featured Janet Leigh in a provocative state of partial undress. As her affair and then her theft of money dramatize, she is "fallen": as an adult on her own in the world, she dirties her hands by engaging in moral compromise and petty criminality. However, the guilt associated with the character is also as superficial and limited as guilt could possibly be. Indeed, despite the mores of 1960, I would argue that the character is rendered more innocent in "giving herself" to Sam before marriage and in committing the naive theft than if she had not done these things. It is as though Hitchcock were trying to push the representation into something as childlike as possible without crossing that line and making Marion either a literal child or a brain-damaged adult. Thus, far from arguing that as a woman her death is more acceptable than that of a man, I am arguing that her femininity in the context of this film adds to rather than subtracts from the pathos of the scene. A woman's death has more pathos, even for a 1960 audience, than that of a man (consider the death of the Englishman in *Secret Agent,* which was already acceptable to audiences in 1936), while it still conforms to some notion of justice insofar as we can ascribe some kind of existential guilt to the adult woman which we cannot to the child. This is, of course, an ironic twist on the double standard in the culture: women's deaths appear more touching than men's and hence more desirable for representation. Nor is it my intention to deny that the prevalence of female corpses in Hitchcock's films reflects an element of sexual aggression present in the filmmaker and in the audience to which his films appealed. Rather, it is to argue that in conjunction with this aggression, and no doubt helping to spur it, is the fact that the female body is more vulnerable in the culture and hence more likely to produce an effect, to make viewers *feel*. In short, the female victim in most Hitchcock films represents that balance between vulnerability and responsibility that does not exist either in the male victim, whom we are conditioned to think of as fully responsible (certainly a destructive illusion in its own right), or the child, whom we know to be wholly vulnerable, that is, not responsible at all.

It is in the context of such a critique that *Frenzy,* one of Hitchcock's last films, can be read as an important departure. The most noteworthy murder victim in *Frenzy* is the liberated woman Brenda Blaney (Barbara Leigh-Hunt), the protagonist's ex-wife, whose gruesome rape and strangulation Hitchcock shows directly on screen without artful camera work or lighting. The character's professionalism and competence have taken her out of that realm of the vulnerable feminine that we associated with Marion Crane. The scene is hard to watch, not because it seems to be taking glee in what it represents but because what it represents is so real, so unaestheticized and unsentimentalized; "among the most disturbing scenes cinemas has to offer."[25] *Frenzy* grapples with changing sex roles and stereotypes while also struggling to bring plotted action into life in the most unmediated way possible. The strangulation scene resembles the scene on the bus in *Sabotage*, only now the film's entire fabric supports the gratuitousness of the death, giving it a context in which it seems not just jarring and unsettling, the destiny of the vulnerable and the weak, but true and inescapable, part of a larger pattern of deaths that will include our own.

Sabotage, then, introduced an event (Stevie's death) that did not conform to its audience's expectations about what kind of things could happen in film, just as it introduced a character (Verloc) who did not conform to its audience's expectations about how people should be in suspense films. Hitchcock helped to create these expectations through his previous films and through the way in which this film had otherwise controlled its meaning. His two subsequent British films, *Young and Innocent* and *The Lady Vanishes,* remedied the problem by returning to more conventional action plots and flat characterizations. However, once he arrived in Hollywood, Hitchcock expanded his concept of the cinematic to better accommodate those elements that had been so jarring to audiences in *Sabotage.*

3 Psychoanalysis versus Surrealism: *Spellbound*

By the late 1930s Hitchcock had reached a career pinnacle in England and, like so many European filmmakers of the period, looked to Hollywood for new opportunities. Yet, despite initial interest from a number of studios, only David O. Selznick seemed to have an idea of how to use Britain's most acclaimed director.

Selznick wanted to wed those elements of action, suspense, and humor that had made Hitchcock's films appealing to a male audience to his own gift for "women's pictures." *Rebecca,* the film Selznick eventually assigned to Hitchcock for his Hollywood debut, had this kind of potential. Based on the best-selling gothic novel by Daphne du Maurier and featuring a neurasthenic Cinderella character at its center, the movie had a guaranteed audience among women. At the same time, it had a solid suspense plot and the potential for capitalizing on a strong male lead. The addition of the Hitchcock name would solidify the mix: the film would be marketable to men as well as women.[1]

Rebecca is the story of a genteel but penniless young girl (Joan Fontaine) who finds herself courted by a handsome widower, the wealthy and eligible Max de Winter (Laurence Olivier). To the surprise of his friends, de Winter marries the girl and brings her back to his family estate of Manderley. There, she finds constant reminders of his deceased wife, Rebecca, and is wracked by insecurity when she measures herself against what she believes Rebecca to have been. This insecurity is fed by the family housekeeper, Mrs. Danvers (Judith Anderson), a woman fanatically devoted to her former mistress. Only when Rebecca's drowned body is discovered and an investigation into the manner of her death is begun does the young Mrs. de Winter discover the truth—that her husband hated his first wife and wanted her dead. In the final scene of the film, Mrs. Danvers sets fire to Manderley and allows herself, along with the house, to be consumed by flames.

In assigning *Rebecca* to Hitchcock, Selznick made a point of insisting that the director remain faithful to the du Maurier novel—a requirement that rankled. Hitchcock had adapted a du Maurier work before (*Jamaica Inn*) and would again (*The Birds*), but in these cases he had diverged freely from the literary source. (*The Birds* is such a radical departure from the original story that one wonders if he was avenging himself on du Maurier for the experience with *Rebecca.*) On the subject of *Rebecca,* Hitchcock later declared to Truffaut: "[Selznick] had a theory that people who had read the novel would have been very upset if it had been changed on the screen, and he felt this dictum should also apply to *Rebecca.*" Explaining why fidelity to the novel was antithetical to his style, he continued: "It's not a Hitchcock picture; it's a novelette, really. The story is old-fashioned; there was a whole school of feminine literature at that period, and though I'm not against it, the fact is that the story is lacking in humor."[2] If Hitchcock was trying to use the medium of film in the male-oriented way that its ideological positioning in the culture seemed to support, then *Rebecca,* as Selznick conceived it, was a regression, a slavish adaptation of a gothic novel. Such novels were seen as the most egregious examples of a literary tradition dominated by a feminine sensibility and point of view.[3] It is noteworthy, in this context, that some feminist critics have singled out *Rebecca* as a film rare in Hitchcock's canon for its exploration of female desire.[4] I would argue that insofar as such an exploration can be said to exist in the film, it must be attributed primarily to the du Maurier novel on which the film was based. As already noted, Selznick hired Hitchcock to provide a masculine infusion to an otherwise feminine vehicle.

That said, however, *Rebecca* remains an interesting film, both in its parts and in its admittedly non-Hitchcockian whole. Despite the Selznick mandate to follow the novel, Hitchcock managed to make many of the individual scenes conform to his cinematic method. For example, there is the memorable shot of Mrs. Van Hoffer (the dowager for whom the protagonist serves as paid companion before she meets Max de Winter) stabbing out her cigarette in a jar of cold cream—a gesture that speaks volumes about the woman's background and character. Or the scene in which the new Mrs. de Winter arrives for the first time at Manderley and meets with her household staff arrayed like an army battalion before her, ostensibly to do her service but psychologically to intimidate her. Some of the film's most effective scenes are silent long shots showing the heroine as a slight, hunched figure, scampering through the massively decorated rooms. Others show her in extreme close-up, bringing us into painful proximity with her furtive eyes and trembling lips.[5]

But *Rebecca* had a greater importance for Hitchcock than as an exercise in such effects. Selznick's requirement that he remain faithful to the novel provided the filmmaker with a graphic lesson in what aspects of literary character could be represented on screen and what aspects, as yet, could not.

A good example of this distinction is reflected in the characterizations of Mrs. Danvers and Max de Winter. In developing the portrayal of Mrs. Danvers, Hitchcock could easily adopt a cinematic approach. The character had been conceived by du Maurier as a kind of priestess to Manderley as it embodied the soul of its former mistress. The "things" of the house could thus serve as physical manifestations of the bond between the two women and as weapons for the destruction of any presumed usurper. This is most dramatically expressed in the film's scene between Mrs. Danvers and the new Mrs. de Winter in Rebecca's bedroom. Rebecca's mirror, brush, and nightgown are each ritualistically displayed and handled. In the process, they become so charged with meaning that they intimidate the heroine into contemplating suicide.

In the case of Max de Winter's character, however, "things" cannot be made to serve character so easily. Indeed, de Winter's true feelings about the things around him are obscured in order to assure the shock value of the climactic scene revealing his hatred for Rebecca. The novel preserved this indeterminacy by filtering the character through the frightened, adoring viewpoint of his wife, but the film could not remain so deeply submerged in a single point of view. (Even *Rear Window,* Hitchcock's most sustained use of point of view, is hardly so complete or intense.) As the story unfolds, we see de Winter in his house, moving among familiar possessions. We watch what appear to us to be events on the level of what narratologists term *histoire*—objective reality, unmediated by some inflected other perception. When the dramatic revelation scene finally occurs, the film lacks the ability to redeem the image of the coldly unsympathetic and capricious man whom we have seen operate up until this point. A similar problem occurs ten years later in *Stage Fright,* when Hitchcock presents a flashback from the point of view of a character who turns out to be the villain. The flashback is a lie and, as Hitchcock later acknowledged to Truffaut, a mistake: audiences felt cheated when their confidence in the reality of the scene was shattered at the end of the film. Something of the same feeling of being cheated occurs when we learn the truth about de Winter at the end of *Rebecca.*[6]

Rebecca resembles *Suspicion,* produced and released a year later, which also attempts a novelistic rendering of character. *Suspicion* suffers from a similar determination to establish, against the grain of the visual image, the innocence of the male protagonist.[7] More interesting than *Rebecca* or *Suspicion*, however, is *Spellbound,* Hitchcock's next film for Selznick (in between he made six films, including *Suspicion,* for other studios). *Spellbound* is thematically, technically, and administratively a response to *Rebecca,* which is to say, it is both a rebuttal of that film and an addendum to it—its elaboration into a form more compatible with Hitchcock's temperament and style. It is also a film that can be said to act out many of the tensions that confronted Hitchcock in coming to America, working for Selznick, and attempting to broaden and revise the subject matter and appeal of his films.

Rebecca was made when Selznick was at the height of his authority and creative power, his decrees shaping all facets of the production. Five years later, when *Spellbound* was undertaken, he was beset by personal and financial difficulties. His control of the later project was therefore less absolute and his interventions more sporadic. The result is a far more uneven film than *Rebecca,* but one that shows the seams of collaboration more clearly, offering insight into how Selznick's style was both evaded by and assimilated into Hitchcock's own. More important for my thesis, this film (along with *Shadow of a Doubt*) marks the beginning of Hitchcock's unencumbered drive to reclaim for cinematic use a novelistic concept of character.

Spellbound's convoluted plot involves an amnesia victim (Gregory Peck)—his name, we later learn, is John Ballantine—who arrives at the mental institution of Green Manors pretending to be the institution's newly appointed head, Dr. Edwards. Upon his arrival, John meets Dr. Constance Peterson (Ingrid Bergman), a staff psychiatrist, and they fall in love on sight. When the police begin to suspect that the real Edwards has been murdered, John, whose amnesia has been triggered by a latent "guilt complex" (the by-product of a childhood accident involving the death of his brother), becomes convinced that he is the murderer. Constance is certain that he is innocent. She hides him at the home of her old psychiatry professor, Dr. Brulov (Michael Chekhov), whom she persuades to help cure him. By decipering one of his dreams, the two psychiatrists are able to identify the ski resort where Dr. Edwards died. Constance takes John to visit the resort and tries to piece together the childhood events that brought on his guilt complex and that now obscure his memory of what happened with Edwards. The experiment is a success; John remembers the accidental death of his brother, his guilt disappears, and his amnesia is lifted. However, the death of Edwards remains unexplained until Constance, returning to her notes on John's dream, deduces that the killer was Dr. Murchison (Leo G. Carroll), the head of Green Manors who was about to be replaced by Edwards. When confronted, Murchison threatens to shoot Constance but ultimately turns the gun on himself.

Leonard Leff has referred to the interaction of Selznick and Hitchcock in the making of *Spellbound* as "a game of cat and mouse."[8] The analogy is an apt one, drawing attention to the maneuvers and countermaneuvers that characterized the two men's work on the film.

The idea for a film about psychoanalysis had originated with Selznick, who had been in analysis for several years. To make a film on the subject was to establish his intellectual credentials and, since the field was a favorite target for ridicule and vulgarization within popular circles at the time, to do some corrective public relations in the process. Hitchcock, for his part, would probably not have been drawn to this theme on his own. Given his ribald and skeptical temperament, his highly guarded (a psychoanalyst would say "repressed") attitude toward personal and emotional revelation, and his preference for action plots and the "gags and bits" that attend them, one imagines that his initial response to the psychoanalytic idea would have been some combination of disdain and embarassment (with perhaps the added observation that the whole thing lacked humor). However, given the cue from Selznick that such a subject be pursued, he immediately went about acquiring a potential story, presumably as a means of assuring himself some control over the project at an early stage. The property in question was *The House of Dr. Edwards,* a lurid popular novel set in an insane asylum and "filled with diabolical maniacs running loose," in the words of one of Selznick's readers in a memo to his boss.[9] It was hardly the kind of story that Selznick, whose tastes ran to the earnest and sentimental, would likely have chosen on his own. But Hitchcock moved quickly, and Selznick was too preoccupied elsewhere to interfere as strenuously as he might have done in the past. After acquiring the rights to the novel, Hitchock hired a writer, and together they drafted an initial treatment that established the basic structure of the eventual film. At this point, Selznick did intervene. He assigned Ben Hecht, already a prominent screenwriter, to develop the script, and named his own psychoanalyst, Mary Romm, as a consultant. Both made valuable contributions. Hecht worked on the dialogue (inserting some topical banter dealing with the public's prejudices about psychoanalysis). He also fleshed out the love story that would ultimately lift the film above its outlandish premise. Romm tightened the psychoanalytic theme and softened some of the cruder Freudian allusions.[10]

During the period of actual production, Hitchcock managed to assert far more autonomy than he had on *Rebecca.* Ingrid Bergman recalled how he shut down the cameras and pretended that a technical malfunction had occurred whenever Selznick visited the set. To minimize postproduction meddling, he refined his famous technique of "cutting in the camera" (what Selznick would refer to as his "goddamn jigsaw cutting"[11]). Nonetheless,

Selznick managed to exert influence during postproduction, eliminating an opening montage depicting life in the mental institution and radically cutting the Dali dream sequence (see my discussion of the final version of the sequence later in this chapter).

Although *Spellbound* is far from an unmitigated success, without Selznick it could have been far worse. Indeed, it seems clear that Selznick made valuable contributions not only to *Rebecca* and *Spellbound* but also to Hitchcock's development as a filmmaker. His contribution can be summarized as follows: he steered Hitchcock toward strong "domestic" narratives (the du Maurier novel; the psychoanalytic theme); he alerted Hitchcock to the challenge of novelistic character (by forcing him to be faithful to the novel in the making of *Rebecca*; by assigning Mary Romm and Ben Hecht to the scripting of *Spellbound*); and he encouraged Hitchcock in a more creative use of the female performer (by suggesting more close-ups of Joan Fontaine in *Rebecca*; by the felicitous casting of Ingrid Bergman in *Spellbound*).[12] *Spellbound* can be read as something of an allegory of the painful, but ultimately fruitful, effects of Selznick's influence. John Ballantine's amnesia causes him to impersonate another man, but in the course of the film, the impersonation is abandoned and his true identity achieved, enriched now through his relationship with Constance. In making *Rebecca,* Hitchcock had been forced, under orders from Selznick, to impersonate Daphne du Maurier. In a sense, he had also been required to impersonate Selznick, who was known for his women's pictures and whose name (and even a photograph of the Tara-like Selznick Studio) was prominently displayed in the film's opening credits (Selznick, Hitchcock acidly explained to Truffaut, was indisputably the rightful recipient of the Oscar for *Rebecca*). With *Spellbound,* Hitchcock returned to the Selznick studio after a five-year absence to make a film in his own style that would carry his own signature (unlike *Rebecca, Spellbound* features Hitchcock's name above the title).[13] The amnesia is lifted, leaving behind rewards: a greater interest in psychological character and cues to the way in which such character might be effectively rendered on film.

The creative tension between Hitchcock and Selznick in the making of *Spellbound* can also be analyzed in more abstract terms as the interplay within the film itself of pictorial and narrative values. Selznick complained that "Hitchcock has a tendency to fall in love with individual scenes and bits of business and to distort story line to accommodate these," while Hitchcock saw Selznick as shortchanging the dramatic potential of the image (he told Truffaut that he wanted Dali's collaboration in order to "convey the dreams with great visual sharpness and clarity, sharper than the film itself").[14] Within the film, the narrative element can be equated with the psychoanalytic theme (appropriately initiated by Selznick) and the pictorial element can be equated with the use of surrealist imagery (Hitchcock's idea, as noted above). Both elements play a role in determining the film's structure and overall effect, and they deserve to be looked at in historical context for the ideological baggage they bring with them. Although both psychoanalytic subject matter and surrealist imagery are highly simplified, even bowdlerized, in the film, what seems important is that they are invoked; they refer us to a cultural context in which these ideas had their source.

Psychoanalysis was dubbed the "talking cure" when Freud realized that he could leave off hypnotizing his patients and let them use free-associative talk to produce clues to the source of their symptoms. Talk, as Freud used it, was a therapeutic method by which unconscious information could be brought to the surface and made available for interpretation. In the gaps and patterns produced by talk, the therapist could help the patient piece together a repressed story and, in so doing, effect a cure. In this respect, psychoanalysis has much in common with novel-writing, and it is no coincidence that it appeared as a science at the time when the novel figured most prominently in Western culture. Novels, as they developed as a genre, moved from being vehicles for plot contrivance in the picaresque adventure stories of the seventeenth and eighteenth centuries, to being vehicles for character elaboration in the nineteenth century. In short, this was a shift in the nature of story: from a record of happenings to a revelation about mind and heart. The novelist emerged in this later context as a mediating consciousness—as the therapist, one could say, for the fictional character. In novels—at least in the realist examples of the genre produced during the nineteenth century—when we have access to the internal lives of characters, we see not what would emerge in the early stages of analysis but something digested and coherent, something like the story that, with the help of the therapist, gets imposed on the analysand's talk to create the representation of a coherent self. For example, in *The Mill on the Floss,* George Eliot's 1860 novel about a young girl's growing up under harsh and unsympathetic conditions during the early nineteenth century, we are given everything we need to make a Freudian diagnosis of the young protagonist, Maggie Tulliver. To be crude about it (and psychoanalytic diagnosis is inevitably crude in its drive to reduce complex behavior to a collection of symptoms), Maggie is a masochist involved in an emotionally incestuous relationship with her brother, probably as the result of guilt developed in her earlier relationship with her father. Although the novel puts a moral spin on her actions, making her self-immolation seem heroic, we nonetheless are given a consistent portrait of early influences and, along the way, a pattern of behavior and set of explanations that all cohere to support this diagnosis. Even ostensibly surprising actions now cannot surprise us. When the character decides to leave the lover with whom she has impulsively eloped and return to her brother's house where she will be humiliated and ostracized, we can accept this seemingly irrational act as consistent with Maggie's psychology. As the narrator explains: "Her brother was the human being of whom she had been most afraid, from her childhood upwards—afraid with the fear which springs in us when we love one who is inexorable, unbending, unmodifiable—with a mind that we can never mould ourselves upon, and yet that we cannot endure to alienate from us."[15] The narrative reads like a venerable analyst expounding upon a patient: it understands details of action as conforming to some pattern of meaning embedded in character.

The relationship between psychoanalytic interpretation and literary narrative is asserted in *Spellbound* through the many references to and images of books and writing in the film. Constance and Brulov both wear eyeglasses to reinforce their link to texts; Constance suspects John is an imposter when she compares the signature of Edwards's book to that of John's note to her earlier that day. The relationship between talk and writing is also invoked in the opening frames of the film, which feature a written text projected on the screen. The text asserts that "the analyst seeks only to induce the patient to talk about his hidden problems to open the locked doors of his mind." When John recites his dream to Constance and Brulov, she takes notes which will help her discover the site of John's memory loss. Later reference to these notes will also clear him of a murder charge.

In counterpoint to this literary notion of identity, the film presents another notion of identity that is visual and symbolic and that draws analogically on surrealist ideas. While the credits pass on the screen as the film begins, behind them is projected the image of a tree whose branches are sparsely covered with leaves, blowing in what appears to be a stiff wind. The image of the blasted tree is a surrealist image insofar as it exists outside of any coherent context or set of relationships. It contrasts with the words in the open book (that follow) in being evocative rather than explanatory, spatial rather than temporal.

The surrealist movement which florished briefly in Paris in the 1920s was an attempt to build artistically on the insights produced by psychoanalysis but, at the same time, to break with the drive for rational coherence—for narrative—that psychoanalysis posited as its goal. Where psychoanalysis filtered the incoherent talk of patients through the mediator of the therapist to produce a story that explained the patient, surrealism sought to reproduce the sense of surprise and incoherence that the mind presents before such consolidation.

As an expressive medium, literature was not well suited to the surrealist agenda. This was because the reader, accustomed to viewing written words within the context of a conventional narrative sequence, was always falling into the trap of imposing such a narrative, even when it was not intended. As for the medium of film (despite such surrealist classics as *Blood of a Poet* and *Un Chien Andalou*), it was too costly and dependent on a large market to be a major outlet for surrealist expression. Because film had early on taken what Christian Metz has termed "the narrative road," it also represented an obstacle to surrealism's antinarrative drive. Pictorial art had none of these drawbacks.[16] Painting was a relatively cheap and convenient mode of artistic expression and had the further advantage of not bearing the weight of narrative associations. Surrealist painters took the symbols and images that psychoanalysis had gathered from dreams and free association—material that psychological novels and psychoanalytic case histories had narratized to present a coherent self—and scattered these about their canvases to produce a new kind of landscape. As André Bazin has noted of surrealist imagery: "the logical distinction between what is imaginary and what is real tends to disappear. Every image is to be seen as an object and every object as an image."[17] The surrealists envisaged a unified self nowhere, but the shards of such a self everywhere—an unboundaried vista where the depth and coherence of the psychoanalytic narrative were replaced by surface and surprise, by effects rather than meanings.

A related point of contrast between psychoanalytic literature and surrealist painting involved their attitudes toward the female subject. Psychoanalysis places special emphasis on the woman as unusually sensitive to emotional experience. Many theorists, of course, have noted the sexist premise of this assumption: that the male psychiatrist (Freud being the paternal precursor) uses the female psyche as the ground for interpretation and theory building. Yet because analytic talk presumes a narrative that can be circulated and learned, there is also a sense in which psychoanalysis provides women with the tools for self-analysis. I have already suggested something along the same lines with respect to the way novels operated in nineteenth-century culture. The most innovative novels were written by men, but in schooling women in a complicated subjectivity, they eventually became associated with female power and threatened the patriarchal institutions and values they were designed to support. Women became novelists in great numbers, and they also became psychoanalysts—Freud himself included a number of women in his inner circle. The paradox of women's relationship to psychoanalysis is articulated in *Spellbound* by Constance Peterson's mentor, the Freud-like Dr. Brulov, whose combined indulgence and dismissal of his former student embodies the attitude of the Victorian father toward his daughter (see chap. 4). "Women make the best psychoanalysts till they fall in love," he tells her, "then they make the best patients." When Constance starts talking about her love for John, Brulov tells her to stop talking "baby talk," the opposite of professional analytic talk but precisely what a psychoanalyst wants a patient to talk in order to gain access to the secrets of the unconscious.

The confusion that psychoanalytic narrative introduces in the positioning of the female subject (Is she the subject of analysis or the subject doing the analysis, or both?) disappears in surrealist art. The surrealist movement was entirely dominated by men (though a number of women "circulated" in the group as sexual objects, a practice that occurs, significantly, in *Rope*). When the female figure appears in surrealist paintings it tends to be represented in odd and distorted ways, often in pieces, as an objectified motif of sexuality. This can be attributed in part to the backlash against that feminization associated with Victorian culture discussed in chapter 1. But I would also connect the surrealist objectification and dismantling of the female figure to a drive to diffuse feeling into the world rather than to contain it in a body—that is, to obliterate subjectivity as we know it. Freud, one might argue, had already initiated this process by seeking to lift repression from the patient (stereotypically, a female hysteric) and to diffuse the power of inner drives by talking about them. But he had also sought to recontain that diffusion in the form of an interpretive text, a diagnosis that narratized the internal identity of the patient. Surrealist art took this a step further—or perhaps one could say, refused the final step—letting the "baby talk" escape the harness of narrative. By populating the world with weird psychic symbols, pieces of anatomy, and everyday objects oddly juxtaposed and charged with emotional meaning as they might come to us in dreams, surrealists dissolved the boundaries of the personal into a communal landscape. Part of this process included the purging of the female sensibility, for women were associated with excesses of feeling and with the psychosomatic illnesses that abounded in late nineteenth-century culture. They were also associated with the confinement of domestic space. To eliminate the woman as subject was thus symbolically to liberate the psyche from circumscription in general. It is in this spirit that surrealists engaged in experiments like automatic writing and collaborative art.[18]

In the context of psychoanalytic and surrealist ideas, early entertainment film was a new kind of hybrid that tied together the strands of narrative and pictorial traditions. It associated itself with a world of visual surfaces, and yet it used narrative to tell a story. As Metz put it, there was a "demand" for narrative; the Lumiere brothers' slice-of-life films had failed to attract large audiences once their novelty wore off. Thus, in keeping with the need to juggle realistic image and story, early film concentrated on plot, linking character to narrative only in the most perfunctory way. Hitchcock's British films—in which characters "rid[e] the roller coaster of plot"[19]—are representative in this respect. *Spellbound* is a turning point because it is the first film in which Hitchcock grapples directly with the paradox of how to render interiority in a medium oriented toward surfaces. He takes a storyline that employs psychoanalysis as a theme and seeks to find visual correlatives for the psychoanalytic narrative. This explains his decision to employ Salvador Dali to create a representation of the protagonist's dream.[20]

The Dali sequence reflects both the creative potential of Hitchcock's concept of the cinematic and its limitations. Taken by itself (and this is further helped if we eliminate the narrative overlay), the sequence has great visual power. It opens with the screen covered with human eyes that dissolve into a representation of eyes painted on a set of large curtains which a man is cutting with an enormous pair of scissors (perhaps an allusion to the eyeball cutting scene from the most famous surrealist film, Luis Buñuel's *Un Chien Andalou*). The focus of the scene is a stylized card game, shot in distorted perspective, that codes a large portion of the film's action in a purely cinematic way. It is decoded at the end of the movie to supply the viewer with a succinct explanation of what happened to Dr. Edwards. This stylized set piece anticipates the more naturalistic set pieces in later Hitchcock films, most notably the apartment set of *Rear Window,* discussed in chapter 6.

But the dream sequence fails because, as Leonard Leff puts it, it does not successfully "bridge the schism between the literal and the metaphoric."[21] The blatant artificiality of the imagery brings its metaphoric function into relief but jars with the narrative thrust of the film as a whole and with the narrative that accompanies the sequence in particular. Indeed, if one attends to the verbal and gestural commentary of the characters participating in the scene, one begins to see why the narrative and pictorial aspects were fated to clash in this film.

As the scene begins, Dr. Brulov takes a chair near John (who is sitting on the sofa, his head in his hands), while Constance moves to a chair behind them and prepares to take notes. As John begins to recount his dream and the Dali images appear on the screen, Brulov interrupts to ask questions or offer abbreviated interpretations. Constance remains in the background. Early in his commentary, John describes the appearance in the dream of a scantily dressed woman who enters the club and kisses the men seated at the tables. Brulov refers to the woman as "a kissing bug" and identifies her as Constance. The film, at this point, temporarily breaks with the dream imagery and concentrates entirely on the discussion of the seated "real" characters. John, accepting Brulov's interpretation, apologizes to Constance for casting her as a "kissing bug" (he repeats Brulov's phrase), and she responds with coy amusement, reassuring him that she prefers this role to others in which her patients have cast her. She then resumes taking notes, while he, obviously buoyed by the exchange, returns with apparent relish to his account of the dream. The Dali visuals now return to the screen.

The interactions among the characters that punctuate the surrealist images in this scene seem to constitute a powerful set of controls, countering whatever disruptive or evocative potential the images may be said to carry. The positioning of the characters asserts a hierarchy (Constance's placement in the background taking notes explicitly subordinates her to the men), and the dialogue they engage in works to hierarchize the relationships still further. The aggression and eroticism of the dream imagery is rhetorically canceled (the term "kissing bug" trivializes and infantilizes the image of the kissing woman), and John recoups the conventional male role of aggressor, compromised by the dream imagery, by apologizing to Constance for casting her as a "kissing bug." This is a confusing apology in itself, since Constance does not actually appear in the dream and the figure of the woman is that of her female patient (some of this confusion can be attributed to cuts that Selznick made in the sequence during postproduction). Framed within the conventionalized interactions and dialogue of the characters, the dream sequence now operates less as a key to the particular psyche of this patient than as a key to the way the film itself operates to reduce male psychology to a circumscribed and interpretable set of meanings (to turn a surreal landscape into a text to be interpreted). At the same time, the visual context in which the dream sequence occurs also works to trivialize the woman and relegate her to the background. In analogous fashion, the narrative overlay so eclipses the images of the dream sequence that they are reduced to aesthetic curiosities.

But in another major set piece in the film, the effect of the visuals is more unsettling. This is the flashback to John's childhood that shows us the traumatic event that initiated his guilt complex. The scene, quite as surreal in its way as the Dali sequence but with the advantage of not overtly breaking with the conventions of realistic representation, shows the protagonist as a young boy, his face contorted in anger or hate, pushing his brother down a sloping front stoop to be impaled on a spike at the bottom. Although the scene serves thematically to redirect our attention from problems in the hero's relationship to the heroine in the present, "solving" his psychic difficulty and lifting his amnesia, it succeeds far less than the dream sequence in bringing the images under the control of the conventional narrative. The strangely truncated violent act, divorced from a context either of the boys' relationship to each other or of parental response, can only raise more questions than it answers. Why does the memory of such a scene free the character from a sense of guilt and how can it be said to relate to the character's position in the present? The scene functions both as an evasionary tactic—an attempt to place the meaning of character safely back into a circumscribed childhood past—and as a filmic "return of the repressed," setting into play meanings that the film cannot adequately accommodate.

The blocked childhood trauma of the male protagonist reenacted in memory is supposed to serve as an explanation for the character's recent behavior, but this explanatory function is compromised by the fact that there is no symmetry between the childhood experience and the contemporary one. Or if there is, it is not pursued because knowing more about the childhood incident would tend to work against the drive of the plot to totally exonerate the character. A similar drive has been noted in the stabbing of Verloc by his wife in *Sabotage,* where the ambiguity of the scene is connected to the need to leave the heroine morally uncompromised. I would argue that the effect in *Spellbound* is less successful because the moral ambiguity that the flashback leaves in its wake is less assimilatable to the notion of male character than it is to the notion of female character. The problem, in other words, is less a function of Peck's acting than of the contradiction posed by the script between a highly charged psychological experience, rendered graphically and requiring a complex self to support it, and the need for the kind of simple innocence that the script requires of its protagonist (and of men in general) with respect to the working out of plot. This contradiction can be said to arise out of an ideological need to understand male aggression as simple and accidental rather than as complex and conditioned, and thereby to separate the heroically constructive results of male action from the disturbingly destructive. The problem with both the childhood flashback and the dream sequence connects directly with the problem they are meant to eludicate—that of male character as a locus for subjectivity.

Spellbound is an ambitious film because it tries to produce a male character of emotional and psychological complexity. It fails in this because the idea of male depth is incompatible with the ethos of classical narrative film, which relies on the active hero to propel the plot and engage the active participation of the viewer in its resolution. John Ballantine functions in the film as a mystery to be solved, and attempts at visual evocativeness regarding his character seem to get in the way of the narrative drive to unravel that mystery and to make it fall neatly within the whodunit plot.

John's psychological limitations might have made for a plodding, emotionally uninflected film, but this is not the result. The reason has to do with the character of Constance. Although relegated to the background in the dream sequence, her role cannot be as neatly contained and subordinated as this iconography suggests (and indeed, even in this scene, we watch her more than her placement seems to encourage). The female character offers precisely what the male character lacks—a connection to a novelistic tradition of subjectivity that can infuse static appearance with psychological suggestiveness. (It is worth noting that *Love Letters,* produced in the same year, employs the amnesia theme but casts according to more conventional gender lines: Jennifer Jones plays the mysterious amnesiac and Joseph Cotten occupies the male active role, helping to resolve her identity. The film is maudlin and predictable in the extreme. It serves to highlight the originality of *Spellbound,* which employs conventional gender roles in reverse of their expected usage and brings into relief their function in representation.)

In an essay on early silent films on historical subjects put out by the Vitagraph Company, Roberta E. Pearson and William Uricchio have argued that "Vitagraph's vision of history also included character psychologization, by which we mean . . . access to the characters' interiority through the externalization of their thoughts and emotions." What facilitated this "psychologization," they explain, is the fact that "historical characters carry an explicit and extensive intertextual baggage that already psychologizes them to some extent."[22] My own argument with respect to the female character in *Spellbound* depends upon a similar sense of the link between subjectivity (what Pearson and Uricchio term "psychologization") and the evocation of a narrative tradition (what they call the "intertextuality" of history but which, I would argue, is more novelistic than historical).

For one thing, the decision to have a psychoanalyst fall in love with her patient thematically enacts a psychological idea of character. This theme dramatizes the disjunction between a surface self (the professional doctor) and a submerged self (the unprofessional life of emotion). The disjunction between surface and submerged or "deep" self was, of course, a central premise not only of psychoanalysis but also of nineteenth-century novels that had evolved into narratives of character—explorations of the invisible terrain of subjectivity. Both forms tended to concentrate on women, whose emotional lives were presumably both more intense and more repressed. By making the psychoanalyst a woman, the film thus heightens the sense of a disjunction in the character between surface and depth. Moreover, in the two instances early in the film during which Constance meets with a patient—first, with the seductive, man-hating Mary Carmichael; then, with the oedipal Garmes—she proceeds, following each encounter, to enact aspects of the behavior she has just seen (her attitude toward men and toward authority is an intellectualized replay of her patients' reactions). In psychoanalytic terms, the patients serve to illuminate her countertransference. In cinematic terms, they become facets of her inner self made available to us in the externalized way that, as spectators to a visual/dynamic medium, we can absorb. This is a far more sophisticated use of psychoanalytic ideas, I might add, than anything that appears in the working out of the plot.

Hitchcock employs other conventions to support the idea of Constance as a psychological subject. Based on a conception of female character familiar to us from novels, we know that as soon as her colleague begins teasing her for being cold, the opposite must in fact be true. Later, when she is harassed in the lobby of the hotel and then rescued by the house detective who takes her for a schoolteacher, the scene turns on the same thematic irony. The idea of propriety that the detective connects with the profession of schoolteacher is nothing but a false front; this very proper professional woman has thrown caution and propriety to the winds, pursuing a man to whom she is not married. In another scene, Constance uses her glasses to evade the gaze of the two male detectives waiting to see Dr. Brulov. They are later shown examining a sultry photo of her and drawing the glasses on the face of the picture to confirm their identification. The glasses once again evoke a disjunction between surface and depth. They suggest the idea of the woman both as a creature of subterfuge and as one unsexed by intellectual work. In both views, the glasses announce that another identity exists beneath them.[23]

Some of the credit for the successful rendering of these effects must be said to lie with the aptitude of Ingrid Bergman's face for evoking them. Robin Wood has written that the "essential Bergman thematic . . . might be summed up in a simple formula: the attempt (usually by men) to destroy Ingrid Bergman's smile, and its final, triumphant restoration."[24] I would amend this to say that Bergman tends to be most expressive when no clear emotion is called for. Her smile has the effect of asserting a highly artificial, though thematically necessary, closure on our sense of a persona that might otherwise lose its anchorage in plot. At one point in the film, for example, Constance is shown with John admiring the landscape. She exclaims, "Isn't this beautiful?" while he gazes down on her and agrees: "Perfect." Selznick later criticized the scene, arguing that to have the characters admire a landscape without showing it was to frustrate and irritate the audience.[25] But the effect seems to be dependent on the absence of a "real" landscape. The scene enacts the point of view of the male spectator for whom the landscape is entirely eclipsed by the female face. Or rather, it is the female who incorporates the landscape into her sensibility so that the male viewer (both inside and outside the film) can now appreciate its beauty by appreciating her. In another such instance in the film, Peck's face is shot moving in toward Bergman's immobilized, illuminated face. Again, he is the admirer, she the radiant envelope for a rich inner life. It should be noted that Hitchcock tried to use Peck's face in evocative close-up as well, but the effect falls flat. Truffaut remarked (commenting presumably on some of these shots) that Peck's performance is "shallow" and that his eyes "lacked expression,"[26] but it seems as inappropriate to fault Peck unduly as it is to praise Bergman unduly. Peck is disappointing in the role because of the difficulty associated with making a male face look full of meaning when its conventional function with respect to the plot is to resolve meaning. The woman's face, on the other hand (and Bergman's is a kind of paradigmatic female face in this regard), receives the camera's gaze without being reduced to a cardboard cutout or a corpse. (Even Janet Leigh's dead eye in *Psycho* carries a residue of this meaning, making for an ironic play on the very effect I am describing.) The female face and body could effectively evoke an idea of subjectivity because women had been the primary subjects of novels and, more narrowly, of Freudian case histories for over a century. Their physical attributes and accessories, when transferred to the screen, were evocative of these literary narratives.

Bergman's evocation of depth in the role of Constance is crucial to the success of *Spellbound.* She convinces us of John's innocence and, more generally (despite a tangled and contrived plot), of the film's worth. At the same time, she is also a potential threat to the film as a vehicle for linear plot development and character revelation. The duality of her role—as both the supporter and the subverter of meaning—is represented with special vividness in one scene early in the film. The scene takes place in the operating room at Green Manors where the patient Garmes is undergoing surgery after a suicide attempt. John, who has come to assist (though why psychiatrists would be performing surgery is not explained), suddenly breaks down as he identifies with the guilt complex of the patient on the table. Before he faints, he pulls off his surgical mask. Murchison, who has been presiding over the operation and will later be revealed as the villain, does the same. Constance, however, remains masked as Hitchcock zooms in for a shot of her wide-open eyes. She is the character for whom the mask cannot be removed, whose depths are infinite and destined always to be at least partially hidden. She stands as the only site of help remaining to John, now revealed to his colleagues as a fraud. But she also stands as the true site of mystery at the center of the scene, usurping the role away from him, whose mystery we are supposed to be concerned with. Throughout the film, she can be said to wear some version of that surgical mask. The focus on her fluid features (swimming eyes, pouting lips, quivering nostrils—and the trace of accent in her voice, a kind of fluid in the domain of sound) produces the impression of something out of focus or not quite there. She emerges both as the ground upon which the male character can regain a solid identity and as that which exceeds such identity and makes it seem only approximate. In the terms of analysis I have engaged in for this book, she is the symbol of a feminized literary tradition first suppressed and now seeking reclamation in a male-oriented visual medium.

In its representation of the male and female subject, *Spellbound* is an experimental work: awkward, overwrought, and just plain silly in places. Yet it is tremendously rich in technical and conceptual possibilities. The film's central weakness—its inability to make the male subject the center of a psychological plot—would be readdressed in later films. After *Spellbound,* Hitchcock's plots increasingly turn upon the ways in which men are tantalized and tortured by a subjective experience associated with women.

The Father-Daughter Plot: *Shadow of a Doubt, Stage Fright, Strangers on a Train*

Critics have long noted contrary and self-contradicting impulses in Hitchcock's films. Lesley Brill explains these impulses in archetypal terms, as the result of the interpellation of mythic motifs. William Rothman sees a drive to both reveal and hide the fact of authorship. Feminist psychoanalytic critics focus on what they see as Hitchcock's ambivalence toward women. What all these approaches share is a basically static understanding of conflict as an oscillation between extremes which seek continually to counter each other.[1] Far from discerning such oscillation, I see a systemic progression in Hitchcock's work. Conflict and contradiction arise not out of a compulsion to repeat but out of a compulsion to make, as he told Truffaut, "a brand-new thing."[2] His use of the thriller genre is thus a scaffold on which conventional elements can be combined in new ways (one might compare this to Shakespeare's manipulation of the sonnet form or Jane Austen's reshuffling of "two or three families in a country setting"). Even in the one case where he uses a plot line a second time, the remake has an altogether different emphasis and raises altogether new issues about character and relationship. (Conceptual differences between the two versions of *The Man Who Knew Too Much* are addressed in chapter 6.)

What, then, is the pattern of Hitchcock's development and why did it follow the pattern it did? I have discussed how a nineteenth-century literary tradition informed his evolving concept of the cinematic. Yet one cannot limit an explanation of Hitchcock's career to formal influences alone. One must take into account the ways that issues arising out of his private life (and the private life of his culture) were brought to bear on his work. In this chapter, I explore the impact on Hitchcock's films of an evolving family dynamic that had its roots in a Victorian family ideal.

Hitchcock was born in London in 1899, a child poised between the Victorian and the modern eras. Queen Victoria died in 1901, and as Virginia Woolf put it, "in or about December 1910, human character changed."[3] Woolf was alluding to the Postimpressionist Exhibition which, she felt, had a cataclysmic effect on culture. She might also have been referring to the advent of film, the first major production of feature films occurring around this period (it was in the winter of 1910, in fact, that D.W. Griffith moved his Biograph Company from New York to California).

Yet despite the changes that accompanied the rise of film, Hitchcock always presented himself as very much in the mold of the bourgeois Victorian. This Victorian demeanor may perhaps be attributed to his lower middle-class Catholic upbringing in which conventional notions about gender roles and social hierarchies, set in place during the nineteenth century, still prevailed. It may also owe something to his ungainly physical appearance—the proprieties of an earlier age serving as a convenient cover for shyness. Ironically, however, the very qualities that attached him to an earlier set of norms and values may also have drawn him to the new medium of film. If the world no longer strictly conformed to a well-defined (Victorian) system of beliefs and if Hitchcock lacked the ability on his own to forge an authoritative presence in his real-life interactions, film provided an alternative arena in which these beliefs and his authority could be asserted.[4]

He began his film career with the Famous Players Lasky Corporation, which had opened a British studio in Islington, a suburb of London. He met his future wife, Alma Reville, in 1921, when she was a script editor and he still a part-time employee at the studio. Only when he had risen to assistant director (a position he achieved through his willingness to learn everything and take over any job when necessary) did he begin his courtship. It was important to him, as it would be to any proper Victorian, to be financially secure and to hold a position superior to that of his future wife. They were married in 1926 after a five-year engagement. Alma seems to have shared many of her husband's characteristics and interests. Self-effacing and industrious, she had been working as a film cutter since the age of sixteen, slowly building expertise and reputation in what came to be known as "continuity" (making sure that the edited film showed consistency and coherence from shot to shot). While she worked within an industry that came to define modernity for the culture, her job was to assure that the films themselves maintained their link to the narrative tradition from which they had sprung.

She went on to perform the work of "continuity" on the domestic front, abandoning her own career to support her husband's. "Our home," she is quoted as saying, "had to be as orderly and tidy as one of Hitch's film sets."[5]

Hitchcock's marriage appears to have solidified his position as a Victorian-style patriarch. This may help account for the way gender roles are represented in most of his early films. The female characters either assist the heroes, as in *The Lodger, Young and Innocent,* and *The 39 Steps* (in *The Lady Vanishes,* the heroine, in a slight variation, must sell the plot to the hero before being able to assist him in solving it), or they provide negative lessons in female self-assertion or desire, as in *Blackmail* and *Secret Agent.* In all these films, the plot eventually carries the male protagonist toward a triumphant conclusion. Pitfalls are mere elaborations toward this end, and even ostensibly freestanding bits of business tend to play a facilitating role. A good example occurs in *The 39 Steps* when Richard Hannay (Robert Donat) finds himself handcuffed to Pamela (Madeleine Carroll). Hitchcock had long entertained an interest in the "problem" of being handcuffed, and the scene gave him the opportunity to indulge his interest as well as exploit the visual humor built into the situation.[6] But *The 39 Steps* also poses a thematic problem that the handcuff bit solves. Pamela is originally represented as hostile to Hannay and has to be converted to his side for the plot to move forward. The handcuff scene thus establishes a comic rapport between the characters so that, once free from the cuffs, the hero can proceed with the heroine's assistance. In other words, the scene operates in the film not to stop or detour the plot, as might at first appear to be the case, but to move it forward and renew our confidence in a successful conclusion engineered by the hero.

An examination of the 1932 release *Rich and Strange* clarifies the way that gender roles assist plot in Hitchcock's early British films. Although the film is uncharacteristic in being a domestic comedy and not a thriller, its direct treatment of the subject of marriage brings into relief the balance of plot and character as it operates in other Hitchcock films during this period. The story revolves around a married couple, Fred and Emily Hill (Henry Kendall and Joan Barry), who temporarily stray from each other but, after a series of misadventures, come to reaffirm their union. Although the film depicts the societal norms which hold women to a higher moral standard than men are held to, it seems to represent this double standard without critiquing it; this is simply the way things are. In keeping with this perspective, Hitchock's use of his female character is relatively simple. Her appeal is piquant rather than mesmerizing, and she supports the plot rather than derailing it in the way later Hitchcock heroines do. The film appears to be a paean to the conventional bourgeois marriage as Hitchcock must have experienced it at the time. He and Alma had been married only six years and had been parents of a daughter, Patricia, for only four (*Rich and Strange* ends, appropriately, with the arrival of a baby).[7]

Seven years later, when Hitchcock began work in America, his family was no longer new. His marriage had settled into a routine and his daughter was approaching adolescence. Patricia turned fourteen when Hitchcock made *Shadow of a Doubt,* the film that initiates a father-daughter theme that figures in many films of the 1940s and early 1950s. She appeared in three of his films, two just prior to her 1952 marriage to an American businessman and one eight years later.

It is not my intention to discuss facets of the father-daughter relationship that were unique to Alfred Hitchcock and Patricia Hitchcock—as no doubt there were many—but rather to point out the generic quality of the relationship, the way in which it traces a trajectory that the family, bred out of a Victorian notion of gender roles, would tend to follow. Because Hitchcock's family evolved while his career as a filmmaker evolved, he was positioned to give cinematic expression to tensions inherent in the conventional life cycle of the nuclear family.

Shadow of a Doubt, his sixth American film, released in 1943, outlines the family dynamic that would be filled in over the course of the decade as his daughter grew into adulthood. In many ways, the film reinforces the conventional view of family life that had been central to *Sabotage*. However, whereas *Sabotage* was concerned with portraying the family as an undifferentiated idea whose betrayal requires swift and certain retribution, *Shadow of a Doubt* concentrates on the dynamic of relationship within the family that both supports and potentially threatens it. Retribution cannot be as simply or as cleanly enacted because the blame is more diffuse. The world, to use the phrase of the detective at the end of the film, "needs a lot of watching"; vigilance rather than justice is required to maintain the family's integrity and security. The call for vigilance recalls Conrad's condemnation of Winnie Verloc, whose rule of life was that "things don't bear too much looking into." Had she thought to question Verloc's occupation and his motives for action, she might have averted the death of her brother. In making *Sabotage,* Hitchcock ignored this cautionary theme in the Conrad novel. If anything, he supported the heroine's apparent unconsciousness of her husband's character and motives in order to simplify her characterization and leave her morally uncompromised. In *Shadow of a Doubt,* he expands his sights to include the question of responsibility in relationship, and he attributes blame not just to the duplicitous partner but to the partner who is duped.

Hitchcock is now supporting a family idea at a different stage in its development, a stage more conducive to psychological considerations. In *Sabotage,* made when Hitchcock's family existed in an ostensibly static form (wife and child were attached to him as clear and willing dependents), the family is an abstract idea to be supported at all costs. In *Shadow of a Doubt,* the family is no longer an abstraction. Its representation seems at least partially the result of Hitchcock's more prolonged experience as a patriarch within a nuclear family and, more to the point, as a father to an adolescent daughter. The film is predicated on the idea that family disruption and betrayal can be assisted by evolving relationships within the family as well as by outside forces, and that internal changes in family interaction are not subject to simple forms of control.

Shadow of a Doubt begins by showing us a man, whom we come to know as Uncle Charlie (Joseph Cotten), stretched out on a bed in a boardinghouse. Outside the window is a seedy cityscape. The next scene is composed of shots that parallel the first ones in structure but contrast them strikingly in tone. A wholesome young woman, Charlotte Newton—"young Charlie" (Teresa Wright), the niece and namesake of the man in the first scene—is stretched on her bed in her family's house on a tree-lined street in the well-tended little town of Santa Rosa, California. She is complaining to her father (Henry Travers), an indulgent figure leaning in the doorway, about a vague malaise. She is critical of the tedium of family life, particularly as this affects her mother, Emma (Patricia Collinge), whom she sees as the martyr to an unrelenting and burdensome routine (she obviously envisages this as her own destiny). Her wish for "a miracle" seems to coincide magically with her Uncle Charlie's decision to pay a visit to his sister Emma in Santa Rosa. We eventually learn, along with young Charlie, that her uncle is a serial killer (he preys on wealthy widows) and that the police have begun to suspect him and keep him under surveillance. He makes several attempts to kill his niece after she confronts him with her knowledge. Finally, in a struggle between them in which he tries to push her off a moving train, she gains the upper hand and pushes him to his death. The film ends with Uncle Charlie's funeral at which the community hails him as a great hero and benefactor. Only young Charlie and her detective-fiancé (MacDonald Carey), watching the proceedings from a distance, know the truth.

The opening scenes of *Shadow of a Doubt* lay out the coordinates of a family plot that plays itself out in subsequent Hitchcock films. The family of childhood has come to seem dull and circumscribed to the adolescent daughter. She wants someone to "save" them—to "shake us all up."[8] As in *Sabotage,* Hitchcock makes the idea of the family unit a central visual motif in the film. A key scene features the usurpation of young Charlie's father, as Uncle Charlie takes his brother-in-law's place at the head of the table. (The deceptively cheerful tone of this scene might be compared with that of the restaurant scene in *Sabotage.* Although the earlier film features a good man in the father-surrogate role, he still functions as a false, or at least a premature, replacement of the real father at this point in the story.) During the dinner, Uncle Charlie singles out young Charlie for special recognition and, later in the kitchen, seals their bond with a ring. The ring-giving scene is perhaps the most unsettling in the film. It is uncomfortable to watch because it makes the relationship between uncle and niece a site of intense emotion without clearly defining it. There is the romantic rhetoric, but there is also the age gap and family connection as well as the confusion produced by the duplication of names. The uncategorizable quality of the relationship is part of its threat, because it suggests that conventional hierarchical and relational cues involving age and sex (cues that suggest a conventional father-daughter relationship) may be disregarded, giving rise to something both freer and more intense. This is suggestive at once of incestuous boundary-crossing and of vampiristic voraciousness (incest and vampire themes figure in the film). The erosion of generational and gender hierarchies, moreover, spells the destruction of the nuclear family, which depends upon such distinctions. The relationship between Uncle Charlie and young Charlie in its disregard of conventional relational boundaries ("We're sort of like twins") thus sets into play that excess of meaning that I have already suggested had evolved within the literary tradition, and that film, as a return to patriarchal control, was designed to suppress. In *Shadow of a Doubt,* Hitchcock is calculatedly offering a glimpse of the disruptive effects of uncontrolled meaning (he had uncalculatedly dramatized those effects in *Sabotage* with his representation of Stevie's death). The film functions as a cautionary tale of how relational distinctions can become blurred and confused within the family if they are not "carefully watched."

The blurring and confusion of roles that begins to occur in the Newton family is stopped when young Charlie discovers that her uncle is a murderer. This is a fact that, like the fact of Verloc's clandestine activity in *Sabotage,* is relayed through the character of a detective destined to be the heroine's husband. (As a professional enforcer of the law, the detective is the "proper" replacement of the father in a conventional family plot.) But the detective is hardly a weighty presence in the film; indeed, he seems even more peripheral than the detective in *Sabotage.* The true locus of authority lies not with him but with the ordering intelligence of the film itself. This is dramatically demonstrated in the scene in which young Charlie has her suspicions confirmed in the town library. Hitchcock shoots young Charlie, after she finds the incriminating evidence about her uncle in the library newspaper, from a high overhead angle that brings home the point of the movie with extraordinary economy and power. The angle and distance of the shot make the library look like a cathedral and Charlie like a puny supplicant. The shot is common in

Hitchcock's repertory to place or sum up a situation.[9] But here it carries special narrative resonance: It casts the filmmaker in the role of the unseen, omniscient spectator—the supreme patriarch—looking down on the daughter, humbled by experience and brought back to the fold. It dramatically conveys to the audience that truth has been found out and the daughter will be saved. In doing this, it also supports the audience's relationship to the plot, for we have suspected Uncle Charlie's guilt all along. In all these respects, it works to reassure us that disorder (madness and murder) can be kept at bay and the family idyll maintained intact as long as "things are carefully watched."

Yet this reassurance is not without its paradoxical implications. The bird's-eye view of young Charlie, while it serves to register an awakening to truth, does so at the expense of the heroine's imagination and desire. It places her in a simple, uninflected position of antagonism to the complex man she has loved. Insofar as our imagination and desire have also been activated—if, for example, we had hoped to see Uncle Charlie vindicated or young Charlie escape life in Santa Rosa—we now must give up on such possibilities and succumb to the inexorable course of the plot. We too have been put in our place.

The paradoxical effect of the overhead shot is to combine the protective gaze with the controlling gaze and to suggest that both spring from the paternal role within the nuclear family. In putting the orderly childhood family back in place, the filmmaker thus becomes like Uncle Charlie, who had expressed nostalgia for the innocent time of his childhood ("It was a wonderful world. Everybody was sweet and pretty then."), but who became the agent of the family's disruption. For while the act of control with respect to a child may be an expression of love, the act of control with respect to a grown woman is an expression of tyranny. And when the woman happens to be one's own child, the question of what it means to be a good father becomes fraught with contradiction. The strong, protective father can become a monster when viewed with the knowledge and perspective of adulthood (the theme literalized at the beginning of *Notorious* and in *Foreign Correspondent,* in which the good father of childhood is unmasked to the adult woman as a Nazi). By the same token, the loving, indulgent father who provides the daughter with freedom may be transformed into the controlling father once the daughter exercises that freedom independent of him. This is precisely the duality present in Uncle Charlie, who turns from indulging to punishing once his niece attempts to detach herself from him and judge him. Indeed, his crimes consist of punishing women—merry widows—who have managed, in his view, to detach themselves from men and to indulge their own desires.

In making *Shadow of a Doubt,* Hitchcock was initiating an exploration of the father-daughter dynamic that must certainly have been influenced by his relationship to his adolescent daughter. By 1949 (the year *Stage Fright* was produced), Patricia Hitchcock had turned twenty-one and begun training as an actress. She had chosen a career that her father ostensibly scorned (given his view of actors as cattle), but that he also indulged, and that no doubt flattered him as a tribute to his influence. He cast her in two of his films during this period, films in which she brought the tensions of her daughterly role into the literal space of his films. What I term the "daughter's effect" grows out of these tensions as they came to influence his cinematic method. During the 1950s, he also took to perverse extremes his habit of cultivating young female actresses.[10] As I discuss in subsequent chapters, these relationships appear to reflect his effort to assimilate the father-daughter dynamic to the romantic plot.

Stage Fright, released in 1950, culminates the line of father-daughter plots in the 1940s films. Significantly, it is also the first film in which Patricia Hitchcock appears. The heroine, Eve Gill (Jane Wyman), is a young drama student at the Royal Academy (where Pat, in actuality, was then a student). The plot revolves around Eve's attempt to prove that her boyfriend, Jonathan (Richard Todd), is innocent of murder. He has come to her in desperation, explaining how his infatuation with a famous singer, Charlotte Inwood (Marlene Dietrich), has caused him to be suspected of the murder of her husband. Charlotte, he says, actually committed the murder herself and persuaded him to help her cover it up. Eve hides Jonathan and, with the assistance of her father (Alistair Sim), gets herself hired as Charlotte's maid. In the process of scouting her rival, she meets the detective investigating the murder (Michael Wilding), who falls in love with her, unaware of her involvement with the case. The final scenes reveal Jonathan as the murderer after all. He tries to elude the police by holding Eve hostage in the Academy theater. After she manages to trick him and get away, he is crushed by the safety curtain, which the police bring down to block his escape.

In his discussion of the film with Hitchcock, Truffaut noted that Jane Wyman bore a striking resemblance to Patricia Hitchcock. At another point in the interview, Hitchcock professed to be mystified as to why he cast Alistair Sim in the role of the father, although the actor bore an equally striking resemblance to himself. As these casting choices suggest, the film is rich in clues to Hitchcock's relationship to his daughter during this period. Thus, for example, the young detective, smitten with the heroine, causes her irritation when he comments that she doesn't "look like" an actress. The remark carries the double implication that she doesn't have what it takes to act and that acting isn't a vocation for a proper young woman, as Eve appears to be, and as Hitchcock no doubt conceived of his daughter. (This was a conventionally

Victorian attitude toward a career on the stage.) The combined nastiness and protectiveness implicit in the comment reflects exactly the dynamic inherent in the paradigmatic father-daughter relationship outlined earlier in this chapter, a dynamic that would emerge more dramatically in Hitchcock's next film.

Wyman's resemblance to his daughter may have accounted for Hitchcock's negative reaction to her performance, which he criticized not on the score of acting but of appearance: "She couldn't accept the idea of her face being in character, while Dietrich looked so glamorous, so she kept improving her appearance every day and that's how she failed to maintain the character." The complaint came at precisely the point when Truffaut remarked upon Wyman's resemblance to Patricia and his "impression that the whole film was somehow a paternal, a family, picture."[11] (He might also have noted that Alma did the adaptation.) Hitchcock's hasty move to criticize Wyman's concern with her appearance suggests that if she were a stand-in for his daughter, she did not altogether fit the bill. He clearly wanted her to present herself as he wanted to see his daughter, as unglamorous and completely subject to his direction. It seems consistent with his comment here that in each of the three roles that Pat played for him he incorporated details of character and appearance that undermined her vanity. In *Stage Fright,* her weight is made the object of gentle humor (her character's nickname is Chubby). In *Strangers on a Train,* her glasses neutralize her sexuality, emphasizing her mischievous, childish nature. Finally, in *Psycho,* her character is represented as vulgar and catty, harping continually on her marriage and her mother. One can't help wondering whether this last role were conceived as revenge against Pat for marrying.[12]

Stage Fright is most interesting, however, in its use of the father-daughter relationship to establish a distinctive structure and tone for the film. It is not that the relationship is central to the plot; one can imagine the basic action transpiring without it. Yet the father's role is emotionally crucial. He grounds the daughter in a way that makes her loyalty to the villain seem less calamitous, even as he abets her in her misjudgment. Indeed, it is the father's presence behind the scenes, one could say, that gives her the confidence and wherewithal she needs to carry out the ruses that place her in danger, but also that finally solve the enigma of the plot and straighten out her loyalties with respect to the villain.

The characterization of Eve's family in this film is comically eccentric, turning on its head the conventionality of the family in *Shadow of a Doubt.* (That this is supposed to be a British family rather than an American one may account for the greater looseness in familial roles. A similar contrast exists between the families in the two versions of *The Man Who Knew Too Much,* discussed in chapter 6.) Eve's mother and father do not cohabit, yet appear to have a congenial relationship. The mother's only apparent fear is that the father, in staying the night, may expect to share her bed. The daughter is equally at home in the society of both parents, though she has a special kinship with her father (her mother is one in a long line of distracted, silly Hitchcock mothers). Eve's comfortable relationship with her father, her creative consort in the plot, suggests the relationship that Hitchcock had with his daughter up until her marriage. (Patricia was known to frequent the sets of her father's films as early as *The Lady Vanishes*.)

The father-daughter relationship in *Stage Fright* also establishes a tone by which the film is able to negotiate a number of tricky thematic elements. Low-key and affectionately ironic, it contrasts the intensity of Charlotte Inwood and her relationships. Charlotte is a narcissistic, exploitative, disorienting presence: a "woman" to Eve's "girl." She has made Eve's boyfriend into her murderous slave, and she even briefly enthralls Eve's father (in a shot where he is shown watching her performance from the wings). When Eve is dealing with events surrounding Charlotte, she is most compromised and confused, having to feign fainting, engage in bribery, and generally lie about who she is and how she talks and dresses. But neither the father nor the detective allow themselves to fall seriously under Charlotte's spell, the suggestion being that, for these characters, Eve's presence is an antidote. The detective doesn't want to listen to Charlotte sing, as if wary in advance of the kind of power such women exert, and the father concocts a strategem (asking a little boy to carry a doll with a bloodied dress up to Charlotte while she is performing) to disrupt her performance and prove her guilt. Hitchcock's staging of the scenes in which Charlotte sings (drawing quite obviously on Marlene Dietrich's persona as a performer in *The Blue Angel* and *Destry Rides Again*) are interesting in the way they too disrupt the performance through shots from the side of the stage or by assuming the point of view of another character. Unlike the usual Dietrich movie, *Stage Fright* contains no prolonged performance scene in which the action is stopped and the audience's point of view is made equivalent to that of a music-hall spectator. The film continually works against the kind of fetishism that theorists have postulated as one aspect of female representation in classical narrative film, an aspect that has been particularly associated with Dietrich. Tania Modleski has argued that this failure reflects the films antifeminist loyalties, despite the fact that a fetishistic portrayal of Dietrich is generally condemned by feminist critics.[13] According to Modleski, Charlotte Inwood represents female self-sufficiency of a kind that the masculine filmmaker and patriarchy in general find terrifying; Eve, she argues, is the figure of patriarchal complicity—the good little daddy's girl. Admittedly, the film discredits Charlotte in every shot while also emphasizing her serpent-like fascination. But one must also remember that the plot moves from a thorough condemnation of Charlotte to a revision of that verdict. She is not, after all, as guilty as the various parties would have us believe (Modleski reads this as a sign of that ambivalence or countercurrent always at work in Hitchcock that prevents him from ever leaving us with a simple female-annihilating message). Moreover, a representation of Charlotte as a threat to patriarchal culture does not seem persuasive, since she is essentially a caricature of a woman produced by patriarchy—and thus quite self-consciously fetishized. Without denying the subversive potential of this kind of excessive representation (which Dietrich always manages to tap), it becomes difficult, given our fleeting access to the character, to take this subversive potential very far (though Hitchcock appears to acknowledge the parodic aspects of Dietrich in some of her scenes, particularly the exchange about the dog that she engages in with the policeman toward the end).

As for Eve, her role cannot be reduced simply to that of patriarchal supporter and apologist. After all, the scheme to discredit Charlotte originates with her, and she enlists her father in the scheme and not the other way around. Moreover, the outcome, while it indicts Charlotte, still more indicts the man in whom Eve has placed her trust. In the film's most extraordinarily unsettling scene, Eve begs Jonathan to turn himself in, drawing on her greatest resources of sympathy and nurturance, though she has just learned that he is a murderer. Instead of responding, he announces his plan to kill her to establish himself as mad and thereby not have to face the charge that the original murder was premeditated. The scene plays as a warning against female overconfidence in men and as a mockery of the supposed strength of female love to bring a man to see the light. A mixture of paranoia and jealousy might be the motives for such a message from a father to a daughter, but also a desire to offer a warning, based on the father's own experience as a manipulator, not to trust the sentimental messages that men may send her. The scene of Eve's final revelation about Jonathan's character is shot with great care and sensitivity: only her eyes are illuminated, wide with shock. (It is the same expression that Patricia uses when, in her role in *Strangers on a Train,* she suddenly "sees" Bruno's guilt. The shot also recalls Ingrid Bergman's eyes above the surgical mask in *Spellbound.*) But the shift from naïveté to cunning is then represented by an equally striking shot of Eve's hands as they approach the tensed fingers of the killer. She tenderly takes those hands and assures him that they can escape together. Then, when she has eased him out the door onto the stage, she shuts the door between them and cries for help. The rush of feeling that had caused her to harbor a criminal and to trust in his innocence has been transformed into guile. She uses tenderness to trick him and save herself. It is an extraordinarily subtle and sad moment of transition, captured through mostly visual imagery, and it is precisely the kind of transformation that a father must mourn in his daughter but also see as necessary for her survival in a predatory world.

Both Eve's father and the detective who falls in love with her are benign, indulgent figures. The detective seems always to be laughing at her, although it is not clear why, since he is not made aware of her ruse until the end. The father tries, not very hard, to dissuade her from pursuing her scheme but, once she is on her way, fully assists her. Thus it is not that Eve represents patriarchal complicity, as Modleski would have it. Instead, she is the product of patriarchal indulgence, allowed room to operate because of a fatherly willingness to provide the rope—rope by which she almost hangs herself. But what ultimately makes the film an expression of a highly evolved father-daughter relationship is its sense that a generational and gender hierarchy is little more than a formality (making it resemble a less intense version of the mutuality that characterizes young Charlie's early relationship with her uncle). There is no sense that the father really knows best. If one were to compare the film's implicit loyalties to that found in nineteenth-century fiction, say in Jane Austen's *Emma,* in which the heroine's misjudgments are also indulged for most of the novel, the difference seems to lie in the fact that Austen has a patriarchal figure, the righteous Mr. Knightley, standing on the sidelines with all the answers and stepping in and taking over in the end. In this film, the father is indulgent to the point of believing the daughter and following her. He possesses no alternative and seems otherwise without occupation. The ability to effect change thus resides in the daughter, who enlists her father as her accomplice.

What keeps the film from realizing the feminist implications of this message lies in its satirical representation of both the daughter and the father. Because the daughter's influence leads her, for most of the film, in the wrong direction, it cannot be said to carry much weight. As for the father, his essential lack of seriousness makes his faith in his daughter less impressive than it might have been. *Stage Fright* is actually the last in a line of films featuring an indulgent father whose lack of power seems a function of this indulgence. *The Paradine Case, Shadow of a Doubt, Spellbound* (in aspects of the relationship between Constance and her mentor, Dr. Brulov), and *Saboteur* (in the relationship between the heroine and her blind uncle) all feature benign father figures, often represented as foolish, impotent, or disabled. Their indulgent attitude, while it tends to be represented as an expression of their love for their daughters (or daughter-surrogates), is also implicitly critiqued as a form of weakness—not only because it leaves the daughter vulnerable to potentially destructive outside influences but also because it entails a delayed repressive response. It requires that the controlling side of the father (in the form of the filmmaker who enacts a return to order and stability) must repair the damage that paternal indulgence has made possible.

Stage Fright is an idealization of family as a retreat from the anxiety of the workaday world—and a retreat from intense feeling itself. The father-daughter relationship is rendered in an uncomplicated way as a chummy alliance. The whimsy of the relationship is so pronounced, its function with regard to the solution of the plot so haphazard and fumbling, that one suspects the structure is being used here with very calculated superficiality, as a way of avoiding an emotional messiness that it displaces entirely onto the figure of Charlotte Inwood (the foreigner and the professional—the figure for whom family is either an opportunist appendage or an encumbrance to be brushed aside). In this respect, it operates rather like *Shadow of a Doubt,* which also introduces disruption into the domestic scene in order to purge it. This is not the case with *Strangers on a Train.* Made a year after *Stage Fright, Strangers on a Train* is a far more unsettling film that develops more fully the paradoxical implications of the father-daughter dynamic.

Strangers on a Train is the story of Guy Haines (Farley Granger), a tennis champion who hopes to divorce his vulgar and promiscuous wife to marry a senator's daughter. On a train trip to his future fiancée's home, he encounters Bruno Anthony (Robert Walker), who seems to intuit Guy's dilemma. Bruno wants his father dead and suggests that he and Guy exchange crimes: he will kill Guy's wife if Guy will kill his father. Guy listens to Bruno's proposal but dismisses it as a joke. He then hurries off the train at his stop, forgetting his cigarette lighter in his haste. That evening Bruno stalks Guy's wife, Miriam (Laura Elliott), at a local fairground and strangles her. The film traces Guy's mounting desperation as Bruno pressures him to complete his half of their supposed bargain. Finally convinced that Guy will not act, Bruno decides to incriminate him by planting Guy's lighter at the scene of Miriam's murder. The film culminates with a suspenseful parallel action scene that shows Guy rushing through a tennis match as Bruno makes his way toward the fairgrounds. Guy and Bruno are finally brought together in a climactic struggle on an out-of-control carousel. Bruno is thrown off and crushed by the machinery. As he dies, his hand opens to reveal the lighter that clears Guy of all charges.

Some critics have argued that *Strangers on a Train* suffers in not having a stronger, more appealing protagonist in Guy Haines. But the weakness of the character is obviously part of the point of the film. Guy is not a throwback to the flat, action-oriented protagonists of the British perod. Nor is his inadequacy a failure on the part of the scriptwriter or the actor. Guy's weakness reflects something realistically wrong with his character, a flaw which opens him to the kind of manipulation the film records. The problem with the character resembles the problem in *Spellbound,* where I argued for the difficulty inherent in representing the hero in psychologically complex terms. In both cases, the inadequacy of the character seems a function of certain ideological constraints on male subjectivity (this is a point discussed more fully with respect to *Rope* in the next chapter). *Spellbound* filled in for the lack of psychological nuance in its male protagonist with its female protagonist, who, as played by Ingrid Bergman, served as the emotional hinge of the story. Hitchcock later complained about Ruth Roman's performance as the love interest in *Strangers on a Train,* as if the right actress might have done for this film what Bergman did for *Spellbound.* But even with Ingrid Bergman in the role, it is doubtful that the effect would have been different. This film's focus lies elsewhere.

The emotional core of *Strangers on a Train* resides in two scenes which, though physically separated within the film, operate as a unit. The first is the scene in which Bruno stalks Miriam at the fairground and ultimately strangles her. The dramatic tension of this scene comes from its aggressive banality. We are made to watch an act of brutal violence perpetrated against an ordinary, flawed human being. The act is made more appalling because we do not feel anything for Miriam but a sense of her childish tawdriness (the equivalent of the fair's honky-tonk music that plays in the background during the scene). We are thus deprived of the moral satisfaction of feeling for a victim who, we nonetheless know, does not deserve to die.

The second emotionally gripping scene in the film carries a different kind of power, yet it does not elicit a conventional reaction either. This involves the wordless confrontation between Bruno and Barbara, the younger sister of Guy's fiancée—the role played by Pat Hitchcock. Bruno has just crashed a party given by Guy's future father-in-law (Leo G. Carroll), where he quickly ingratiates himself with two older women by launching a titillating discussion of murder. In the course of the exchange, the camera moves closer to the characters and positions itself in a series of shot reverse-shots, alternately behind Bruno's shoulder and between the backs of the two women across from him. The sense is that we are standing in these alternating positions: on Bruno's side as his consort, and opposite him on the side of the women. Eventually, Bruno offers to demonstrate to one of the women how easy it is to strangle someone. With her delighted cooperation, he puts his hands around her neck. At this point, we are shown Barbara entering the frame of the scene, in Bruno's line of vision and behind the two women. As the demonstration proceeds, the camera backs up, now assuming Bruno's point of view entirely and bringing Barbara squarely within his field of vision. His hands are on the woman's neck, but he is gazing straight ahead, transfixed by the image of the standing girl whose glasses recall the glasses Miriam wore when he strangled her the day before at the fairground (Hitchcock had filmed Miriam's murder as an image reflected in the lens of her fallen glasses). The music of the fairground is inserted to denote Bruno's memory of the murder, and the camera moves in for a close-up of Barbara's frozen face, the glasses giving her eyes a dreamlike, doubly distanced appearance. She seems as much transfixed by Bruno as he by her. As the older woman begins to gasp and struggle, the camera now shifts from Barbara to a close-up of Bruno's hands which have tightened around the woman's neck. Finally, he faints, his hands are pried away from the woman's neck, and he is carried out of the room. The crowd now moves away, and Barbara is once again "revealed," still transfixed, but now slightly bent forward.

The emotional exchange between Bruno and Barbara in this scene is a kind of perverse play on the idea of love at first sight. The original fairground scene also parodied romantic convention, as Miriam, attracted to Bruno on sight, coyly leads him on. With Miriam, however, adolescent courtship was being parodied, with the murder made to resemble a malevolent child's play on an established rite (the reflected image of the strangling in the lens of Miriam's glasses flattens and stylizes the effect). With Barbara, the quality of play has disappeared. Indeed, the intensity of the later scene suggests that it is a corrective to the frivolous tone of the earlier scene. It is not just an opportunity to rattle the villain and give Barbara a clue to his guilt; it is also an opportunity to avenge that original murder through an ingenious turning of the tables of who's in control. In this respect, it seems to enact metaphorically the way in which power gets redistributed within the family once the father-daughter dynamic has evolved to a certain point. Barbara's presence within the frame of Bruno's vision produces the impression that he is really trying to strangle her, but her figure is also a figure of recognition and hence of judgment. She terrifies Bruno by her presence (by reminding him of his murder victim, she is like a ghost), but her presence is equated with her gaze. Does he see in her a resemblance to the murdered woman, or does he see in her a recognition of his seeing that resemblance? The two acts, that would logically occur consecutively, are represented, by virtue of the concentration on Barbara's eyes as the point of resemblance, as occurring simultaneously.

A precursor to this scene is the scene in *Sabotage,* discussed in chapter 2, in which the wife, holding the carving knife, looks at her husband. He seems to read her intention, rises, and tries to take the knife from her. In the ensuing struggle, he is stabbed. The scene is ambiguous. Does he recognize her intention to kill him and, for this reason, try to take the knife from her? Or does his own sense of this possibility cause him to struggle with her and be stabbed by accident? Hitchcock seems to suggest a simultaneity of recognition: she thinks of killing him at the same time that he thinks that she is thinking of doing so. He plants the idea in her head at the moment that she plants the idea in his. By showing no particular expression on the faces, instead concentrating the camera on the hands, the bodies, and the knife, Hitchcock is able to retain this ambiguity. In *Strangers on a Train,* he does the same by keeping the two characters' faces locked in a frozen mutual gaze while showing us Bruno's fingers gradually tightening around the neck of the older woman. The final effect of the scene between Bruno and Barbara is that Barbara has been violated (her hysterical breaking down with her sister and Guy in the next scene is like the aftermath of a rape). But she has also broken through the armor of the villain; she sees this man as he is, and her gaze can, at least temporarily, put him to rout (Bruno loses control of himself, then faints).

Significantly, Barbara had refused Miriam her common humanity earlier in the film and was chastised by her father for her insensitivity. What connects both responses—the earlier brash dismissal and the later horrified recognition—is that in both scenes the daughter speaks or sees what must not be spoken or seen, or what others fear to speak or see. In the first case, she says what the others really think about Miriam (opposing the proprieties embodied by her upright father), and later, she stands for the victim and metaphorically sees through her eyes in her confrontation with Bruno. She has been cast as the complement to the father's word and vision, the one who, once empowered to assert autonomy, is capable of returning his gaze and, hence, of editing his power and even revising his vision. (This dynamic has been anticipated in *Shadow of a Doubt* when young Charlie ceremonially descends the stairs, displaying the ring that her uncle knows she can use as evidence against him.)[14]

The father-daughter interplay that operates at the center of *Strangers on a Train* is wholly absent from the Patricia Highsmith novel on which the film is based. In the novel, Guy becomes so enmeshed with Bruno that he is willing to perform his side of the imagined bargain and murder Bruno's father. When Bruno accidentally dies, Guy is devastated at the loss of "his friend, his brother" and acknowledges that Bruno "had borne half his guilt."[15] Highsmith's focus on the pathological bonding of the two men leaves all other relationships in the background. In the film, Ann's family is placed in the foreground. Guy and Bruno find no point of mutual recognition that carries anything like the emotional power of the scene between Bruno and Barbara.

Donald Spoto has referred to the "malevolent humor" that occurs in the confrontation scenes between Barbara and her father in the film and what they suggest of possible real-life confrontations between Pat and Hitchcock:

"Her frequent remark—'Oh come on, Daddy . . . ' must have brought a smile to the faces of the crew."[16] Yet he fails to connect these scenes of malevolent humor to their mirror scenes of malevolent violence, first between Bruno and Miriam (where humor does figure, alongside the horror, in the form of a nasty glee at Bruno's manipulation of Miriam's sluttishness) and between Bruno and Barbara (where all glee has disappeared). If the scene between Bruno and Barbara is a metaphor for Hitchcock and his daughter's mutual recognition on the set, it suggests that the daughter's gaze is intimidating to the father, capable of stopping him in his tracks or, more creatively, of making him rethink his approach.

That Pat Hitchcock intimidated her father during the making of this film, even as she served as a creative influence, is suggested by the practical joke that he is said to have played on her during production.[17] It seems that during the filming of the fairground scene Pat begged her father for a ride on the ferris wheel. He finally agreed, then stopped the wheel when she was at the top, turned the lights out, and went off to film his next scene in another part of the grounds. Spoto reports that Pat was hysterical with fear when she was finally brought down. The "joke" yields wonderfully to interpretation in the context outlined above because it so neatly plays on the dynamic of the father-daughter relationship. The little girl begs her father for a ride, trusting in his indulgence and protection, both of which, in this joke, are maliciously withdrawn. The idea gets translated, I would suggest, into the elaborate merry-go-round scene at the end of the film (which Hitchcock took pains to shoot) where children are represented as terrorized by the out-of-control ride. The malevolent joke Hitchcock played on his daughter while filming and the rendering of the out-of-control carousel within the film can be read as his symbolic retaliation for the fact that his daughter was now no longer a little girl, no longer completely dependent upon him for her physical and emotional well-being. Although still ostensibly under his protection (working for him, after all, and still living at home), she was nonetheless capable of judging him, all the more so in that she was placed in a position, as an actress in his film, of seeing him work. But insofar as the ride also serves to kill the villain who had himself, like Hitchcock, been recognized by the daughter, it is a symbolic revenge that strikes both ways. It chastens its creator even as it expresses his anger. By the same token, it must be noted that the daughter is herself no simple victim in this dynamic. Pat Hitchcock can be said to have activated her father's resentment and instigated his malicious trick against her by playing at being a child again—by begging for the ride (much as, within the film, Barbara "brings on" Bruno's brutality by having been the one to say earlier on that Miriam deserved to die). Both father and daughter, according to this reading, are operating in terms of a dynamic that must, on both sides, edit and revise itself. The simpler relationship of authoritative, doting parent and adoring, dependent child must evolve into a more complicated and mutually threatening relationship. For the father, the fear of seeing the daughter as an adult is the fear of her judgment, while for the daughter, the fear of having to be an equal is the fear of losing the father's indulgence and protection.

A series of publicity photos during this period shows Hitchcock strangling a bust of his daughter.[18] The photos express Hitchcock's ambivalence. They relay a mixed message of hostility toward and pride in his daughter. Miriam is that aspect of the daughter which arouses hostility. In her nasty dealings with Guy in the record shop and in her immature behavior with her two male dates at the fairground, she is the daughter envisioned as a sexually precocious, mocking child. Any suggestion of sexuality emanating from one's child would, according to the Victorian father's view, be seen as indecent not only because it would activate the incest taboo but also because the sexualized child can be understood as the knowing child—the child capable of returning the gaze of the father and appraising him "objectively." Unsurprisingly, the joke Hitchcock played on his daughter during the filming is not without sexual resonance. It recalls a scene from *Mr. and Mrs. Smith,* a very uneven screwball comedy which Hitchcock made nine years earlier as a favor to Carol Lombard. In the scene in question, the heroine (Lombard) gets stuck with her new fiancé at the top of a ferris wheel in the midst of a downpour—one of a series of mishaps that will eventually lead her back to her husband. In the film, the stalled ride and the downpour on top of it are forms of comic retribution for potential sexual misconduct. The idea of sexuality farcically quenched must have remained associated with the ride for Hitchcock (in this sense, it functions like the glasses Pat wears in the film to undermine her appeal). In short, the practical joke that Hitchcock played on his daughter during the making of *Strangers on a Train* can be seen to do double duty, reflecting the double bind in which the father of the adult daughter finds himself. He seeks to deny the daughter the pleasures of childhood, punishing her for no longer being a child, while he also thwarts her in the pursuit of "thrills," as these might be symbolically understood as adult (sexual) pleasure.

Ultimately, the character of Miriam and the character of Barbara seem to be drawn out of a mix of affection, fascination, fear, disgust, and anger. Bruno's successful attack on the one and his foiling by the other can be said to trace the story of Hitchcock's own journey with respect to his daughter as an autonomous figure tied to him in essential ways.

During the period in which the father-daughter relationship was evolving in the terms I have outlined above, Hitchcock's technique was undergoing a corresponding development. He was becoming less interested in creating thrills and more in producing the prolonged quality of suspense of his best films. The difference might be summed up in a contrast between the shock of the villain's missing finger in *The 39 Steps* and the shock of Bruno's appearance in his father's bed in *Strangers on a Train.* In the one case, Hitchcock takes the hero and the audience off guard by displaying an unexpected physical deformity that carries with it an explicit meaning. This is the man the hero was warned to avoid; he is now in mortal danger. The scene in *Strangers,* however, occurs after an elaborate preparation of what Hitchcock called "suspense effects."[19] The final surprise of finding Bruno in the bed is the biggest, but unlike the earlier surprises, which merely shocked, this one raises a host of questions relating to the characters' motives and state of mind. How did Bruno know Guy was not prepared to shoot his father (since we ourselves were unsure of Guy's intention)? Will Guy shoot Bruno now? What kind of threat does Bruno represent to Guy? In short, Hitchcock has attached to this "suspense effect" a more indefinite sense of threat that is based on our awareness of the overdetermined nature of experience. This indeterminacy grants the audience an expanded, more personalized role in the creation of meaning.

In many of the films that followed in the 1950s, Hitchcock achieved both an increased control and an increased loosening of control—a greater assertion of himself as a creative director and a greater trust in the power of the performer to produce certain powerful effects through movement, dress, intonation, and qualities of presence. In conjunction with this came a greater trust in the audience to respond correctly to his films, to recognize him as "master" (in Rothman's terms), as "father" in my terms—and, by recognizing him, to be assigned a position of relative equality to him. These films, in their stress on atmosphere and the resonance of performance alongside tight plotting and ingenious camerawork, fully integrate the cross-gendered, cross-generational dynamic of the father-daughter relationship at its most developed within the nuclear family. Hitchcock's films of the 1950s are the closest he ever came to reclaiming for cinema a psychological concept of character.

5 Digression: *Rope, I Confess*

It is a commonplace in film theory that the woman in classical narrative film performs the role of the object of the male gaze, "the ground of representation, the looking glass held up to men."[1] Hitchcock's films of the Hollywood period are primary examples referred to by the pioneers of this theory. They point to his preference for the chiseled blond, a cultural stereotype of female desirability, and to the manner in which he filmed women during his Hollywood period: a fetishistic concentration on parts of the female body and on female accessories, and prolonged close-ups of the female face.

However, such readings ignore the qualifying influence of tone and context in these same films. The ideas of female emotion, intuition, and imagination had evolved into a narrative of femininity during the nineteenth century. Although that narrative reduced the woman to a prescribed role, the elusiveness of the coordinates involved and their connection with subjectivity through the elaboration of literary texts (and the teachings of psychoanalysis) also made the notion of a circumscribed role seem inadequate and artificial. And since visual representation could not begin to represent this narrative directly, the female image could, by simply invoking the literary narrative, escape the control to which film might otherwise condemn it. The pressure of a narrative of femininity (and the related drive to represent a novelistic concept of character) is increasingly felt in Hitchcock's films of the 1940s and 1950s, a pressure that I have called the "daughter's effect" insofar as it can be associated with his daughter's now-mature presence not only in his household but on the sets of his films. Patricia Hitchcock was bred to a conventional female role, but she was also entangled with her father's identity in a way that could not be resolved through standardized distancing and objectifying techniques.

If we switch the vocabulary, another dimension may be added to this argument. Claude Lévi-Strauss's model for elementary kinship systems assigns the woman the role of exchange object between men, initiating an ordering process that he posits as the origin of [patriarchal] civilization.[2] However, as I have argued at length in my 1991 book, *The Daughter's Dilemma,* Lévi-Strauss's model must be amended at a certain juncture in the history of the family and of representation, when the woman's position as exchange object becomes complicated by the idea of consciousness. Novelistic fiction and the science of psychoanalysis both posited a concept of the subject as inaccessible to complete representation and they associated this internalized subjectivity primarily with women. The generic aspect of exchange was thereby undermined as women became conceived of as unique individuals. This modern female subject, though developed as a support for the nuclear family, thus emerged as a threat to role hierarchies within the family and to patriarchal supremacy more generally. Early narrative film emerged in this context as a source of control and ideological reclamation, a way of reducing the woman to an exchange object—making her a prize or source of trial by which male worth could be established and his authority reinforced. The archetypal image of early silent films is the maiden in distress, tied to the railroad tracks, awaiting salvation by the hero who, to save her, must engage in a race with the oncoming train (this archetypal scene also seems designed to activate and assuage male anxiety about the advance of an intimidating technology, of which film itself is an example). As plot lines evolved, films borrowed from novels the triangular structure that set a woman between two men.[3] But where domestic novels focused on the female consciousness struggling to make the "right" choice (her choice becoming a reflection of her moral judgment and insight into character), films tended to use the woman as an occasion for the men to prove themselves with respect to each other. During Hitchcock's British period, films such as *The Lodger, Secret Agent, Sabotage,* and *The Lady Vanishes* (each of which involves the heroine throwing over her fiancé or husband for the hero at the end) seem designed along these lines. The heroine's primary structural importance is to help enforce what Eve Sedgwick has referred to as the "homosocial bond": the hero's entrenchment in masculine identity through his assumption of a hierarchical relationship with another man.[4]

When the psychological associations attached to the female image (the residue of a superseded literary tradition) manage to enter these films, they are contained within strict limits and for definite ends. In *Blackmail,* for example, the artificial amplification of the word "knife" during a breakfast table conversation (a scene that renders the heroine's traumatized emotional state after she has killed the man who attempted to rape her) is dramatically effective. But since no attempt is made to elaborate the female characterization consistently, the scene becomes noteworthy mostly as a technical experiment (indeed, it is the one scene invariably referred to when *Blackmail* is discussed or when mention is made of Hitchcock's early sound films).[5] Similarly, *Sabotage* contains the psychologically charged scene in which Mrs. Verloc stabs her husband with a carving knife, but it too fails to illuminate the woman's character sufficiently. Thus the scene appears to serve the characterization only incidentally; its central purpose is to resolve the plot conventionally (to make the act of murder an involuntary act that allows the heroine to be acquitted of a crime, leaving her free to remarry). Both these films, like others in Hitchcock's early repertory, recognize the psychological possibilities of the female character only at discreet moments in the narrative in order to serve other ends.

But after Hitchcock arrived in Hollywood and fell under the influence of David O. Selznick this began to change. A specialist in women's pictures, Selznick encouraged the director to make greater and more creative use of the close-up of the female face. By insisting upon a "faithful" adaptation of the literary source in the filming of *Rebecca,* Selznick also helped Hitchcock achieve a greater appreciation of the limitations of cinematic representation with respect to inner states of mind and emotion. In *Spellbound,* this appreciation was reinforced by the felicitous casting of Ingrid Bergman. Hitchcock now began to use female appearance and role associations more systematically. Because his own daughter launched her acting career at this time, it seems likely that her image was also associated in his mind with that of the women he was filming.

Significantly, it was also during this period that the fetishistic aspects of the woman's presence begin to emerge in his films (this is the period that theorists use in expounding their ideas about the male gaze). The coincidence is logical enough. As the woman is granted a psychological presence, she is also fetishized, as if to counter what otherwise promises to upset the traditional gender hierarchy. The conflict between a literary and a cinematic use of the woman thus gets translated from the thematic level to the level of the image itself: the close-up of the woman's face, body, or accessory can serve alternately, and sometimes simultaneously, as both a fetishistic, reductive image and as an evocative image carrying an "excess" of meaning.[6]

Most of Hitchcock's films of the 1940s and 1950s maintain the structure of having two men with a woman between them, but it is now less clear what

Sabotage. Mrs. Verloc carves the roast.

Spellbound. Ballantine "unmasks" during surgery.

All photos from the Museum of Modern Art, New York.

Spellbound. The "kissing bug" appears in Ballantine's Dali-designed dream.

Shadow of a Doubt. Murderous Uncle Charlie greets his unsuspecting relatives.

Stage Fright. Father and daughter share a lighter moment.

Strangers on a Train. Bruno pursues Miriam at the fair.

Strangers on a Train. Bruno demonstrates his strangling technique.

Rope. Rupert sets the metronome—a symbol of the film's orderliness.

I Confess. Father Logan's depth of emotion is supported by the visual emblems of his vocation.

Rear Window. Doyle and Lisa face off.

The Man Who Knew Too Much. Mother and son do their number.

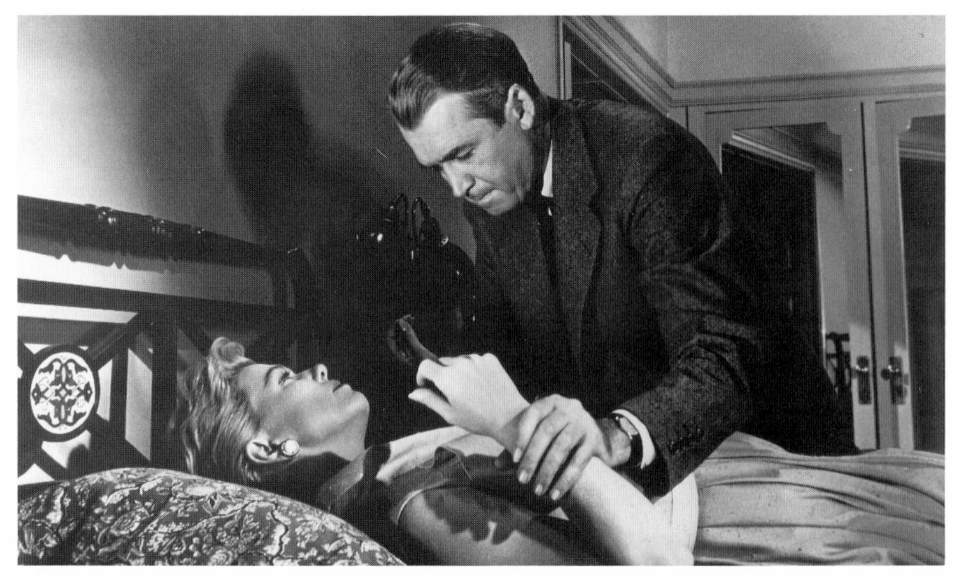

The Man Who Knew Too Much. Ben subdues Jo after sedating her.

The Wrong Man. Rose cracks up.

Vertigo. Who is Judy?

Psycho. The policeman stops to interrogate Marion, but his gaze registers nothing.

Family Plot. Fran, disguised as a traditional Hitchcock blonde, inspects the latest ransom.

role the woman is intended to play. Is she an exchange object for the characters and a source of erotic projection for the spectator, or is she a mediator, a consciousness capable of shaping merit, bringing villainy to justice, and leading the audience to a heightened consciousness of how it responds to experience? In these films Hitchcock seems to be struggling to balance the two aspects of the feminine image, one as fetish/object of exchange, the other as consciousness/mediator of action and meaning. In *Strangers on a Train* these two conceptions of the woman are actually split into two women, one calculatedly designed to symbolically avenge the other. Miriam's grotesquely fetishized image, flattened into the most abject object of exchange between Bruno and Guy, is reconstituted in the image of Barbara later in the film. Watching Bruno pretend to strangle another woman, Barbara stands transfixed. Her face fills the screen not as a fetish object but as a "consciousness" capable of affecting the male subject and thereby shifting the course of action. Here in the most literal manifestation possible is an expression of the "daughter's effect."

In the 1940s and 1950s there was an enormous double burden placed on the female role in Hitchcock's films, and films of the period can be read as his attempt to cope with that burden both in his use of the female image and in his related thematic representation of the heterosexual relationship. Each film of the period seems another attempt at working out a balance. Yet in the midst of this effort to produce a satisfying and workable gender complementarity, two films stand out as exceptions—attempts to rethink the problem from a new angle. *Rope* and *I Confess* are notable for dropping the woman out of the male story. An examination of these films tells us about some of the ways in which Hitchcock sought to substitute for the woman's role in his films. To the extent that they failed to hold an audience and were criticized by Hitchcock himself, they can also tell us how much Hitchcock and the culture he served depended upon the particular structure and meaning that the woman's image brought to his films.

Rope, produced and released in 1948, concerns the murder of a young man by his two friends, Philip (Farley Granger) and Brandon (John Dall). They have been inspired to perform the deed by the teachings (though without the knowledge) of their former prep school teacher, Rupert Cadell (James Stewart). Rupert had taught his students a radically elitist philosophical doctrine. The great man, according to this doctrine, dares to act above the petty rules of society. The weak and insignificant can be sacrificed to the interests of and at the whim of the strong. As tribute to his own audacity, Brandon arranges a dinner party to be held following the murder, to which he invites Rupert. He also invites the victim's parents and fiancée. As a special touch, he has the meal laid out on the very trunk in which the body is hidden. Ultimately, Rupert guesses what his former students have done and, after expressing horror and outrage at the deed, calls the police.

As if driven by an effort to escape the female evocativeness that threatened to engulf his previous films, Hitchcock seems to have made *Rope* to excise that complicating element—the mediating woman—and to return to a direct scrutiny of the homosocial bond. Yet the film subverts its own enterprise from the start. By making the male characters murderers, it ensures that the dream of unmediated male alliance will not capture the sympathy of the audience. It is little wonder that Hitchcock later disassociated himself from any investment in the film, claiming it to be a "stunt . . . I really don't know how I came to indulge in it."[7] The phrasing here suggests not only that the film was a mistake, but that it was a moral mistake—an "indulgence" that might be compared to Rupert's indulgence in philosophical rhetoric within the film. Given this perspective, the film must be understood as leading back to the path from which it represents a temporary detour—that of the heterosexual romance plot.

The central action of *Rope* occurs as the film begins (even as the credits are running). Philip and Brandon are shown strangling their friend David behind the drawn blinds of their apartment's living room. What we have then is a monstrous act performed before we even have a chance to know the characters or the circumstances. We quickly learn that David has been murdered in cold blood by these young men. Their motive is merely to prove that they are capable of doing it and to mark their victim as an inferior being. If we return to the basic assumption of feminist film theory, that the woman's image serves to provide the male spectator with a sense of mastery and superiority, then the act of murder suggests itself as the substitute for male voyeuristic satisfaction with respect to the woman; that is, without a woman to look at, a man needs to commit murder. In Lévi-Strauss's terms, this is to say that women are indeed ordering functions in society, and without them, men regress into barbarism. Both of these conclusions are appropriate glosses on the crime in question, and yet they fail to address how it is that the woman is able to lift the man above monomania and barbarity. Something must be brought to bear on the man through the woman's presence that makes him different from Brandon (who, of the two men, is clearly the most fully "behind" the crime). We are brought back to the more evolved concept of the woman as a consciousness serving to direct and shape the development of male subjectivity. Again, an example can be taken from *Spellbound.* If we were to consider the premise of that film's plot logically, leaving out the emotional element that Constance brings to it, the childhood accident which John seeks to remember (his involvement in his brother's death) supports an assumption that he is guilty of the more recent murder of Dr. Edwards. In other words, the murder on the ski slopes appears to be a simple case of repetition compulsion. But Constance's faith and love construe things otherwise and force the film to support the conviction of John's innocence. Her presence, then, produces that "swerve" in meaning (analogous to the swerve that John enacts on the slopes when he pushes her out of danger and thereby proves his innocence), severing the logical connectedness of past and present and insinuating a new meaning between them. In short, she creates the idea of an unconscious, of a buried meaning that contradicts an apparent, surface meaning. Through her, therefore, he is able to rise to the occasion, to be a man other than the one that he would have been without her. In *Rope,* by contrast, Brandon is subject not to mediation but to influence. He has committed the crime after following the doctrine taught to him by Rupert. The idea of an unconscious, contradictory meaning that insinuates itself against the grain of logic and literal meaning is absent from that relationship. Male-to-male influence in this context functions as a linear impetus not only to action but to an idea of the subject conceived only in terms of imitation. There is no deviation possible, no unique self, no "swerve."[8]

I have suggested earlier that the potential for this kind of male subject began to be bred out of the separate-spheres ideology of the nineteenth century, as men became increasingly alienated from a world of relationship and feeling. *Rope* postulates such an alienated world and also seeks to uncover the kinds of influences that feed it. The film is permeated with images and allusions to books—no other Hitchcock film makes books so literally present on the scene. But the literalness of their presence seems directly connected to the kinds of books they are—to the literalness of their message, so to speak. The books invoked throughout the film (and presumably present on the dining-room table for David's father, a book collector, to peruse) constitute the ideas of men like Rupert put into writing. They pertain to the moral and political philosophy that Rupert taught the boys in prep school (he now publishes philosophical texts: "not what *you'd* read," he explains to one of the women present). This philosophical tradition stands in counterpoint to the novelistic tradition that I have referred to throughout these pages. Whereas nineteenth-century novels strove to depict character as driven by multiple, often contradictory, motives, nineteenth-century philosophy sought to give voice to "truth," either in the form of reasoned argument or by oracular pronouncement. These texts were concerned not with subjectivity but with objectivity, or at least with "transcendent subjectivity," in which the world could be entirely shaped in one's own image. The distinction connects again with the Victorian notion of separate spheres where novels were associated with women and nonfiction prose with an elite male readership. (The film suggests a similar distinction, with popular film falling on the side of novelistic fiction. At one point, the women are shown chattering about Hitchcock's recently released *Notorious,* while Rupert listens with amused contempt.) Both Nietzsche and Carlyle decried a "feminized" culture that had lost touch with an ideal of manly heroism. Both philosophers wrote in aggressively oracular styles, and their work was used by Nazi propagandists as rationalizing texts. (Nietzsche and Nazism are referred to in the film on separate occasions.)

Rope explores these ideas thematically and also on the level of its form. Hitchcock, like Brandon with his dinner party, has organized the film with virtuoso precision. Everything conforms to an artful design: the stylized plotting of movement, the careful orchestration of talk, the layout and appearance of the set (for example, the artifical balustrade that is painted near the door of the men's apartment, the horizontal expanse of blinds that disguises what would otherwise be a window directly opposite and parallel to the view afforded the audience of the film's action, and the metronome on the piano that Rupert sets in motion at one point). The famous "ten-minute takes" are the most dramatic examples of this design (the takes actually vary considerably in length, but the fact that they tend to be referred to as "ten-minute takes" testifies to the success with which Hitchcock was able to promote the idea that the film was designed according to a perfectly calculated plan). As it is, the absence of montage enacts what Truffaut refers to as a director's "dream of linking all of a film's components into a single, continuous action."[9] Such a dream assumes that the filmmaker can operate unencumbered by contradiction and qualification. Montage, after all, is a form of visual qualification; it asserts that something happening in one place or from a particular perspective can have an influence on how we understand what is going on elsewhere. As Hitchcock explained and the actors amply testified, the filming of *Rope* involved elaborate planning and demanded the tedious and often contortionist accommodation of all variables to the imperatives of the camera.[10] This tendency to control is always present in Hitchcock's films but it gets countered in other films of the period by the overdetermined associations that tend to attach to the female image and role. Given the emphasis on the sterile effects of male influence in this film, it seems fitting that most of the takes end with the camera centered on the back of a man's suit. The effect is to emphasize the dark, uniform expanse of that apparel—the sense in which every man present is some form of imitation or facsimile of the others and, as a result, dependent for his identity on distinctions based on power. (It is noteworthy that Rupert suspects foul play when he is given David's hat by mistake.)

So seamless is the mesh of form and content in this film that we might be liable to forget the murder we saw enacted in the opening frames were it not for the presence of Rupert Cadell. He exists on the scene as a qualifying agent, an ongoing reminder of the gap between what is going on in this film and what should be going on. Rupert's role as the man who solves the crime but who also instigates it is crucial in establishing our point of view not only on the events but also on the notion of character from which the events can be said to spring. Having the audience know of the crime while Rupert only gradually comes to suspect it creates an added sense of irony to our view of the character. We can continually measure his philosophical postures against the real effects we know them to have produced. As a result, we can be in no danger of succumbing to the imitative attitude of Brandon.

The full revelation of Rupert's function in the film occurs in the final scene. He has finally learned what his former students have done, and he breaks into a passionate exposition, directed at them but staged like a classroom lecture, in which we are positioned with Brandon and Philip in the role of students. Only now, the teacher has abandoned his earlier manner of ironic superiority for a moralistic, self-justifying tone—the tone of the pulpit and the confessional, not the philosophy lectern: "You've given my words a meaning that I never dreamed of. And you've tried to twist them into a cold, logical excuse for your ugly murder. Well, they never were that, Brandon, and you can't make them that. There must have been something deep inside you from the very start that let you do this thing. But there's always been something deep inside me that would never let me do it."

As he speaks, Rupert's voice is shrill and self-righteous, showing evidence of the hysteria that Robin Wood refers to as underlying all Stewart's performances for Hitchcock.[11] This is not the voice of authority but of authority made vulnerable, opened up, so to speak. It is the voice of someone *lacking* "something deep inside" him (to turn his own words back on himself). As the parallel structure of his statement exposes ("There must have been something deep inside you . . . but there's something deep inside me . . ."), Rupert is like his students with the difference that they have committed murder and he has not. He goes on to accuse the two men of "sterility"—implying that the "something deep inside them" to which he has alluded accounts for both their ability to commit murder and their inability to love. He, presumably, could not murder and *is* capable of love, though there is no indication that he is loving anyone at the moment. What accounts for the difference between them? Only that the "something deep inside" his students that has led to murder is actually something *outside* them: Rupert himself. In his hierarchical relationship to them, they don't know *not* to take him literally. He spurs them to turn words into action. Rupert, however, is different in that he is a man uninfluenced by other men. This constitutes his hubris but also his vulnerability—there is no higher authority by which he can invest his ideas with the force of truth. Indeed, part of our sense of Rupert's likeability throughout the film comes from what Thomas M. Bauso has called his "essential lack of seriousness about his ideas." Cadell's earlier talk is, according to this critic, "a comic performance enacted for the benefit of his appreciative audience, particularly Mrs. Atwater, who laughs delightedly at his trivializing of the subject."[12]

The two conceptions of character, one embodied by Philip and Brandon, the other by Rupert, reflect the duality present in narrative film with respect to the male character. The genre of narrative film developed in part to counter that feminization of culture associated with a novelistic tradition. Film sought to totalize an approach to experience that psychological narrative, with its assumption of a split between conscious and unconscious, had deconstructed. In this attempt at unification, film resembles Brandon, whose values are a textbook of patriarchal convention: he favors action, doctrine, manipulation of women, and a narrative that eliminates ambiguity and nuance in the realm of character. Brandon reflects the part of Hitchcock that drew him to the gimmicks and simple plot lines of early narrative film—that part of him which sought a sense of mastery both of vocation and, more generally, of values which, by the end of the nineteenth century, had become confused and dislocated by a "sexual anarchy" (the novelist George Gissing's phrase) fueled by an evolved literary tradition.[13]

What *Rope* also shows, however, is the inadequacy of such a conception of character to a narrative designed to entertain an audience and to challenge the creative resources of a filmmaker. The gimmickry of *Rope,* like the gimmickry of some of the British films, becomes in this context an artificial effort to generate challenges which are lacking in the conceptual domain of character. Rupert is Hitchcock's surrogate in acknowledging the limitations of his professed loyalties and beliefs and in making that acknowledgment part of an evolution in method. Just as early narrative film directed an increasingly alienated male subject to a form of narrative representation that accommodated character, albeit in a simplified form (in counterpoint to nonfiction prose in which the concept of character is eliminated), Rupert is directed through the film narrative to a new appreciation of the limitations of his own character—of the inadequacy of the narratives he has at hand to give it shape. Watching Rupert operate from our position of greater knowledge dramatizes the mechanism by which narrative produces character without resolving it. Male character is represented as a "lack" which the female image, when conceived of as a fetish, works to complete (in the way murder completes Brandon). But when the female image is conceived of as harboring a consciousness, it works instead to launch a male character into the realm of subjective process. Bauso's observation that Rupert's performance seems enacted for the benefit of Mrs. Atwater is on target. The instances in the film when he seems most at ease and least in earnest about his philosophical position occur when he is interacting with the women at the party. They are his complements, the vehicles through which his words find their "proper," rather than distorted, meaning. They assuage the "lack" in him not by disguising it but by putting it into play. Stanley Cavell has argued that the qualities of vulnerability and suffering that attach to the Stewart persona "admit him to the company of women."[14] The Stewart persona needs to engage with women not so much to triumph at their expense, as Mulvey would have it, as to enter into an exchange with them. Thus, though the point of view of this film coincides with that of the active male, the subject is conceived of as pertaining to both male and female—impossible without their complementary relationship. Stewart is the ideal Hitchcock hero because his halting speech, awkward, jerky movements, and confused manner dramatize lack and discontinuity. He is constituted as a fully conceived subject only in interaction with women, while women are made to exceed the object role by being inserted into his narrative. He activates the suggestion of depth in his female counterparts through a kind of complementarity that builds on nineteenth-century role complementarity, focusing it into the arena of subjectivity.

In the context of such a reading, the homosexual subtext that the film carries (and that was quite explicit in the original play based on the Leopold and Loeb case) becomes a convenient conceit for dramatizing the absence of sexual role complementarity. It functions for the film rather the way Nietzschean philosophy functions for the characters in it, as a purely theoretical set of coordinates on which the action is grounded. The film does not condemn homosexuality or Nietzschean philosophy. What it does condemn is a certain kind of relationship to these ideas (a "delusional" relationship in the terms of film theory), that would find in them a whole meaning, an answer that blocks out other, alternative forms of interpretation and relationship. Homosexuality thus becomes a code for the homosocial bond rather than the other way around—a way of imagining the world with the women dropped out. *Rope*'s failure to appeal to a mass audience and Hitchcock's after-the-fact dismissal of it as a "stunt" (a statement that recalls Rupert's dismissal of his ideas at the end of the film as not intended to be taken literally) is evidence that the film did not evoke a sufficiently evocative text to give these men's action a tragic resonance. The only audience capable of championing the film (aside from theoreticians who would appear to be attempting to reduplicate the error that the film takes as its subject) are individuals or groups who can fill in for the film's "lack" by the infusion of their own more humanly inflected story.[15]

If *Rope* attempts to eliminate the female position from its world, *I Confess,* made four years later, seeks more ambitiously to substitute for it. The plot revolves around the crisis faced by a young priest, Father Michael Logan (Montgomery Clift), when a man who works for him (O.E. Hasse) admits during confession to a murder. Constrained by the confidentiality of his office, Logan cannot tell what he knows, even when he is accused of committing the crime himself. The film chronicles his ordeal as he stoically maintains silence even as he is tortured with accusations and humiliating details from his past.

The film's effect turns on the unspoken mental anguish that the priest must suffer.[16] Hitchcock had tried to evoke something of the same effect with Gregory Peck in *Spellbound* and with Louis Jourdan in *The Paradine Case.* Clift's features resemble those of Peck and Jourdan—as well as those of Henry Fonda in *The Wrong Man* (where Hitchcock's intention has shifted, as I discuss in chapter 7). Clearly, the filmmaker had in mind a paradigmatic male face when he attempted to render psychological depth quite as much as he had in mind a paradigmatic female face for that purpose. Jourdan had the advantage of Peck in being supplied inside the film with something on which to hang his baleful looks: *The Paradine Case* evokes a narrative of military duty and feudal devotion. However, since the object of the servant's devotion in the film is dead and most of the action transpires in a courtroom, the visuals that would have solidifed these encoded texts are not sufficiently present. *I Confess,* by contrast, succeeds where both *The Paradine Case* and *Spellbound* fail. Its encoded text is the iconographically rich one of Catholicism, and Hitchcock exploits it in almost every shot. Each close-up of Clift's face eventually pans down to his robes or up to the architecture of his church. Even the landscape of Quebec, with its precipitous view into the valley from the mountain, contributes to this spiritual iconography. Hitchcock had tried to use the Dali visuals to evoke Peck's character in *Spellbound,* but the result had been flat-footed and hokey. This was because the narrative overlay destroyed the evocative effect of the images and because the male character could not support the weight of a complex subjectivity. Instead, as I have argued, it was the female character in that film who captured the visual space by invoking a literary narrative pertaining to the internal life. Ingrid Bergman's face and wind-blown hair as she looks ecstatically out onto the landscape during her walk with Peck deserves comparison to similar shots of Clift gazing up at the cathedral ceiling or out into the city stretched below him.

It is worth noting that *I Confess,* as if intent on ridding itself of competing meaning, makes a point of denigrating the romantic plot associated with the female role. The most awkward sequence in the film is the flashback encounter between Logan and his former girlfriend Ruth (Anne Baxter) before he became a priest. It is shot in soft focus to stress its sentimental unreality, and the narrative it contains is equally saccharine and unconvincing: a sudden rainstorm forces the couple to spend the night together and presumably to consummate their relationship. Logan is then called off to military service. When he fails to write, she marries someone else. The flashback seems to be included in the film to bring home the triteness and pseudo-mystery of romantic love as a contrast to the importance and real mystery of Logan's present spiritual vocation (which, of course, entails celibacy).

Problems with *I Confess*, helping to account for why it is the only explicitly Catholic film in Hitchcock's canon, reside in the difficulty a non-Catholic has understanding the priest's struggle. Hitchcock admitted as much to Truffaut in discussing his disappointment with the film: "To put a situation into a film simply because you yourself can vouch for its authenticity, either because you've experienced it or because you've heard of it, simply isn't good enough." And, he subsequently elaborated, "We Catholics know that a priest cannot disclose the secret of the confessional, but the Protestants, the atheists, and the agnostics all say, 'Ridiculous! No man would remain silent and sacrifice his life for such a thing.' "[17] In other words, the cues to a narrative which are unavailable to direct representation cannot effectively evoke that narrative unless one has been conditioned in its iconography. In arguing for a Catholic subtext in other Hitchcock films, Rohmer and Chabrol cite, among their examples, the scene in *Notorious* in which Alicia Huberman (Ingrid Bergman) is shown being looked at by Devlin (Cary Grant) while the cross on the top of the Sugarloaf mountain in Brazil is seen through the window of the plane in which they are flying.[18] Yet Bergman's face dominates that scene; the spiritual evocativeness of the cross feeds into the feminine image rather than the other way around (unless one happens to have the Catholic narrative at the center of one's consciousness while watching the film, as Rohmer and Chabrol obviously did). Although the literary text to which the female image refers may have been no more directly known to Hitchcock's audience than the Catholic text behind Clift's features, its conventions had permeated the general culture to a far greater degree. Indeed, film itself, by so effectively representing the woman as the object of the male gaze, had helped to publicize these conventions even though its initial ideological function was to thwart them.

Rope and *I Confess* both lack the kind of general allusiveness that would make them accessible to a mass audience. In the case of *Rope*, references to a buried narrative are nonexistent (or at least too incomplete to be convincing if one tries to unearth a text of homosexual alienation). In the case of *I Confess,* the Catholic subtext is too dependent upon conditioning in religious lore and ritual to be accessible to a mass audience. In both films, moreover, Hitchcock seems to have taken pains to efface the female presence in the context of the issues raised, thus eliminating what in other films constituted his most powerful affective symbol. In *Rope,* the housekeeper, Mrs. Wilson (Edith Evanson), is not presented as charming or wise. If we compare her depiction to that of the nurse, Stella (Thelma Ritter), in *Rear Window,* we see how the same kind of character can be rendered more appealingly (significantly, the few sequences that show Mrs. Wilson being teased by Rupert are closest in tone to the later film). In *I Confess,* the killer's wife does take heroic action in the end (in a scene reminiscent of the averting scream in the 1956 version of *The Man Who Knew Too Much*), but she has, up until this point, been eclipsed by her husband and the inanimate edifice of the church in whose corners she shrinks (her job is to cook and clean). In both *Rope* and *I Confess,* the conventional romantic role is also reduced to a marginal satirical portrait, romance being inconsequential or diversionary within the interests of these plots. Ruth, in *I Confess,* is a married woman engaging in a self-indulgent nostalgia for past romance; Janet, in *Rope,* has been the girlfriend of three men in the film (if one includes the body in the trunk), reflecting a fickle and perhaps mercenary nature. Some suggestion is made that she has matured and will now become a better partner to Ken, her former boyfriend, but since Brandon has arranged the match, this may simply be Hitchcock's way of wholly discrediting the idea of a romantic plot (what he does through camerawork in *I Confess*). Indeed, within the larger narrative of the film, Janet functions as little more than scenery—a structural as well as a thematic "exchange object." Both Ruth and Janet have a pinched and physically uncomfortable look—their dresses are too tight without seeming sexy—as though they are being literally pressed out of the films to make room for concerns (male philosophy in one case; male spiritual vocation in the other) that by definition will not admit them.

The failure of *I Confess* at the box office seems to have effectively put an end to Hitchcock's search for an alternative to the female image in his films. Theorists have noted a tendency in modern culture to replace the idea of God as essential "other" by the idea of Woman.[19] The singularity of *I Confess* in locating a priest in the iconic role suggests that Hitchcock was temporarily resisting this conception of woman, which he had already begun to embrace in films like *Spellbound* and *Notorious*. Although the conception of woman as the site of that mystery traditionally ascribed to a spiritual being is obviously delusionary, it has the virtue of placing the male subject in a humbler, more open relationship to his role. Its humbling effects (assisted by the "daughter's effect") are seen in Hitchcock's major films of the 1950s. But this is also a threatening conception, one liable to reactivate male insecurity and generate the kind of backlash that Hitchcock later represented in *Psycho*.

The Daughter's Effect: *Rear Window, The Man Who Knew Too Much*

In trying to position Hitchcock with respect to his time, one is drawn in two directions. He was at once a latter-day "eminent Victorian," the stereotype of bourgeois caution and conventionality that Lytton Strachey and fellow modernists satirized and relegated to the dust-heap of culture. By the same token, in choosing film, the medium that "had superseded the novel in line with historical necessity,"[1] Hitchcock was more modern than Strachey and his circle, who remained attached to the written word.

The difficulty of locating Hitchcock is compounded further by the way in which he conceived of the cinematic with respect to the literary. On the one hand, he sensed from the beginning the potential distinctiveness of film as a medium of expression and seemed to scorn any suggestion that literature should be "faithfully" adapted to the screen ("What I do is to read a story only once, and if I like the basic idea, I just forget all about the book and start to create cinema"[2]). On the other hand, much of the impetus behind his technical development seems have been a drive to find cinematic expression for values associated with the nineteenth-century domestic novel. It was not the thematic content of these novels that can be said to have influenced him (or at least not thematic content understood in any literal way, as his disclaimer about story adaptation indicates), but rather the moral, imaginative, and psychological elements associated with novelistic character.

Hitchcock called *Rear Window* (released in 1954) his most cinematic film. It is also, according to the terms I discuss in this book, his most literary.

It represents an almost perfect merging of a narrative of action and a narrative of character. Although it maintains the problem-solving male protagonist at its center, it charts his development as a uniquely psychological subject under the cover of a suspense plot.

L.B. Jefferies (James Stewart) is a newspaper photographer laid up with a broken leg. Nearing the end of his convalescence, he is bored and restless and has taken to passing the time stationed before his window, watching his neighbors in the apartment buildings across the way. One night, he is struck by the suspicious behavior of one of these neighbors, a traveling salesman named Lars Thorwald (Raymond Burr). He eventually concludes that Thorwald has murdered his invalid wife. The plot develops as Jefferies tries to prove his suspicion and convince others of Thorwald's guilt. These include his detective friend, Doyle (Wendell Corey), the insurance company nurse, Stella (Thelma Ritter), and his girlfriend, Lisa Freemont (Grace Kelly). Stella and Lisa are eventually convinced. Doyle remains skeptical until he witnesses Thorwald's attack on Jefferies at the end of the film.

Jefferies's voyeuristic preoccupation with his neighbors has been pointed to by Laura Mulvey and subsequent feminist critics as an example of the male scopophilic drive upon which classical narrative cinema is built. "In a world ordered by sexual imbalance," explains Mulvey, "pleasure in looking has been split between active/male and passive/female. The determining male gaze projects its fantasy onto the female figure, which is styled accordingly."[3] The designation of Jefferies as the embodiment of the patriarchal gaze hardly requires disputing as the film's point of departure. In the early scenes, Jefferies is pictured as a kind of grabbag of conventional male characteristics, all of which support Mulvey's depiction of "a world ordered by sexual imbalance." His penchant for action and adventure is relayed through visual clues in his apartment and is underscored by his refusal to be "tied down" in marriage. He leers at the the voluptuous spectacle of the neighbor he dubs "Miss Torso," while his early interactions with Lisa show his unreflecting support for a conventional hierarchy that places men above women. (He refers slightingly to her work in fashion without questioning his own interest in sports and war, and he denigrates her opinions through rhetorical ploys of sarcasm and dismissiveness.) At this juncture, Jefferies can be compared to Rupert Cadell in *Rope* (also played by Stewart). But, though *Rear Window* starts with a character as benighted as Cadell, this film seems intent upon taking the concerns of the earlier film further. It attempts to answer the question that *Rope* implicitly raises; namely, how does one bring about that receptivity to difference and contradiction that the male subject, as stereotypically defined, tends to resist? How, in other words, does one create "subjectivity" out of conventional male identity? Both *Spellbound* and *Notorious* represent their male protagonists as firmly entrenched, if flawed, vehicles for action and authority. The romantic unions at the end of these films are designed to suggest an abstract idea of wholeness (the women acting as a kind of prosthetic unconscious for the men). *Rear Window* proceeds under the assumption that a man must be constructed as a subject—must be equipped with a narrative of identity—for the idea of relationship to be realistically proposed. (In the second part of this chapter, I describe how Hitchcock's 1956 remake of *The Man Who Too Much* tackles the female side of relationship.)

The film first arouses our expectation that this will be a conventional action thriller and then quickly thwarts that expectation. After an initial crane shot of the courtyard that pans several of the apartment windows giving us only a glimpse of their occupants, the camera settles into a close-up of Jefferies's sleeping face. The shot announces this to be the face of the film's hero—we assume that he will awake and "activate" the plot. But this initial shot, which serves to whet our appetite for action, is followed by a second panning shot that, after returning to a close-up of Jefferies's face, now tracks from the face to the body, revealing the "punch line": the leg cast. This tracking shot announces the constraints under which the film operates. After all, what can be done with a hero in a toe-to-thigh cast, confined to a wheelchair? Unless the film is structured as a flashback (which the theatrical realism of the opening shots belies), it seems to undermine its potential to entertain us even before it begins.

The sense that the film is suffering under a handicap as a result of its protagonist's handicap is developed in subsequent scenes involving Jefferies. His crankiness and frustrated maneuvering in his wheelchair, his angry conversation with his boss on the phone, and his annoyance with Lisa's ministrations announce that he has lost access to the kind of role he normally plays—as hero in a conventional action plot. "If you don't pull me out of this swamp of boredom, I'm gonna do something drastic . . . I'm gonna get married," he warns his boss on the phone. "Then, I'll never be able to go anywhere." The meaning seems to be: "I might as well get married since I'm already trapped inside a domestic plot." Ironically, of course, he appears to have no knowledge of what such a plot would look like (as his equating of marriage with boredom and not going anywhere indicates). He can only fall back on a vaudevillian repertory to fill the gap of his inactivity: the farcical business with the wheelchair and the back scratcher, the sarcastic cuts at his visitors, and the bellyaching on the phone to his boss.

Critics of the film have noted that Jefferies's position as an invalid confined to his apartment metaphorically duplicates the female position in culture. Hitchcock made a point of comparing Jefferies to Mrs. Thorwald in his discussion with Truffaut.[4] This feminization has generally been seen as producing a retaliatory response in the character, as posing a threat that exaggerates the castration anxiety inherent in masculine identity formation, hence making Jefferies a kind of exaggerated masculine prototype.[5] Yet what Hitchcock manages to do in the early scenes is to use the resistance of the character(and of the spectator) in order to more clearly delineate a starting point for the formation of the character's subjectivity.

That there is resistance is understandable. Jefferies's condition is defined as a curtailment of his freedom—a reduction in the external stimuli to which his past life had given him unlimited access. In the nineteenth century, an ideology of repression had created psychological character, as it were, by default.[6] Individuals were associated with subjectivity to the degree that they were denied access to the world at large, hence the tendency to equate subjectivity with women. In line with this reasoning, we can see how cinema's unlimited access to visual material removed a constraint in the realm of representation that resulted in a loss of complex definition for the self. As Christian Metz has noted, "any paradigm in film is very rapidly overwhelmed because the filmmaker can express himself by showing us the diversity of the world."[7] The self was the nineteenth-century paradigm *par excellence*: character acted as the generator for narrative. With the rise of narrative cinema, narrative had to be generated out of the very thing that had overwhelmed character: "the diversity of the world." The broken camera and photograph of a burning sports car that we are shown in the opening tracking shot of Jefferies's apartment reflect a "flat" identity linked to conventional cinematic realism—a character established by random engagement (one could say "crashes") with "the diversity of the world." Jefferies's present circumstances, by contrast, involve a recycling through the same routine and people, distilling patterns of response that would never have emerged in his former, more physically active life. (Hitchcock's frequent decision to impose limitations on his filmmaking—the most extreme examples being his decision to confine himself to a single set in *Lifeboat* and to eliminate montage in *Rope*—may be understood as a form of self-imposed limitation, akin to what he imposes on Jefferies, for the purpose of finding new patterns of meaning in scripts and performances.)

The film also demonstrates how the seeming freedom of Jefferies's past life (represented inside the film by his friend Doyle) is actually composed of its own kinds of constraints. One feels that Doyle is *obliged* to be flippant with men and condescending with women, as though these behavioral tics come with the job of tough police detective. Jefferies, a photojournalist by profession, seems similarly compelled to stress the exoticism and danger of his assignments and to marginalize other, less "manly" aspects of his work (like the fashion photography that Lisa would like him to do more of). Where behavior is so rigidly linked to a prescribed gender role, to be forced to modify one's behavior as Jefferies is as a result of his broken leg could be enormously liberating, though it might at first be experienced as the direst calamity.[8] A comparison to Hitchcock's own situation once again suggests itself. Donald Spoto refers often in his biography to Hitchcock's obesity as an obstacle to conventional male behavior. For example, it hampered his confidence with women and inhibited his physical activity (even keeping him from service in World War I). His career in film can be intepreted, at least in part, as a form of compensation, a way of vicariously living the life that his physical condition thwarted. However, what began as compensating activity eventually yielded new avenues of expression. In this sense, Jefferies's evolving subjectivity can be said to collapse Hitchcock's evolution as a filmmaker: from conventional action plots (vicarious enactments of his masculine role) early in his career, to plots like those in *Rear Window,* in which the action serves only as a container or cover for issues of character.

Jefferies's handicap is, of course, only the precondition for the story of his subjective development. It is his relationship to something outside himself—in this case, the apartment buildings that enclose the courtyard which his window overlooks—that produces him as a subject. Hitchcock's own remarks are helpful in elucidating this point: "*Rear Window* was structurally satisfactory because it is the epitome of the subjective treatment. A man looks; he sees; he reacts. Thus you construct a mental process."[9] "Looks", "sees," "reacts"—the terms can be analyzed sequentially to explain how the film works to solder the protagonist into a new subject position: to "construct," in Hitchcock's words, "a mental process."

What, first of all, does Hitchcock mean when he says that "a man looks?" Many critics have limited their reading of the film to a commentary on the "look." According to this reading, the film is on archetypal example of classical narrative cinema that works to bring the (paradigmatically male) spectator into identification with the camera's look as it doubles for his own act of perception. This produces an illusion that the spectator is bringing the film into being with his look, and this illusion of action is reinforced, or "sutured," through identification with an active hero within the film.[10] Although Hitchcock's films have been used as prototypical examples of this suturing technique, his movies never enact the process with the kind of completeness that is often assumed. Or perhaps it would be more correct to say that it is not always the same ideological position that is being sutured. In *Rear Window,* the parallelism between Jefferies's state and that of the audience becomes uncomfortably close, and the illusion of action, instead of being reinforced, is undercut. For example, Jefferies's awkward maneuvering in his wheelchair, persisting throughout the length of the film, is a continual reminder to him and to us that looking is emphatically not acting. At the same time, it cannot be said that Jefferies's look is without power. It not only helps to solve a murder, it also initiates the process by which he becomes more than the generic male identity that he seems to be when the film begins. In short, the protagonist occupies an unconventional relationship to both action and spectatorship: the film unmasks the illusion that makes us feel that our looking is a form of acting at the same time that it breaks down the preconceived notion that looking is necessarily an inferior mode of dealing with experience.

The tendency to place acting above looking with which the film takes issue can be correlated with a tendency to demarcate the look itself. This demarcation appeared in the eighteenth century when the invention of the microscope radically enlarged the possibilities of what could be seen in the natural world.[11] The rigors of method soon enforced a distinction between informative looking (which assumed a distance between the observer and the thing being looked at and which suggested a moral or instrumental end) and pleasurable looking (which drew the observer into the experience with no ostensible end but the experience itself). This distinction parallels distinctions that patriarchal society more generally enforced between acting and looking, distinctions which carry more categorically absolute implications such as serious and trivial, useful and useless, real and illusory, sacred and profane, and of course, male and female. The fact that women became the principal subject of scrutiny in the realm of psychiatric medicine in the late nineteenth century helps account for the field's initial lack of credibility. Freud tried to address the credibility problem by insisting that his work conformed to a rigorous method and had serious goals. In the introduction to his Dora case history, for example, he explicitly condemns those "many physicians who (revolting though it may seem) choose to read a case history of this kind not as a contribution to the psychopathology of the neuroses, but as a *roman à clef* designed for their private delectation."[12] Yet Freud's focus on female sexuality, being culturally associated with noninstrumental, pleasurable looking, ensured that many physicians *would* approach the case histories as pornography rather than as science. At the same time, the very fact that psychoanalysis chose to direct its gaze at female symptoms, otherwise ignored or scorned in the culture, was to invest them with an unprecedented importance. As I have argued elsewhere, Freud's endeavor was anticipated and reinforced by the development of the novel, a genre that from its origins blurred the distinction between instruction (involving detachment from what was being described) and distraction (involving investment and implication in what was being described). And once novels had become focused on the internal workings of character, the confusion escalated. It became more difficult to label someone good or bad, to determine whether an experience was important or trivial, to decide what was action and what was merely background description and filler. Finally, it became more difficult to maintain assumptions about female inferiority when the female character was the focus of attention and concern.

Early narrative film sought to retrieve old distinctions by repartitioning the look: narrative related to male action, spectacle to female character. The observer, instead of being drawn into a narrative of character, as was the case with the novel, remained detached from the image-spectacle of character, associated with the woman, while being drawn into the narrative of action associated with the male hero. Hence, looking could be made to feel like acting and the negative associations of looking could be purged. Hitchcock's films, though they initially hold to this distinction, progressively erode the partition separating action and character by manipulating the spectator's look. Dating more or less from the beginning of his Hollywood period, Hitchcock began to use the image of the woman to evoke a lost narrative of interiority (as I discuss in chapter 3 on *Spellbound*), and to use the narrative of action to code for an interior journey. This tendency is most fully realized in *Rear Window.*

In *Rear Window,* the look of the character is an analogue for the look of the spectator. We come to appreciate the potential power of our own look, to recognize its connection to the way we generate meaning and feeling, by watching a story unfold out of Jefferies's look. Significantly, point-of-view editing—equated with Jefferies's look—does not begin until his conversation with his boss on the phone, when his gaze first wanders distractedly to the windows across the courtyard. And the first direct link between what he sees and what he is saying occurs when that gaze falls on the Thorwald apartment. "If you don't pull me out of this swamp of boredom, I'm gonna do something drastic . . . I'm gonna get married," he warns, the statement obviously triggered by what he has just observed of Thorwald's oppressive domestic life. If we return to an examination of the second panning shot early in the film, we note that the Thorwald apartment was left out, the sole cut in what would otherwise have been a continuous take. This omission makes the appearance of Thorwald in the first point-of-view shot seem that much more like a subjective incantation. This is not to say that Jefferies "produces" the Thorwald plot by force of his imagination (as has been suggested), only that he is uniquely positioned to fasten his look there (both literally, in having his window directly opposite the Thorwalds' window, and psychologically, in possessing points of identification with both the wife and the husband). Subsequent interactions with Stella and Lisa add context to Jefferies's interest in the Thorwalds, although his gaze continues to wander to other windows as these happen to correlate with his mood or situation. Then, after a fight with Lisa, he embarks on the night-long surveillance of the Thorwald apartment. He now wants to see better and more: he switches to a camera with a telephoto lens and then to binoculars. The Thorwalds have ceased to be a gloss on Jefferies's random fears and frustrations and have become a source of sustained curiosity, a spur to narrative. The more prolonged and continuous point-of-view editing tells us that the protagonist has found an external object through which his character can be anchored in place and through which the work of subject formation (what Hitchcock terms "mental process") can begin.

The "look" establishes a relationship between the character and the object of his gaze—between the idea of the self and something outside the self. But there its job essentially ends. It cannot render a "narrative of character"; it cannot show a subject engaging in complex thought and feeling. As the beginning of *Notorious* attests, strict point-of-view editing can actually have the opposite effect, rendering the character whose point of view we see more remote and enigmatic—not a subject, but a registering object like the camera (a stance that Jefferies tries to imitate unsuccessfully in his final confrontation scene with Thorwald). What Hitchcock refers to as the next stage in the construction of a mental process ("a man . . . sees") superimposes a narrative onto the look. "Tell me what you saw, and what you think it means," Lisa demands portentously as she is about to be drawn into Jefferies's interpretation of events. Her statement, punctuated by a fade, effectively cuts the film in half. At this moment, Lisa is the audience's surrogate, about to be convinced of what, up until now, she has been skeptical. She brings into relief Hitchcock's method of answering the question of what it means to "see with" a character within a cinematic context. The question can be posed as follows: since narrative cinema, by definition, narratizes visual images produced from the point of view of the camera/filmmaker, how can a film lend credence to a character's point of view within the film and yet distinguish it from the point of view of the film as a whole? Hitchcock solves the problem by giving us one piece of visual information that Jefferies (who has fallen asleep at his post) does not have: a woman coming out of the apartment with Thorwald early in the morning. This visual detail does not so much destroy Jefferies's credibility as an observer as it places us at a distance from him and turns us from an audience that shares in his vision to one that needs to be convinced.

Jefferies's initial attempt to superimpose a narrative onto his look is a rather crude matter of establishing a relationship between two observations: Thorwald's nocturnal comings and goings and the absence of Mrs. Thorwald in her bedroom the next morning. Although the internal logic of this narrative is sound, it is vulnerable to attack from the outside. Locate Mrs. Thorwald alive, and her husband's nocturnal behavior ceases to matter. Lieutenant Doyle has no problem locating Mrs. Thorwald in the country (we already suspect we have located her through our access to the visual detail that Jefferies missed—the woman leaving the apartment with Thorwald early in the morning).

Jefferies becomes more persuasive, however, as his narrative is elaborated—as it seeks to maneuver around or incorporate ostensible obstacles. This includes his own creative bypassing of Doyle's proof. Why, he asks, would she send a postcard from the country saying she had arrived safely when she had spoken to him over the phone? Can we trust the landlord's observations if he has never before seen Mrs. Thorwald? He also becomes more persuasive as he deploys other kinds of evidence. When Lisa asserts that no woman would willingly take a trip without her wedding band, he listens, consults Stella ("I'd sooner cut off my finger," Stella confirms), and is satisfied, based on this unorthodox verification, that the evidence is sound. In a subsequent scene, he has his conviction strengthened by his ability to interpret empty space: he notes that Thorwald is the only neighbor who doesn't come to the window when the body of the little dog is discovered (killed because "he knew too much," he and Lisa postulate).

Jefferies constructs his narrative about what happened in the Thorwald apartment based on imaginative supposition and interpretation that gains credence as it becomes more linguistically "filled in." His detective friend Doyle constructs his counternarrative through an opposite strategy: disqualifying possibilities and deflating potential meanings. The two methods of "seeing" suggest the distinction between literary and cinematic representation. Doyle's literal-minded action-orientation aligns itself with narrative film, which tends to consign what it cannot represent visually to the realm of unreality. Jefferies's approach aligns itself with novelistic narrative in its elaboration of an unseen context for the image (and sometimes, as in the case of Thorwald's absence at the window and Mrs. Thorwald's absence in the apartment, in its elaboration of an unseen context for an absent image). Jefferies's form of seeing derives from the idea of the self as hidden and "deep." It assumes that only through imaginative projection can we hope to decipher the motives that drive individuals to act as they do. Projection carries the danger of twisting all evidence to conform to a paranoid or eccentric vision of reality. Doyle's form of seeing, by contrast, is based on an idea of the self as a function of surface reality, derived from general rules and norms (most men leaving their apartment with a woman early in the morning would be leaving with their wife)—*It* carries the danger of discounting anything that is not statistically prominent ("It's a thousand to one shot," he says of the murder). Hence victimized invalids like Mrs. Thorwald, who have no power and no visibility in the world, can, by Doyle's method, be easily substituted for by imposters and can disappear without leaving a trace. Both forms of seeing have their place in the search for meaning (Doyle's method might have benefited some of the mistaken identity cases that scatter other Hitchcock films). But since this film is concerned with the growth of subjectivity, Jefferies's form of seeing is favored above Doyle's.[13]

Finally, the last stage in the cinematic construction of a "mental process" involves the way Jefferies "reacts." Reaction, as it applies to this film, must be equated, at least in part, with *emotion,* since emotion is precisely what the conventional male subject is constructed to deny. Recent scholarship pertaining to male subjectivity has placed the issue of emotional responsiveness at its center, connecting the inability to feel with the inability of power to examine itself.[14] Unsurprisingly, therefore, the release of emotion, both in Jefferies and in the audience (for whom he serves as a surrogate), seems to involve the disturbance of what Eve Sedgwick has referred to as "the homosocial bond"—that network of relationships among men that form the bulwark of patriarchal power.

The pivotal scene that enacts this disturbance and sets the stage for Jefferies's affective awakening occurs when he and Lisa meet with Doyle to discuss their theory of the murder. The two men have already engaged in verbal sparring during their previous two encounters, but the tone has been amiable (we learn in passing that Jefferies and Doyle had served together in the war, a detail that reminds us that in the lexicon of masculinity actions speak louder than words). In this scene, however, the tone is different owing to the presence of Lisa. Doyle arrives while she is in the kitchen, but he hears her singing and glances suggestively at her open overnight case (displaying the nightgown and slippers that she exhibited to Jefferies earlier as a "preview of coming attractions"). When she appears, he is openly leering. Either unconscious of his look or in the manner of a woman used to being looked at this way, Lisa hands each man a glass of brandy and then, somewhat smugly, delivers the proclamation: "We think Thorwald's guilty."

When Lisa returns after leaving to get her own brandy from the kitchen, the three figures arrange themselves in a triangle with Doyle at the center. All three are swirling their brandy, though Lisa swirls her glass with the most ease and confidence. Caught up in expounding her theory to Doyle, she stands quite close to him, cradling her glass comfortably with one hand and gesturing animatedly with the other. At one point, she even touches his arm with her free hand, and he looks down to where she has touched. Her presence is clearly distracting him, making it hard for him to focus on his own argument and on his friend, Jefferies, whose peripheral role in the scene is reinforced by his lower position in the wheelchair. The camera, in other words, has identified Lisa both as an object of desire and as a threat and irritant to Doyle.

But how are we, the audience, expected to react to this identification? From Doyle's entrance up until this point, we are, indeed, oddly positioned with respect to point of view. Some of the shots are from Jefferies's point of view, others from Doyle's. The overall effect suggests that Jefferies knows precisely what his friend is thinking, having thought that way himself, but that he is, for the first time, uncomfortable with this knowledge. His continual, though rather lame, warning to Doyle ("Careful, Tom") is translatable as "Don't let yourself think what I know you are inclined to think." Critics have argued that Lisa occupies the role of a sexual fetish for Jefferies in the film, but it seems to me that this scene serves to put Doyle in the place where Jefferies had been and to mark a parting of the ways.

After Lisa's assertion about Thorwald's guilt, Doyle draws both of them out, appearing to be interested in their new theories about the murder. Then, suddenly, he slams the door in their faces. "Lars Thorwald is no more of a murderer than I am," he declares with brutal satisfaction. Doyle's reaction here pushes the woman aside, asserts a homosocial bond with Thorwald, and challenges Jefferies to take his place within this alliance. As the scene proceeds, Jefferies moves over to the window, refusing that alliance but also, significantly, withdrawing from the fray and allowing Lisa and Doyle to stand in more direct confrontation.

The scene works brilliantly to diffuse the spectator's resistance to the new kind of alliance that is being formed between Jefferies and Lisa (just as an earlier scene worked to diffuse our resistance to the idea of an invalid hero). Doyle's lust for and distrust of Lisa are being explicitly represented (and even activated in the audience to the extent that the camera encourages us to see Lisa as Doyle does) only to be dismissed as the "wrong" response. In this, we are like Jefferies, caught on the cusp of two perspectives. The scene ends with Jefferies and Lisa together near the window, allied against Doyle, who sits near the center of the room in self-satisfied but uneasy isolation. Iconographically, the figures now arrange themselves in what might be taken as a form of ironic cultural commentary: a man in a wheechair and a woman balance a man possessed of all his powers. But Doyle's insinuating looks, smarmy allusions, and brutal verbal sallies have already tipped the balance away from him. And in the event that we are still unsure of our loyalties, Hitchcock delivers a final touch: as Doyle prepares to leave, he takes a quick (manly) gulp from his brandy snifter, only to spill it down the side of his mouth and on his shirt (a counterpoint gesture to Lisa's poised and balanced swirling of her brandy). He has now been rendered ridiculous. Although Doyle has come to impart what appears to be definitive information discrediting the murder theory, this is all but lost in the gender dance of the scene. Ultimately, the scene works to build the audience's support for Jefferies's theory by emotionally discrediting its antagonist. In the next scene, when the little dog is found dead, we are prepared to accept unequivocally Jefferies's argument that Thorwald's failure to appear at the window is evidence of his guilt.

The scene with Doyle is the first of three scenes in which Jefferies's subject position is solidified through the way he "reacts." In this scene, as I have noted, he is situated outside of the direct confrontation between Doyle and Lisa (the sign of his rupture with Doyle but also of his unwillingness to side with Lisa). The audience is called upon to guess his actual feelings (to project its own feelings onto him). However, in the later scene, when Lisa is trapped in Thorwald's apartment, Jefferies's emotional response, implicit but largely taken over by us in the earlier scene, is explicitly represented "as frantic self-forgetful concern."[15] Stewart's face is extraordinarily expressive in this scene, almost to the point of recalling the libretto acting of silent film. But instead of appearing hokey and artificial, the exaggerated emotion works dramatically; we have been set up for it, so to speak. Lisa's errand (to find Mrs. Thorwald's wedding band) recedes into the background, both literally, in the way the scene is shot, and conceptually, in the sense that we are less interested in it than in Jefferies's reaction to it (just as, in the earlier scene, Doyle's information is eclipsed by the dance of emotional loyalties that the characters perform). Unable to act, Jefferies can feel. Indeed, it is his inability to act that has, to some extent, produced his ability to feel. That Hitchcock wished to make a point about his protagonist's emotional responsiveness seems clear when we consider that the scene is a marked departure from other depictions of emotion in Hitchcock films. Generally, as I have noted earlier, he preferred to impute the emotion through a blank face rather than through overt facial contortion, tears, or other outward signs (for example, Mrs. Verloc's face before stabbing her husband in *Sabotage* is unreadable, as are Eve's wide-open eyes as she stares at the killer at the end of *Stage Fright*). Moreover, Jefferies's emotional ordeal is triggered by Lisa's physical bravado, dramatizing a temporary reversal in conventional gender alignments relating to feeling and action.

The culminating "reaction" in Jefferies's story occurs when he directly confronts Thorwald. This scene condenses the paradoxes relating to male subjectivity that the film has raised and sought to resolve. Thorwald, alerted to Jefferies's surveillance, has now tracked him down. Alone in the apartment, Jefferies can only sit helplessly waiting, the echo of the killer's footsteps drawing ominously and inexorably nearer to his door. When Thorwald enters the room, however, the mood shifts. The man stands in the doorway, a very human figure, and speaks rather than acts. "What do you want from me?" he demands plaintively. "Say something. . . . Tell me what you want." Against all expectation, we are made to feel for the speaker. One thinks of Thorwald earlier, glimpsed serving his peevish wife; no doubt it was a question he often posed of her. Since the image of the nagging wife had initially drawn Jefferies into identification with Thorwald, it is as though we are being asked to duplicate that initial sympathetic identification. The difference now, of course, is that the question "What do you want from me?" is being posed of another man. It not only suggests that the speaker is being harassed, but that he is being betrayed by a brother. "What do you want from me?" implies that Jefferies has breached Thorwald's privacy, trampled on a male perogative that he should understand. What emotionally draws us in the question lies precisely in the way it conflates our conventional loyalties with our newly acquired distrust for authoritative judgments and our enhanced ability to "feel" (acquired during the confrontation scene between Doyle and Lisa). Jefferies's silence, reinforced by his shadowed, seated posture, is offputting because it suggests the detachment and omnipotence of the conventional male role that he has forfeited up until now.

Rapidly, however, the film repositions us. Thorwald's plaintive questioning gives way to an attack, a graphic reminder—indeed a reenactment—of the crime he committed against his wife. One could even say that Jefferies's silence has been a strategy to provoke the reenactment by revealing the nature of the man before him—a man who deals with frustration through violence. Yet at the same time that the attack destroys our sympathy for Thorwald and reactivates our sympathy for Jefferies, it also contravenes the authoritative effect of his silence. The silence now ceases to be the expression of judgment and power and becomes the silence of the trapped victim (just as Lisa's attack by Thorwald was experienced by us as silent because her screams could not be heard). The clutching and clamoring that occurs during the attack, filmed in accelerated action and focusing on the thrashing limbs, suggest a rape.

Jefferies's confrontation with Thorwald operates as a complement to the scene in which Lisa made her first appearance in the film. There, a shadow was shown to fall over Jefferies's sleeping face as her face, in a slow-motion effect, appeared bending forward to kiss him. Thorwald's attack is both a reversal and an extension of that earlier scene with Lisa. The protagonist himself is now in shadow; he is not sleeping but awaiting his visitor in a state of heightened consciousness. The encounter takes the form not of a slow-motion kiss but of an accelerated-motion struggle. The visitation embodied by Lisa, represented as a dreamlike vision from which the protagonist could awake, is now a visitation with which he must engage. In terms of cinematic representation, this is not so much a case of a "return of the repressed" as it is a moment of coalescence: the point where the character is activated as a subject. A literalized, emotionally fraught identification with the woman's position of the kind Jefferies is now forced to experience marks the moment when the construction of his "mental process" is complete. Being made to feel as a woman feels appears to be the closest thing to enacting a subjectivity for a man within the bounds of classical narrative film. The scene ends with Jefferies being pushed out the window and breaking his other leg—a result that assures him a continued stay in the "feminized" state that initiated his investment in this narrative of domestic violence in the first place and led him to become its victim.

Donald Spoto has argued that *Rear Window* is a lesson in introspection, with Jefferies's window-shopping a metaphorical fulfillment of Stella's remark that "sometimes we should get out of our houses and look in."[16] But such a reading assumes that there has been all along something for Jefferies to look into. As Peter Middleton has argued in his discussion of masculinity and subjectivity in modern culture, where masculinity has been defined as an active and externally directed expression of power, "the inward gaze is a vacant one."[17] What this suggests is precisely what *Rear Window* demonstrates, namely that the representation of male subjectivity must also be its construction. This process functions as a reversal of Freud's famous dictum of "making the unconscious conscious"; it requires instead a making of the conscious into the unconscious. In the struggle with Thorwald, Hitchcock manages to represent the idea that the hero is doing battle with the prototype of masculinity that he once was, infusing that entitled, aggressive position with the position of its "other," producing an identity that is no longer uninflected or "vacant." The cinematic function of Lisa in the film (her character, significantly, is absent from the Cornell Woolrich story on which the film is based) becomes clear: she acts as a beacon of subjectivity to which the male character must, through the circuit of plot, arrive.

Of course, the scene also ends with Jefferies vindicating his theory, bringing the murderer to justice, and triumphing over his complacent male friend. In short, despite his feminization, the trappings of masculine power and success remain intact and are even bolstered. This seems to me both the greatest and the most problematic achievement of the film. For, as the confrontation with Thorwald demonstrates, the assumption of an imaginative and moral position that refuses the homosocial bond can only be pushed to a certain point. The power of judgment is weak and without staying power when it does not have the force of patriarchy behind it. (The law that comes to Jefferies's rescue did not, it must be remembered, save Mrs. Thorwald.) Deprived of the backing of authority, the silence of the judge becomes the silence of the terrorized, the victim, the woman. If the male subject exerts his power in silence and detachment, the female subject exerts her power in talk and relationship. But it is not an equal match, and it is necessary to recruit the forms of the law—men like Jefferies—over to the other side. Hitchcock's films are themselves examples of such recruitment—of action plots wedded to psychological dramas. His films reshape public attitudes by keeping one foot in the world that they seek to revise. Critics have often maintained an analogy between Jefferies's relationship to what he sees and the filmmaker's relationship to the material from which the film is shaped.[18] However, Hitchcock seems to have produced less an analogue for his filmmaking than a myth about the genesis of a subjectivity akin to his own. Perhaps we are meant to conclude that the best way for Jefferies to "act" at the end of the movie is for him to become a filmmaker.

In the final scene Jefferies, with both his legs in plaster casts, is shown sleeping facing away from the window, with Lisa stretched out on a couch reading beside him. The scene marks the end of the action plot. Jefferies's position, with his back to the apartment windows, announces that the set has retired its role as a bridge between the external world and the internal life of character. The final vignettes in the windows can be construed as dream point-of-view shots, not Jefferies's any longer, but the filmmaker's (or some self-parody of the filmmaker), who has abandoned access to his protagonist. Likewise, the relationship between Jefferies and Lisa has been resolved only so that it can now take its own course. Lisa's presence on the couch, her uncharacteristic casual attire, and her maneuver with the book (she is reading *To the High Himalayas,* which she puts away to take up a copy of *Harper's Bazaar*) are ambiguous elements that escape narrative enclosure.[19] It is no wonder, given Hitchcock's desire to render cinematically what cinema seemed designed to ignore or suppress, that two years later he tried to represent a viable couple (that entity that promises to exist after Jefferies wakes up) much as he had tried to represent its precondition—the construction of a mental process for the male protagonist—in *Rear Window.*

Rear Window is Hitchcock's midcentury triumph of a cinematic method producing a literary end—a male action plot and point of view made to yield a narrative of character that had come, through novels, to be associated with women. His remake of *The Man Who Knew Too Much* (released two years later) goes one step further. It brings female subjectivity into the realm of action, where it becomes instrumental in the working out of the plot. The film also attempts to produce a workable model of sexual role complementarity, where *Rear Window* concentrated on the formation of a male subject and left the life of the couple outside the bounds of representation.

In the majority of his films, Hitchcock maintained the rule that had operated in nineteenth-century fiction, that marriage serve as the limit toward which the action tends. "The appeal of courtship over marriage as a literary subject is obvious," explains the literary critic Carolyn Heilbrun; "there is built in like the equipment in modern kitchens, suspense, danger, thwarted hopes, and a clearly understood reward." By contrast, she continues, "nothing so well marks [the modern] period as its refusal to take marriage for granted or to be content only to hint at its defects."[20] In this regard, classical narrative film, with the possible exception of screwball comedy, is a throwback to the Victorian narrative tradition in its favoring of the courtship plot with its "built in equipment." Hitchcock generally conformed to this formula except when he wanted the marriage itself to pose a mystery or constitute an obstacle (as in *Rebecca, Suspicion, The Paradine Case, Under Capricorn, Dial M for Murder,* and *Marnie*) or when the film was a clear deviation from the convention: *Easy Virtue, Rich and Strange,* and the early version of *The Man Who Knew Too Much* were done early in his career before he had solidified his style; *Mr. and Mrs. Smith* was done as a favor to Carol Lombard, and *Rope* and *I Confess* were experimental films predicated on replacing women with other things. But the 1956 version of *The Man Who Knew Too Much* is exceptional in not conforming to either category. It does not make the marriage a source of suspense, but neither does it represent an obvious departure from the Hitchcock style. When released, it was well received by a mass audience but little commented upon by critics, who tended to prefer the 1934 British version. While remaining within the bounds of the familiar and the conventional, *The Man Who Knew Too Much* thus makes forays into unconventional territory without announcing the fact. It emerges, from a vantage point of forty years later, as Hitchcock's critique of 1950s America on its own terms.[21]

The movie centers on an American family, Dr. Ben McKenna (James Stewart), his wife, the retired singer Jo Conway (Doris Day), and their son Hank (Christopher Olsen), who have embarked from Paris, where Ben had attended a medical convention, for a vacation in North Africa. The film opens with the family on a bus entering Marrakech. On the bus, a misunderstandng with a local Arab (Hank accidentally knocks off the veil of the Arab's wife) brings them into contact with a Frenchman, Louis Bernard (Daniel Gelin), who conciliates the dispute. Jo finds Bernard's interest in Ben and his evasiveness about himself suspicious, but Ben dismisses her suspicions. The next day, the McKennas visit the city's marketplace with the Draytons (Bernard Miles and Brenda de Banzie), a British couple they had met in a restaurant the night before. Suddenly, a fracas erupts in the bazaar, and Bernard, dressed as an Arab, staggers into the scene with a knife in his back. As he dies, he crawls toward Ben and whispers an enigmatic message about a plot to assassinate a foreign official in London. Later, when Ben is being questioned by the police, he learns that Bernard was a French agent working undercover. He also learns that the Draytons are actually behind the assassination plot and that they have kidnapped Hank to prevent Ben from revealing Bernard's message. The remainder of the film takes place in London, where Ben and Jo use Bernard's dying words as a clue to finding their son. Through their combined efforts, the assassination is averted and Hank is rescued.

The early scenes in *The Man Who Knew Too Much* show Jo and Ben exhibiting stereotypical gender-linked behavior. Jo reacts with nervous suspicion to Bernard and the Draytons when she first meets them; her husband paternalistically tries to calm and correct her. Female emotionalism is countered by male logic. Yet the conventional associations we are encouraged to draw from these reactions (confidence in Ben, dismissal of Jo) are also qualified by certain elements in the presentation. For one thing, the thriller genre requires that something unexpected happen, thus undermining Ben's complacency and supporting Jo's suspicions. For another, there is a hard-nosed, confident quality about the character of Jo McKenna as played by Doris Day that makes it harder to gauge how we are supposed to react to her. She bears no resemblance to the silly mothers of *Shadow of a Doubt, Strangers on a Train,* or *Stage Fright,* all of whom are older, frumpier, and more peripheral characters. But neither does she produce the kind of visual evocativeness associated with Ingrid Bergman and Grace Kelly, actresses clearly marked for the courtship plot. Bergman and Kelly are the symbols of a subjectivity situated within a male plot structure whereby the domestic sphere is conceived of as a mysterious and rather threatening place which men must be enticed to enter. Doris Day's Jo does not need to conform to this model because she has already produced what the other films make their goal, namely the domestication of the male protagonist. Ben has married her, settled down, and fathered a child. What then remains to be done? On a literal level, the film offers a rather lame version of the courship plot by including the fact that she wants a second child and he doesn't (that is, that his domestication is not complete). But this suggestion of something unfulfilled in the marital scenario is obviously different in kind from the desire that propells the male protagonist in Hitchcock's courtship-driven films. Instead, whatever friction may be said to exist between husband and wife in this film seems to derive from the routine nature of their relationship and to raise practical questions implicit in the overdetermined last scene of *Rear Window.* Questions such as: Where does authority lie in the family? What is the place of subjective experience? How are logic and emotion, one conventionally associated with men, the other with women, to be configured with respect to each other for the family to "work?"[22]

Jo and Ben are presented in this film as what Max Weber called "ideal types" of mature gender roles in conventional 1950s terms. Their typicality is highlighted by the way Hitchcock frames them as the American couple within two sociologically contrasting contexts: the Arab culture, with its exaggerated, formalized enactment of male domination and female subordination, and the British culture (or, at least, all we see of it) represented by Jo's wisecracking theater friends, whose amorphously defined roles and relationships constitute the other extreme. The delineation of a paradigmatic American family gains a historical dimension, moreover, when we place this film beside the 1934 British version. The earlier film draws the family as a dramatically eccentric unit (and Jo's theater friends may be an oblique derivative of this earlier representation): the mother is a sharpshooter, the father, an amiable gentleman of leisure, and the child (a girl in this version), a somewhat irritating gadfly whom both parents treat with amused nonchalance. The British version suggests a more flexible concept of family—which may well be the case for the period, or at least for Hitchcock at this point in his life—but can hardly be said to constitute, as has been argued, a more radical critique of gender roles than its successor.[23] In the earlier version, the looser role structure operates in the service of what Selznick termed Hitchcock's "bits of business"; it cannot really be forced into the mold of social critique (Hitchcock commented that the earlier film was the work of a talented amateur[24]). In the later version, by contrast, the delineation of an ideal type of the family, although it may reflect a greater entrenchment of gender stereotyped role-playing in the society, has the virtue of being such a systematic representation that even minute deviations become perceptible and potentially significant in their long-term implications. This is perhaps why the later version of *The Man Who Knew Too Much* has steadily gained in critical reputation. The further away one gets from it, the more it becomes possible to connect it with social changes that occurred in American society a decade later.

Assuming that the film attempts an anatomization of the nuclear family, the behavior manifested by the husband and wife in the early scenes deserves close attention. Contrary to most commentators, I do not think Hitchcock wants to depict a marriage in crisis when he shows Jo nagging, poking fun, and aggressively disagreeing with her husband.[25] The friction discernible in the couple's interactions early in the film seems intended, like the characters themselves, to be typical: to evoke the routine, everyday sense of how marriage "feels," as well as to alert us to the more general systemic sense of how couples come to negotiate within their roles a workable, if often strained, partnership. The plot of the film, then, becomes a matter of demonstrating how the qualities attached to conventional role behavior can be creatively deployed, their relative priority revised, without damaging the basic formula of male-female complementarity.

A key scene that demonstrates the film's method occurs in the restaurant where the McKennas first meet the Draytons. Much of the scene is centered on the difficulty Ben has sitting and eating in proper Arab style. The elaborate business relating to his awkwardness and discomfort, included ostensibly as a comic diversion, actually serves to present us with two contradictory ways in which Ben's character can be viewed. These are, in fact, two perspectives on masculinity that the film struggles to assimilate within its model of marital partnership. On the one hand, in a limited context (which I would equate with our attitude at the moment the scene is transpiring), Ben's inability to sit on the floor and eat the chicken with one hand largely supports his conventional role as a figure of authority in the film. The situation places emphasis on his height, on his impatience with the trivial aspects of daily life (also to be read as the customs of other "less civilized" peoples), and on his loftier priorities (he does not care about manners; he just wants to eat). His wife's behavior, as it differs from his in this context, merely supports the conventional doctrine of separate spheres in which women concern themselves with trivial and domestic matters, men with issues that are really important (as a surgeon, he is, after all, confronted with matters of life and death on a daily basis).

On the other hand, Ben's behavior in the restaurant can yield another meaning, because his ineptitude here foreshadows his errors later in the film. It suggests his inflexibility and his inability to think and act outside of established patterns. It also emphasizes the very limited technical skills that his work has focused on to the exclusion of other, perhaps closely related, skills (one would think that a highly trained surgeon would be able to eat chicken with one hand). Finally, the scene has another function, overlooked in recent criticism: it softens the representation of the character, balancing the conventional attributes of masculinity against a countervailing humanity suggested by his discomfort and ineptitude. In this sense, the scene functions like the broken leg that handicaps Jefferies to an ultimately positive end in *Rear Window.* When Ben is confronted the next day with the reality of his son's kidnapping, we sense his genuine confusion and frustration, what might be called the magnified image of his inability to eat the chicken in the restaurant. He even acknowledges this confusion in one of the more moving moments in the film, when he announces to Jo during their drive back from the police station: "I don't know what's the right thing to do."

Significantly, however, the statement is made before Jo knows anything about the kidnapping. Only after he has prevailed upon her to take tranquilizers (against her inclination) will he embark on an explanation that begins with his announcement that she was "right" in her assessment of Louis Bernard (he repeats this twice for emphasis before breaking the news of the kidnapping to her). The pattern of his statements is worth examining more closely because it reveals issues relating to marital hierarchy and the place of emotion within this hierarchy which will be reformulated as the couple grapples with crisis. Ben's insistence that his wife take the pills—an insistence that the film takes pains to dramatize—is framed by two statements that express his failure to know "right," once in the past with respect to Louis Bernard, once for the future with respect to his son's situation. The sedating of his wife coincides with his (twice-repeated) pronouncement that she, by contrast, was "right" in her assessment of Bernard. The effect is to connect the wife's rightness with the husband's wrongness and make her sedation appear an effort to "right" that imbalance. So long, it seems, as the woman is felt to be wrong, she can be corrected by male authority. When, however, she is right (i.e., when her reaction coincides with events), she becomes a threat to masculine order and action; she undermines the logical pursuit of solutions or, on a more abstract level, she undermines or perhaps confuses the male sense of his own rightness and power. She must be put out of play.

The scene in which Ben argues with his wife to take a sedative before telling her about the kidnapping of their son enacts a struggle for control at the heart of the film: What kind of sensibility is to prevail in the representation of this story? That this is represented as a struggle, even as the husband wins in the particular case, alerts us to a potential revision in the positioning of the two roles and the related forms of representation that correspond to them (just as the couple's earlier quarreling alerted us to a potential, if unrealized, equality in the couple's perceptions about things). Ben, literal and linear-minded, damping his wife's more volatile sensibility, might be compared to the spirit of classical narrative film seeking to subdue novelistic, psychological character as this threatens to overwhelm and subvert the requirements of plot. Ben's insistence seems predicated on what is best for Jo and more generally for the family (Jo's hysteria would delay him in devising a plan of action). And yet, as orchestrated, it is hard to know for sure the cause of Jo's muffled hysteria—is it the news of the kidnapping or the recognition that she has been sedated and thus made incapable of a clear response? (A similar confusion of cause and effect is present in the stabbing scene in *Sabotage*.) The confusion relayed by this scene also has larger symbolic implications: Does male mediation of female subjectivity actually produce that subjectivity? Something of the same question was raised in my discussion of the evolution of the novel, where I explained how male novelists gave impetus to a domestic novel form, refining and empowering a female "central intelligence" that ultimately became a threat to patriarchal culture. Film (a restraint put in place to damp this feminization) serves, in Foucaultian terms, to incite a new, elaborated form of that which it was designed to suppress. Once the struggle between male objectivity and female subjectivity can be so ambiguously represented, assumptions about the two extremes of relating to experience have become fair game for manipulation and revision. Robin Wood has noted that Ben embodies the idea of male authority as it struggles to stave off its own hysteria, his large figure always on the verge of toppling—the literal fear experienced by his character in *Vertigo*.[26] Thus Ben himself can be said to project onto his wife the hysteria that he fears will overcome and incapacitate him. The sense of a repressed emotion is in fact dramatized from the moment Ben hears of his son's kidnapping, beginning with the close-up of his hand grasping and riffling the telephone directory, through his stoical journey back to the hotel, culminating finally in the scene where he sedates his wife and scuffles with her when she realizes what he has done. In this last instance, the act of sedating Jo and forcing her to lie down is as much a reflection of his panic as a prophylactic measure for hers.

Although Ben succeeds in subduing his wife and himself in this scene, the rest of the film replays the scene in new contexts in which the balance of power has altered. The first stirrings of change are discernible in the next scene. It begins (after an exterior shot that tells us night has fallen) with Ben packing his son's clothes in the darkened hotel room. The care with which he puts the little suit jacket and slippers into the suitcase belies his clumsiness in the earlier restaurant scene and contrasts with his jumpiness (culiminating in the scuffle with his wife) in the previous scene. Reflected in a mirror at which he glances is the prostrate body of Jo as she emerges from her drug-induced sleep. The scene recalls the nature of Ben's profession: as a surgeon, he is used to anesthetizing people in order to perform his job. In this case, however, the variables have been changed to emphasize the small-scale, technical side of the husband's activity. Moreover, the separation between the man's work and the woman's body also brings into relief the difference between the situation of surgery, where the site of intervention is, literally, the prostrate body, and the situation here, where the site of intervention is not at hand and is, in fact, unknown. Not only does Ben have no idea where his son is being held hostage but the very act of trying to find him poses risks: the boy must be rescued in such a way that he will not be harmed. In this context, Jo's body, instead of seeming incidental to the male activity (Hitchcock now crosscuts between Ben's packing and Jo's immobilized, but now conscious, figure), becomes weighted with potential significance. The conventional priority of the positions of the characters (Ben standing, Jo lying down) have been altered.[27] We are dealing with action and spectacle, figure and ground, not as hierarchical functions but as two dimensions of a task that lies ahead. In the remainder of the film the female character is given an instrumental role in the plot, not, as in the original version, by simply making her capable of conventional male action (being able to handle a gun and hit a target under pressure), but by linking her action to psychological and emotional aspects of character. These are the qualities that film had traditionally marginalized with respect to an action plot. Their deployment now in the service of such a plot constitutes a tour de force of what I would call gender choreography.

The scene in Albert Hall during which Jo screams and averts the assassination of the foreign dignitary is a replay of the earlier private struggle between husband and wife in the hotel room. Only now the scene is designed to grant each partner a role rather than to put one partner out of play for the convenience of the other. Instead of being together in a bedroom, Ben and Jo are now separated in a public auditorium: he is running, opening the doors of the private boxes seeking the gunman, while she remains immobilized at the back of the orchestra in a state of mounting panic, watching the gun, which is aimed at the foreign minister, emerge from behind the curtain in the balcony above. Her scream coincides with Ben's opening the right door. His scuffle with the gunman in front of the balcony now replaces the earlier scuffle with her in front of the bed. Both her panic and his, suppressed and turned in against each other before, has, in this scene, been given play in the service of the plot. The assassination attempt and the gunman become the intermediaries by which his action and her emotion can find a functional release.

In the climactic scene soon afterward, the same pattern is enacted, only this time with more focus and deliberation. Jo, at Ben's instigation, maneuvers an invitation to the embassy where they believe Hank is being held hostage. Once there, she agrees to perform for the prime minister and his guests. Her singing carries to the upstairs rooms, where Hank recognizes her voice and whistles the tune back to signal his presence. Ben hears and, catalyzed by Mrs. Drayton's scream (she thinks that her husband is coming to kill the boy), breaks down the door.

The final rescue—Ben's aggressive action in response to a woman's emotion—recapitulates the Albert Hall scene, which recapitulates the sedation scene. That earlier scene can now be read as the blueprint for the rescue, a blueprint that also demonstrates how much has changed in the balance of the husband-wife relationship. Gender roles continue to reflect stereotypical characteristics, but the heriarchy associated with these characteristics is no longer in place. The emotion, repressed in the earlier sedation scene, has now been activated to achieve a functionally liberating end.

The sedation scene is thus the originating pattern for gender role behavior—the template on which the couple's future is to be mapped. That other scenarios could emerge from that pattern is clear if we consider the stabbing in the shower in *Psycho* and the rape-strangulation in *Frenzy,* where the woman is simply annihilated at the hands of the man. What seems to make possible the revival of the couple as complementary partners in *The Man Who Too Much* resides in the way Hitchcock was able to narratize the woman's role through her connection with her son. This relationship is represented in an earlier scene in the hotel room in which Jo and Hank are shown singing together. Our initial tendency is to dismiss this mother-son duet as a cloyingly sentimental diversion. Taken out of context, it does indeed resemble a number out of a second-rate musical comedy. It begins as Jo moves about Hank's room while he sits on the stool in front of the bed. She hums absentmindedly (the song is the saccharine "Que Sera Sera"); he then begins to sing; then she sings; then she sings and he whistles; and finally, they sing the last refrain together and dance. This coordinated musical dialogue is accompanied by little orchestrated acts of maternal ministration: she prepares his bed, throws him his slippers, takes out his bathrobe and helps him into it. Meanwhile, Ben is shown in the other room knotting his tie in front of the mirror and reacting with amused dismissiveness ("He'll make a fine doctor"), while Bernard is seated on the balcony far behind him. We, the audience, are situated like Bernard (with other things on our mind) and are encouraged to react, like Ben, with a sense of indulgent superiority and to assume that the scene has been included to give Doris Day a chance to sing. (When Bernard shows interest in Jo's singing, we are inclined, like Jo herself, to suspect ulterior motives.)

Yet what had seemed trite and insignificant while it was transpiring acquires genuine pathos after the fact. For when the duet is reinvoked in a new context at the end of the film, it becomes a code for a mother's love for her son and for the horror of their separation. The closest thing to the emotional impact of the song at the end of *The Man Who Knew Too Much* is the dinner table scene at the end of *Sabotage,* where the sight of Stevie's empty place recalls the earlier dinner when Stevie was alive and present. Here, too, Hitchcock had encoded a narrative of maternal love (in this case, really sisterly love) into the film in order to invoke it later. But *The Man Who Knew Too Much* is able to duplicate the emotional effect while gratifying its audience with a happy ending because it employs its female character differently. Here is where Doris Day's qualities as a performer are of special importance. There are obvious pitfalls attached to casting a well-known singer such as Day in a dramatic thriller and then actually having her sing. But Hitchcock seems not only to have been attuned to these pitfalls but to have self-consciously exploited them to further his ends.[28] Since her role is to disrupt the action at designated intervals, her voice supplies a concentrated form of intervention. Even if Grace Kelly or Ingrid Bergman were able to sing, I suspect they would have been less effective in the role of Jo than Day because their physical evocativeness would have been distracting. Day serves Hitchcock as the embodiment of a femininity that is not diffuse and atmospheric but materially instrumental in the working out of the plot.

Ultimately, this recruitment of emotion to the side of plot salvages the idea of the nuclear family. As the McKennas, now reunited, hurry into the hotel room, displaying themselves to their debauched British friends, they resemble the preserved specimens of big-game animals that decorated the walls of the taxidermist, Ambrose Chappell (the false lead whose shop Ben visits when he first arrives in London). Here is an American family "saved" for the inspection of a curious audience. In this preserved family, the female role has been given more play but has remained tied to a conventional model of male-female complementarity and has served the ends of the patriarchal plot. In this way, the film represents the other side of the experiment of *Rear Window,* where the male protagonist is transformed into a subjectivity but manages, nonetheless, to do the conventional male job of solving the murder. Both films reflect Hitchcock's understanding that conventional roles must be revised to accommodate the complex demands of modern life: women must be given more access to a world of action; men, more access to a world of feeling. Yet while both films make role revision serve the old model of family and couple, they raise questions about the future. To allow female emotion to be attached to a narrative that is no longer buried but crucial to the resolution of the action is also to give it an unprecedented importance, liable to upset the complementarity of gender roles. It is also liable to challenge the dominance of plot over character, hierarchy which is the cornerstone of visual realism and the means by which narrative film first established its hegemony within the realm of representation.

The image of mother and son singing together in *The Man Who Knew Too Much* suggests a new relational configuration that comes to the fore in Hitchcock's films of the 1960s, eclipsing the "daughter's effect." Critics have noted that this is the sole film in Hitchcock's repertory that renders a mother in a wholly positive light. In other films, when the woman emerges from daughterhood into motherhood, she becomes an uncontrolled subjectivity, a creature who, in the mind of her son, is at best out to embarrass him, at worst to destroy him. We are back again to where the impetus of narrative film can be said to spring, in a defense against the threatening power of female subjectivity (originally associated with novels). In *The Man Who Knew Too Much,* the son is a boy and not a man. In *Psycho,* he is a man in a state of arrested development. *Psycho* might be termed Hitchcock's imagination of Hank McKenna's future in a world where his mother has escaped the control of his father and where traditional controls on plot, character, and relationship have been eased by a filmmaker who has likewise forfeited his paternal role.

However, before that vision crystallized, Hitchcock made *The Wrong Man* and *Vertigo,* films that deconstruct earlier notions of plot, character, and relationship, and provide an opening for the emergence of a new configuration.

7 Transition: *The Wrong Man, Vertigo*

The *Wrong Man* and *Vertigo,* released in 1956 and 1958 respectively, are important transitional works in Hitchcock's repertory. Both show the filmmaker cutting loose from the novelistic and familial influences that informed his earlier films and that were the legacy of Victorian culture. Hitchcock's move to Hollywood in 1939 and the influence of David O. Selznick initially gave new form and vigor to this legacy. But Hitchcock was also an observer of the American scene, and he found in the images and social conventions of mid-twentieth-century America a means of representing changes in himself. By the early 1960s, the conditions of Hitchcock's life in America had led him to abandon a Victorian notion of character. *The Wrong Man* and *Vertigo* can be read as two stages in a process of letting go. They represent a bridge between the character-centered films of the 1940s and 1950s and the character-effacing films of the 1960s and 1970s.

The Wrong Man is based on an actual case that Hitchcock read about in *Life* magazine. It tells the story of Christopher Emmanuel Balestrero, known as Manny (Henry Fonda), who lives modestly with his wife Rose (Vera Miles) and two sons in Queens, and works as a musician at the Stork Club in Manhattan. One day, he visits the local insurance company with the intention of borrowing money on a policy to pay for his wife's expensive dental work. As he waits to complete the transaction, he is mistakenly identified by employees as the man who had robbed the company at gunpoint some time before. When other merchants in the area who had been robbed by the same man confirm the identification, he is booked and jailed. The second half of the film records Manny's efforts, once out on bail, to find witnesses to testify on his behalf. It also chronicles the mental breakdown of his wife, who irrationally blames herself for his ordeal. Finally, when his prospects look especially bleak, his mother urges him to pray, and as if in answer to his prayers, the real criminal is caught. At the end of the film, a written text superimposed on the screen assures us of Rose's recovery and the family's resettlement in Florida.

At its release, *The Wrong Man* was widely publicized as an authentic rendering of a true story. Publicity posters for the film proclaimed it to be "the first Hitchcock film taken from life. Every twist and turn of it is true," and Hitchcock himself makes an unprecedented appearance on screen before the film begins, announcing that "this is a true story—every word of it." In his later conversation with Truffaut, he repeated the claim, insisting that the drive for "authenticity" had motivated him throughout: "Everything was minutely reconstructed with the people who were actually involved in that drama."[1] He even let it be known that Vera Miles bought her wardrobe for the role at the thrift shops where Rose Balestrero had shopped.

Nonetheless, claims of truth and authenticity must be taken with a grain of salt. The actual case as reported in the *Life* magazine article did not follow the inexorable downward spiral that the film records.[2] Indeed, the film can hardly be said to reflect a documentary approach. Despite the on-location footage and sparse dialogue, the images are as artfully arranged and the structure of the plot as schematic as any in the Hitchcock repertory. Bernard Hermann's score and Robert Burks's cinematography both contribute substantially to setting a mood for the film, and the use of black-and-white film stock at a time when color had become the norm suggests a calculated pursuit of effect (to be employed again in *Psycho*). Hitchcock is reported to have told Burks that he "wanted it to look like a newsreel shot,"[3] though even this claim is disingenuous when one considers the inordinate use of crosshatched shadow—an effect which consistently invokes the dominant theme of imprisonment and, more melodramatically, of crucifixion.

In fact, what *The Wrong Man* does is manipulate familiar Hitchcockian techniques, images, and themes to suggest a realistic treatment. Picturesque locales, lavish color photography, glamorously turned-out performers, exciting action punctuated by humorous business, and, of course, a piquant love interest—elements that were central to the appeal of *To Catch a Thief,* released the year before—are all subverted or eliminated. This reflects more than a simple attempt to deglamourize the film and thereby produce an illusion of reality. The reversal of conventional effects that characterizes *The Wrong Man* strikes at the literary core of Hitchcock's cinematic enterprise. Hitchcock's drive of the 1940s and 1950s was an attempt to reclaim novelistic (that is, psychological) character for cinematic representation and to accommodate gender complementarity to this reclamation process. *Rear Window* was about the construction of subjectivity for its male protagonist, while *The Man Who Knew Too Much* meshed the gender characteristics of the couple. *The Wrong Man* reverses the drive of both these films. It moves relentlessly to strip the protagonist of an active identity without substituting a compensating subjective identity. By the same token, female subjectivity, as embodied in Rose, becomes an encumbrance rather than an aid to the protagonist and to the working out of the plot. In discarding the notion of character and couple that had increasingly lent weight and complexity to his Hollywood films, Hitchcock sought the cover of documentary realism. The claim of realism acquitted him of responsiblity for a change in perspective, a change which he must have realized would be unpopular with his traditional audience and which he was perhaps not yet prepared to own, even to himself. Hitchcock also distanced himself from the film after it was made. "The industry was in a crisis at the time," he explained to Truffaut, "and since I'd done a lot of work for Warner Brothers, I made this picture for them without taking any salary for my work. It was their property."[4] The statement can be compared to disclaimers made about *Rope* (where he attributed the film's peculiarities wholly to his experimentation with technique). *Rope,* however, stands out as an isolated experiment, while *The Wrong Man* sets the direction for the remainder of his career. Among subsequent films, only *North by Northwest* is a throwback to the style and tone of his earlier Hollywood films.

The lengthy opening sequence of *The Wrong Man* deserves examination for the methodical way in which it both invites and subverts our expectations about meaning. As the credits begin, we see the elegantly dressed patrons of the Stork Club dancing and sitting at tables. The music, produced by a small band at the back of the room, is a lively rhumba. Watching these opening shots, one imagines that the hero and heroine will be drawn from the couples on the dance floor or seated at the tables. As the crowd thins to suggest the hour is getting late (an effect obtained through a series of lap dissolves), this impression is reinforced: one of the few remaining couples will surely be the focus of the narrative. But once the credits end, the camera shifts to the band, formerly only glimpsed in the background, where Manny is playing the bass fiddle. After teasing us with one more shot of the remaining couples in the club, the camera returns to Manny as the music ends, taking him as its object. It records him putting aside his instrument and walking away from the band area and out the door. He says goodnight to the doorman and walks briskly to the subway entrance. The camera follows, and we are once again given a false lead as two policemen on their beat stroll behind Manny, the backs of their dark uniforms symmetrically placed on either side as though about to close in for an arrest. But as Manny descends into the subway the policemen are cropped from the shot, obviously continuing on their way on the sidewalk. There is a quick overhead shot from the top of the subway steps showing Manny at the bottom, then a shot of him on the platform as the train arrives. As he takes a seat inside, he pulls a newspaper out of his pocket, turns briefly to the racing page, then to an ad for a Ford automobile showing a family around a car and the title "Family Fun," then to another for New York Savings Bonds. In a close-up of his face he glances somewhat furtively to the side for a moment and then turns back to the racing page. The train stops, and we see him emerge and enter a subway coffee shop. He converses briefly with the man behind the counter and orders a cup of coffee (the exchange indicates that he is known to stop here at this hour). He takes the coffee to a nearby table and returns to the newspaper, this time taking out a pen and marking the list of horses on the racing page. The next shot shows him on the sidewalk, approaching his home. He mounts the steps, takes a milk bottle from the stoop, unlocks the door, and enters the dark hall. He looks in at the first door, where two boys are shown sleeping in one bed, smiles slightly, then continues down the hall, depositing the milk in the refrigerator. Finally, he slips into his bedroom. The shot is dark for a second, then the room is illuminated—the light switched on by his wife, who is lying in the bed, kept awake by a toothache. Only now, as his conversation with her begins, do we finally learn the true nature of the man whom the camera has been so doggedly tracking up until now.

What we learn about Manny is decidedly at odds with the impression that the opening sequence, with its virtual absence of dialogue, has created. Each image registered by the camera has been charged with potential dramatic meaning that we reflexively fill it in based on our conditioning in the conventions of the suspense film. The Stork Club is a posh night club and Manny's association with it casts an aura of glamour onto him (his familiarity with the doorman reinforces the sense of his insider status). The scene with the policemen creates a vague climate of suspicion, and the maneuver with the newspaper on the subway suggests that this man is a gambler with something to hide. The service in the coffee shop ("The usual?)" supports the idea that he "hangs out" there, and, of course, his marking of the racing page reinforces the suggestion of morally dubious behavior. There is even a portentousness about his entering his house at such a late hour, especially given the muted score and the emphasis on darkness and shadow (although the milk bottle that he picks up outside the door begins the countermovement that will be completed when Manny begins his conversation with his wife and reveals himself to be a wholesome family man).

As we watch Manny, we expect to find something that will justify our interest in him and set the plot in motion. The effect resembles that of the first panning shot in *Rear Window* that settles on Jefferies's sleeping face and causes us to expect his awakening to coincide with the activation of an exciting narrative—an expectation thwarted when the second panning shot ends by tracking from the sleeping face down to the leg cast. The effect of the camera's concentration on the details of Manny's trip home also resembles the false suspense moments (Hitchcock called them "suspense effects") that spotted earlier films (the use of the threatening dog on the stairs in *Strangers in a Train* prior to Guy's entry into Bruno's father's bedroom, for example). But here the context has been stretched so that not only is the particular supposition that the image evokes revealed to be false, but also the very terms under which we have been operating to deduce meaning are revealed as false. In other words, the signifiers we are shown do not fit into the master narrative that we have been made to anticipate. This, you may recall, was the way Doyle responded to experience in *Rear Window.* Whereas Jefferies sought to build meaning by extrapolating from the visible to the invisible, Doyle stubbornly opposed this: "Did you ever own a saw?" he asked, refusing to see Thorwald's saw as different from anyone else's. This literalizing tendency is the premise of a documentary approach to experience, which announces in advance that what will be represented will not fit neatly within a narrative structure—the importance of "things" being not in what they suggest about what we don't know but in what they are in themselves. Meaning gets constructed by induction, by simple accretion, rather than by deduction. However, what keeps *The Wrong Man* from fully conforming to this documentary method is that its thwarting of narrative meaning is ultimately a form of foreshadowing for a more all-encompassing narrative of mistaken meaning. The details of Manny's homeward journey are not arbitrary; they are signifiers that help explain how he will be interpreted by other eyes later. His admission to occasionally playing the horses leads the detectives to see him as a gambler, his association with the Stork Club suggests to them that he is a "high-roller," and his family responsibilities and debts are used to support a portrait of a man desperate for money.

Focusing on the surface details of this man's existence is conducive to a narrative supporting his guilt. In life, surface meanings in a case like this tend to work in contradictory ways, some signifiers supporting guilt, others innocence. In *The Wrong Man,* however, Hitchcock is concerned with a series of accidents in which the accrual of meaning occurs in the mistaken direction only. The initial impetus that appears to set the faulty interpretation of Manny in motion involves a number of coincidental elements: his need to borrow money on his wife's insurance policy, his entrance into the company's office with his hand in his pocket, and his slight resemblance to the man who had robbed the company. Yet even if these occurrences precipitate the plot of mistaken identity, it is questionable whether they are enough to keep that plot on course. What seems to have made this possible is something about Manny himself—something in his self-presentation. Whenever he is shown alone or interacting with strangers, his body is remarkably still, his face without apparent expression. The impassivity of his manner supports our interpretation without offering a corrective as the interpretation continues to take shape. This is what fuels our speculation about his possibly illicit activity early in the film. The effect is repeated in the insurance office where, by simply standing and waiting his turn, he attracts the nervous attention of the female clerk. Hitchcock stages the scene with this contrast in mind: the jumpy tremulous reaction of the woman (who gathers other women to her, all of whom quickly dissolve into a similar hysteria) against Manny's stoney-faced immobility. He is the tabula rasa upon which the clerk projects her imagination of excitement and danger. The scene bears comparison to the recognition scene in *Strangers on a Train.* The close-up shot of the clerk as she stares at Manny (eyes panicky behind glasses, lips parted, body temporarily paralyzed) resembles the close-up of Barbara (played by Hitchcock's daughter) as she "saw" the true identity of the villain in the earlier film. Only here, of course, the woman recognizes the wrong man, a fact that Hitchcock takes care to bring home to us at the end of the film when the same woman meets Manny's gaze after she has identified the "right" man—her look no longer one of emotional intensity but of guilt and embarrassment.

Why does Manny's tentative figure and impassive face produce this kind of false recognition in those who look at him? The answer seems to be a function of what it is his self-presentation "really" means. In other words, there is a connection between the "wrong" identity ascribed to Manny and his "right" identity. The very details that at first encourage us to produce a false narrative can actually be shown to produce a true one if we apply a consistently opposite interpretation. Thus, for example, Manny's work at the Stork Club is not to gain access to the "fast lane" but to provide for his family, despite the late hours and the long commute. (Indeed, his lawyer notes that the club will vouch for his character at the trial.) The marking of the racing sheet that initially looks like a guilty act is, we later learn, only a game which, when he explains it to his wife, becomes a tribute to his self-control and his sense of responsiblity concerning how to use his money. Similarly, the coffee at the diner, far from being the expression of possibly illicit solitary habits, becomes, retrospectively, a way of dramatizing Manny's later assertion to the detective that he doesn't drink. In short, although the trip home first encourages us to read Manny as the detectives will do, it also subsequently acts to discredit the detectives' interpretation and to refer us to another narrative, that of the exemplary family man. The correct reading of the details of Manny's homeward journey shows him to be not only *not* guilty—a condition he shares with the other mistaken identity heroes in Hitchcock—but also profoundly innocent.

Manny's innocence has important implications for the structure and style of the film. Mistaken-identity victims in earlier Hitchcock's films always harbored some guilt and could therefore be said to reap some form of justice in the ordeals they were made to suffer. Guy Haines is the most extreme example, but a suggestion of guilt clings even to Father Logan in *I Confess*. Manny's fate, however, is wholly unwarranted. On the one hand, this can be understood as Hitchcock's way of dramatizing the basically flawed nature of human justice (and, if one is convinced by the ending, the role of faith in bringing about individual salvation). Yet while this may thematically explain the unrelenting quality of Manny's ordeal, it does not explain the peculiarly unsettling quality of the characterization on us and on others within the film. To explain this, it becomes necessary to link the very exemplary nature of Manny's life to the fact of his victimization.

It seems that in performing his roles of husband, father, and son so well, Manny has disappeared within them. Our tendency to read illicit meaning into the Stork Club, the racing sheet, and the diner are all attempts to affix a "masculine" plot of adventure and irresponsibility—recalling the life that Jefferies of *Rear Window* led prior to his accident—onto Manny's life. Instead, these same variables bespeak a narrative that goes unnoticed because its continuity suggests repetition rather than linear progression of the kind we are conditioned to want from our heroes. The "outside" world, the symbolic site of action and variety within the lexicon of narrative film, is not really available to Manny. It exists only as a passage back to a domestic space. The image of the subway train and of the tunnel that Hitchcock films stretching in front of the train expresses the idea vividly, as does the image of the house whose door Manny must unlock to enter. (It is as he fumbles for his key, in fact, that the detectives first arrest him.) In *Rear Window,* Jefferies, cut off from a life of action due to his accident, is compelled to find a domestic plot and to fashion a subjectivity within it. Manny, by contrast, has already been conditioned to a variety of constraints so that the imposition of another does not produce resistance, only a numbing fatigue: when released on bail, his overwhelming need is to sleep.[5]

Hitchcock takes pains to dramatize the way an absence of resistance in the character is taken advantage of, first through the imposition of a false identity, then through the physical humiliation of booking and imprisonment. The film chronicles, with excrutiating deliberation, the process of incarceration: the fingerprinting, the emptying of the pockets, the physical search, and finally the removal of the tie—the last access to a means of self-assertion—

before the actual jailing. This sequence is, to my mind, practically unwatchable, both tedious and painful at the same time. Yet Hitchcock later remarked to Truffaut that this was the portion of the film he was most proud of, frankly acknowledging his emotional investment in it: "I did fancy the opening of the picture because of my own fear of the police."[6] This, then, is the enactment of the nightmare-fantasy in which Hitchcock as a child was locked up in the local prison at his father's orders. Critics of the film, including Truffaut, argued that it was unrealistic in failing to register the emotion of the victim. But Hitchock's point appears to be that he was reenacting a childhood event (or fantasy about such an event)—and it is a characteristic of the child that it cannot take in and hence cannot resist, either physically or emotionally, what is happening. We may recall that an early, unpopular death in Hitchcock was the death of the boy in *Sabotage.* Part of the different kind of discomfort one feels in watching the first half of *The Wrong Man* is connected to the fact that this is not a child but a grown man suffering a similarly gratuitous victimization. During his ordeal, Manny is continually ordered, as if he were a child, to remove his hat. He is also addressed, like a child, by his first name—a name which itself suggests his status as an infantalized man.[7]

The Wrong Man depicts a condition of vulnerability and helplessness for its male protagonist that can be said to correspond to the self-conception that led Hitchcock into filmmaking. His career in film was his defense; it gave him access to technological expertise and to a means of manufacturing fantasies in order to bolster his fragile and insecure self-image. His personal story can be connected to the larger story of patriarchal culture as it too sought to bolster itself against an increasingly powerful feminine literary culture. Narrative film shaped the world to the male gaze and clarified and empowered that gaze in the process. *The Wrong Man* depicts a world where such shaping is absent. It is what the man fears he could be reduced to were the magnified images of the movie screen not present to convince himself and others of the importance of his role.

Although the fantasy of being locked up that the film records seems to have its roots in Hitchcock's early life, *The Wrong Man* can also be said to encode a crisis occurring at the time the film was made. Indeed, it may be a personal crisis that Hitchcock was invoking when he referred so unconvincingly to a crisis in the industry. America's devotion to conformity, its drive for material success, and its support for rigid stereotypes and conventions appear as central themes in Hitchcock's films of the 1950s, but only in *The Wrong Man* do they emerge as overriding, destructive forces.[8] The film seems to mark a pivotal moment in Hitchcock's development, a moment when his social observations became extensions or analogues for stress in his personal life.

Two scenes are especially revealing with respect to this self-conception. The first introduces Manny to us as the film's protagonist. The camera, having concentrated on the elegantly dressed patrons of the Stork Club, cuts to him in the shadowed background space where the band plays. He is shown in profile, holding the bass fiddle, mechanically doing his job. The glamour and festivity of the club are rendered in contrast to his status behind the scenes, present but virtually invisible to those whom he is entertaining. The second noteworthy scene takes place when Manny is brought up before a group of police officers to be registered prior to his arraignment. He stands on a bare platform, an oversized microphone practically obliterating his features. He is told curtly to remove his hat, is asked to recite his name and address, and is perfunctorily dismissed.

These scenes can be read as metaphors for the filmmaker's conception of himself in the eyes of his audience. One scene equates with a sense of invisibility, the other with a sense of callous misrecognition. (Hitchcock's unusual appearance at the beginning of the film on an empty sound stage both invokes and seeks to counter the scene in which Manny is displayed but "misrecognized" by the audience of police officers[9]). In Hitchcock's British films, character asserted itself: the look that would seek to misrepresent met resistance. Richard Hannay in *The 39 Steps* is the early prototype of the active, resisting hero. Faced with being misread by the world, Hannay determines to find the real villain and prove his innocence. But if such a character reflects Hitchcock's newly empowered self-conception at the outset of his career, then Manny is his disempowered self-conception at a later point. Manny offers no resistance to the look of the sales clerks, merchants, detectives, and policemen, and they are free to impose the meanings they choose. When not being misread, he simply fades into the background, content not to be looked at at all—hidden in the shadows behind the bass fiddle at the Stork Club and shuttling home from work underground.

The shift in vision registered in *The Wrong Man* is also connected to an apparent loss of faith in the power of the couple to sustain meaning in the face of adversity. In the 1940s and 1950s, Hitchcock introduced the woman's responding gaze (what I have termed the "daughter's effect") as a complement and corrective to male action. In *Spellbound,* Constance's power to revise meaning saves Ballantine. Barbara's look at the villain in *Strangers on a Train* causes him to lose control and resets the balance that will lead eventually to a just resolution of the plot. Francie's (Grace Kelly) brazen come-ons to Robie (Cary Grant) in *To Catch a Thief* ultimately help to clear him of robbery charges while they also "catch" him in marriage. Manny's wife originally seems to occupy a role like that of past Hitchcock heroines. She is determined to counteract the world's misidentification of her husband, overcoming her shyness in order to call a lawyer to defend him and eagerly grasping at the leads they can pursue together to prove his innocence. But as his tentative efforts at action prove futile against the crushingly authoritative and indifferent social bureaucracy, her emotional support wears itself out. "How do I know you're not guilty?" she asks as she sinks into depression and paranoia, finally turning against herself all the energy that would otherwise have been directed to prop him up and stare down his accusers. Ben's sedation of Jo in *The Man Who Knew Too Much* was an enactment of power relations within the couple that was gradually revised in the course of that film. But Manny's initial character is too tentative and feeble to warrant this kind of revision. Indeed, the institutionalization of Rose after her breakdown can be viewed as a kind usurpation of what in the earlier film was Ben's role. Society, in the form of the psychiatrist, takes over from the husband the management of the wife. It is as though the more democratic conception of the couple that is achieved at the end of *The Man Who Knew Too Much* exists at the outset of *The Wrong Man,* but with the result that the couple can no longer endure as a functioning complementary structure in the face of crisis. His plodding activity and her wellspring of imagination and feeling—plot and character—now exist without recourse to each other.

The film returns in the end to a superficial assertion of old values in order to produce a sense of closure: the right man is ultimately caught, and Rose, we are told in the written text superimposed on the screen, recovers. Yet these events, detailed in the final minutes, seem unconvincing and incidental to the larger feel of the film. The right man appears as though in answer to Manny's prayers, a highly contrived implication in a film that has not previously invoked religion except as a source of imagery. Rose's recovery is even more untenable because the film fails to represent it visually. The last dramatic scene in the film occurs when Manny visits Rose in the mental hospital. He is positioned between the dark, huddled figure of his wife in the corner and the cheerful, white-garbed nurse at the door. Hermann's emotional score swells in the background. This is about as far from a documentary scene as one can get, and yet it is also aggressively subversive of classical cinematic convention. It shows the wife refusing her complementary role in the couple and hoarding her subjectivity. "It's fine for *you,*" she intones in response to the news that he has been acquitted, a statement that opposes the marital convention whereby what's fine for him is also fine for her. The scene also depicts the world "outside," in the figure of the waiting nurse, as another version of the authority figures who have victimized Manny. Here, authority is masked by a certain routinized optimism and cheerfulness ("Your husband's going now, Mrs. Balestrero. Couldn't you speak to him? He brought you good news."), but it remains programmed and impersonal. Beneath the pleasant rhetoric is the order that Manny leave (like those earlier orders that he take off his hat). The two women in the scene thus merely duplicate the two kinds of looks—one unseeing, the other misrecognizing and potentially oppressive—that have been directed at Manny from the beginning. When the film moves in again to salvage this vision of indifference and menace with its written text, assuring us that Rose recovers and rejoins her family in Florida, we are made aware of how much such endings owe to a literary tradition where male action and female subjectivity were conceived of as each other's reward. The superimposed written text represents Hitchcock's way of fulfilling the studio's demand for a happy ending, but he manages to get the last image for himself (in cinema, this is obviously better than getting the last word). This is of a family, filmed in very long shot, strolling down a Florida street. The image both glosses the written text and unsettles it. For how do we know that these are the Balestreros any more than the detective knew that Manny was the "right" man? On the other hand, the distance at which we are placed from the figures recalls the documentary premise of the film, suggesting that these are, in fact, the real Balestreros (as opposed to the actors who played them) and, as such, prefer to remain in long shot, having returned to the background where they feel safe: better to be invisible than to be misrecognized and coerced. But surely, however we interpret this last image, an ending in which the principal players are calculatedly reduced to pinpoints on the screen says something about the future of character for this filmmaker. The way has been prepared for *Vertigo,* a film in which Hitchcock continues to dismantle the nineteenth-century legacy of character and gender complementarity without resorting to the pretense of documentary truth.

Vertigo is the story of a San Francisco police detective, Scottie Ferguson (James Stewart), who, in the course of a rooftop chase, discovers that he suffers from vertigo. Having resigned from the force because of his disability, he agrees to do some private investigative work for an old school friend, Gavin Elster (Tom Helmore), who wants him to follow his wife Madeleine (Kim Novak) and explain her strange behavior. Madeleine seems to be haunted by her great-grandmother, Carlotta Valdes, a woman whom local lore says went mad and committed suicide. Scottie becomes infatuated with Madeleine and is both caught up in and determined to cure her of her delusions. He takes her to a historic mission that she associates with her ancestor's death in an effort to convince her that she is safe, but she suddenly breaks away from him, rushes up the stairs of the mission tower, and apparently throws herself off. Neither we nor Scottie see her jump, because his vertigo keeps him from following her to the top. Afterward, he suffers hallucinations (strangely resembling those Madeleine claimed to have suffered) and sinks into depression. One day, he spots a woman on the street—a shop girl named Judy Barton—who bears a striking resemblance to his lost love. He becomes obsessed with making the vulgar Judy over into the refined Madeleine. We learn early in their relationship (through a voice-over delivered by Judy) that the two women are, in fact, the same and that Scottie has been the victim of an elaborate ruse orchestrated by Elster to cover up his wife's murder. However, Scottie only realizes the truth toward the end of the film. When he does, he drags Judy back to the mission tower, where, under his hysterical questioning, she admits everything and pleads for his forgiveness and love. Just as we feel that a reconciliation might happen, she is suddenly startled by the appearance of a dark figure mounting the stairs of the tower (the figure happens to be a nun from the mission), and she falls to her death. Scottie remains standing at the edge, looking down in anguish, but with his vertigo apparently cured.

The opening scenes of *Vertigo,* with their quick pace, witty dialogue, and lush color photography, bear more of a resemblance to the opening of *Rear Window* than to the drab and humorless landscape of *The Wrong Man.* The appearance of Stewart in the leading role also makes us expect that this will be another film about self-improvement. The first scene, a chase over the roofs of San Francisco, establishes an antecedent life of action and danger for the hero like that which the photograph of the burning sports car established for Jefferies in the earlier film. The next scene shows Scottie visiting with his friend Midge (Barbara Bel Geddes), who, like Lisa Fremont at the beginning of *Rear Window,* cares more for the protagonist than he does for her. Scottie also complains of the corset he wears for his sprained back. "Tomorrow's the big day [when the corset comes off]," he announces to Midge at one point, recalling Jefferies's anticipation of being liberated from his leg cast.

But these correspondences to the earlier film are false leads, versions of the suspense effects Hitchcock enjoyed setting in the path of his audience. Their falseness lies in giving us a message out of sync with a film no longer interested in affirming an idea of the self and of the complementary couple. The opening scene is not a simple reference to reckless action designed to provide a contrast to the subjective exertions of the invalid to follow. It is an invocation of existential horror. The chase is almost immediately eclipsed by the image of Scottie, having lost his footing, hanging to the roof of the building. His glance downward in panic is what appears to trigger an attack of vertigo which in turn triggers (not in a causal but in an associative sense for Scottie) the death of the policeman who tries to rescue him. Hence the encoded equation: "action" leads to "abyss" leads to "vertigo" leads to "death." Midge, who appears in the next scene, is not, in this context, introduced as the heroine in disguise, a girl destined to be "reseen" by a more mature hero later on. She is the woman whom we soon sense he cannot love;

her literalism and practical sense are the antithesis of what he is searching for after his harrowing ordeal. As for the corset, it is incidental. Not the sprained back but the vertigo has caused Scottie to retire from the police force and abandon his ambition to be chief of police.

Scottie is suffering not from a temporary handicap but from a condition with no apparent cure. In this, he resembles Manny, whose daily life with its tedious routine and financial burdens is such a condition (the subway tunnel and the locked house being the metaphorical images to express this). Yet *The Wrong Man* is far narrower in its focus than *Vertigo.* Although Manny can be equated with Hitchcock and with 1950s masculinity in general, the film's insistence that it is based on a true story provides an escape from its harshest and most general implications. At the end of *The Wrong Man,* the correct man is apprehended, a substitution of right for wrong that Hitchcock emphasizes by filming the criminal in long shot superimposed upon a close-up of Manny's face and then by showing the figure move toward the camera until his face entirely fits and replaces Manny's in a dissolve. Even if we remain skeptical about the institutions of justice portrayed in the film, justice is enacted in this shot, which expresses the idea both of divine intervention (Manny has just been shown reciting a prayer in front of a picture of Jesus Christ) and of intervention by a seer filmmaker. Indeed, in billing itself as a true story, *The Wrong Man* becomes its own proof that truth exists.

Vertigo abandons the true-false structure of *The Wrong Man* and, in the process, makes explicit the underlying skepticism about meaning that *The Wrong Man* hints at but draws back from. Manny is imprisoned and then finally liberated. Both states, while they suggest his status as a pawn to forces outside him, also suggest the continued existence of a framework within which truth and falsehood, justice and injustice, can be distinguished. Scottie, by contrast, moves on uncharted terrain, navigating his own search. He announces to Midge his intention to "wander" and then decides to follow the wandering Madeleine. It becomes difficult to imagine an end to this kind of aimless, circuitous movement.

Much of the effect of *Vertigo* is a result of its artificial presentation, which, unlike the insistence on realism in *The Wrong Man,* works to confuse the boundaries of the real and the dream and to disorient us with respect to conventional coordinates of plot development.[10] Concrete explanations of how things happen are calculatedly marginalized. For example, we never learn how Scottie got down from the roof to which he was clinging at the beginning of the picture; or how Madeleine was able to bypass the hotel clerk who claimed not to have seen her enter; or what Judy's role in planning Madeleine Elster's death actually was. Yet even obviously explanatory shots—like that in the redwood forest that locates Madeleine leaning against a tree after she seemed to have magically disappeared—do not have the effect of cancelling the original enigmatic impression. Nor does the later explanation that Judy is really Madeleine dissipate the confusion of identity surrounding the character. The question of meaning is detached from the literal and causal, so that even when logical explanations are given, they cease to be fully elucidating. The opening credit sequence encodes the film's open-ended project: it begins with a close-up of a generic woman's face, tracks in to the pupil of the woman's eye and then produces the graphic image of a spiral emerging from the eye. The image raises the questions: who is this woman (we try unsuccessfully to connect her to someone inside the film), and what does she represent (that is, what narrative attaches to the spiral that emerges from her eye)? Where the first question is akin to the question posed in *The Wrong Man* and correlates with the film's concern with a literal series of impersonations (Judy pretending to be Madeleine pretending to be Carlotta), the second refers to the subjective narrative attached to each of these impersonations, culminating finally in the unanswerable question: who is Judy?[11]

What initially draws Scottie to accept Elster's request to investigate his wife appears to hinge on Elster's question: "Do you believe that someone out of the past, someone dead, can enter and take possession of a living being?" Scottie says no, but his manner announces that the question has drawn him in: he is ready to take on the job that he had earlier refused. According to Spoto, Scottie is "a man drawn ineluctably into the past"[12]—but it would be more correct to say that he is a man seeking a past in another to compensate for the lack of one in himself. In *The Wrong Man,* Manny's routinized existence reflected the absence of a narrative of subjectivity (a past encoded in the unconscious that would have given inflection to his behavior). Hitchcock makes the same point about Scottie with more dramatic immediacy in the opening scene of *Vertigo*: a male prototype of action, a detective (one recalls the active, literalist Doyle in *Rear Window* as a possible precursor), is brought face-to-face with the abyss. There is a strikingly cartoonish quality to this scene. The criminal is dressed in white, the policeman in black, but they otherwise share a square-jawed physical resemblance. Scottie, by contrast, wears a gray suit (his face softened as well by his gray hair) and seems to be distinguished from the other two figures as the odd or extra man, the "real" one, lagging behind their highly conventionalized chase. When Scottie loses his footing and clings to the edge of the roof, their function as metaphorical reflections of himself becomes clear: one falls to his death (the fall will be reenacted as his own in a dream later), while the other races off out of sight (that part of himself that symbolically "gets away" and will be tracked for the remainder of the film). In presenting the chase in a highly condensed, surreal form early in the film, Hitchcock has abandoned all interest in its conventional function as a hinge for plot. *Rear Window* used the chase motif, in Jefferies's pursuit of Thorwald, to lend structure to the story. *Vertigo* introduces the chase only as a point of departure, an event which produces the "condition" of the protoganist. After the opening scene, the protagonist abandons pursuit of the "right man" and soon embarks on the alternative project of trying to plumb the meaning of a woman.

Hitchcock summarized the film's theme to Truffaut as the story of a man who "wants to go to bed with a woman who's dead; he's indulging in a form of necrophilia."[13] But Madeleine appears to be possessed not so much by a nineteenth-century woman as by a narrative of subjectivity associated with such a woman. The painting displayed in the museum and the grave located at the local mission are fragments of that woman's narrative. Scottie makes it his job to piece these fragments together, to learn the whole story. He finally gets this from a local bookseller, Pop Liebl: Carlotta Valdes, the old man tells him, was a beautiful but poor woman taken up by a wealthy man who later abandoned her and took away her daughter. Driven mad with grief, she killed herself. The story might be the plot of a George Eliot or a Thomas Hardy novel. However, it was not the plot but the emotions and imaginings that the plot encouraged that constituted the lure and the threat of novels within nineteenth-century culture. It is this subjective aspect of narrative that Scottie is seeking. Madeleine thus becomes for him the carrier of the subjective content of a lost text, the physical embodiment of a psychological narrative. This is the role that Hitchcock had assigned to women in many of his most successful Hollywood films. But where these films had employed the image uncritically, *Vertigo* deconstructs it.

Feminist critics who insist that Scottie's love of Madeleine is based on a patriarchal power fantasy are right, but they miss the countervailing impulses at work in the obsession. What appears to be propelling the protagonist in this film is the sudden recognition of a "lack" in himself—that abyss that stretches dizzily beneath him as he hangs from the building. Once that recognition is experienced, Scottie gives up his old job and his competitive aspirations without apparent regret. With Madeleine, he seeks a relationship that, while it holds to hierarchical aspects of gender complementarity, also includes a desire for the "daughter's effect," for self-revision.

Although an important portion of the film records Scottie's efforts to refashion what is apparently another woman into his lost love, it has been overlooked that Scottie has himself been refashioned in his relationship with Madeleine. His response to meaning has been altered. The basic skepticism and sarcasm with which he approached life, the hallmark of his early interactions with Midge, have fallen away. He is willing to feel deeply and to be tolerant of the irrational and the ambiguous. What enrages him in the end is the revelation that the woman whom he has allowed to refashion him is actually a male construction.[14] Indeed, not just Madeleine is constructed by Elster, but the story that she requisitioned as her own (Carlotta's story) is constructed by men: Elster, Pop Liebl, and the museum curator are its narrators. This is a deconstructive insight of sorts into the way nineteenth-century male novelists can be said to have constructed female subjectivity and then passed it on to filmmakers like Hitchcock as the real thing. The revelation that other men have shaped Scottie's fantasy places him—and by extension, Hitchcock—in precisely the position of imitative subordinate that constituted Brandon's role with respect to Rupert in *Rope.* Insofar as the audience is made to share Scottie's desires, it is placed in this position as well.

The revelation to the audience that Judy and Madeleine are the same person might seem intended to take us out of the spiral in which we have been confined with Scottie. But the revelation also draws us into that spiral on another level by making us want Scottie to love the "real" Judy. In Judy, the film continues to hold out the hope that an authentic self exists. She is represented as the opposite of the woman whom we learn has been constructed by another man. In keeping with the technique already explored in *The Wrong Man,* whereby an illusion of reality is created through the negation of a fictional convention, she appears more real and unmediated than Madeleine or even Midge (a male imitation rather than a male construction, who presents herself as Scottie's buddy and whose rule of life seems to be to keep a stiff upper lip). But, of course, Judy is no less a construction than Madeleine. Her behavior is dictated by what predatory urban life requires of the poor shop girl, and her appearance is more overtly designed to attract men than Madeleine's. Indeed, part of Scottie's drive to transform her involves toning down the heavy make-up and explicitly sexy clothes. Knowing that Hitchcock's feminine ideal was the polished type represented by Grace Kelly, we can see how calculatedly Judy has been designed as the antithesis of that ideal. The paradoxes of her self-presentation are multiplied if we also consider the actress behind the role. Novak, discovered by Columbia Pictures as a replacement for Rita Hayworth, was by most critical standards a bad actress. Her "badness" consisted of a false elegance of manner and a kind of breathy socialite diction (it is quite possible that Novak was imitating Marilyn Monroe). As Madeleine, Novak's affected style fit well with the character of a constructed ideal. As Judy, she appeared to overlay a false elegance with a false vulgarity—the layer of artifice doubled rather than halved. We get an almost painful sense of a bad actress striving to be real, more exposed as a bad actress but also appearing more real in being so exposed. But, in trying to glimpse the real Novak, the Novak without the veneer of acting altogether, we find ourselves not closer but farther away from what this might be. Ultimately, we must ask what the idea of a real woman behind the actress really means—whether such an idea is anything more than the idea of Madeleine cherished by Scottie. We seem only to be able to talk in terms of the good or the bad actress, turns of the screw on the imagined idea of a real person behind the acting.[15]

In *Marnie,* made six years after *Vertigo,* the protagonist explores his wife's past and gives voice to the desire: "I want to know what happened to the child, the little girl, the daughter." The plea expresses both the particularized desire of Hitchcock, the father of a daughter grown up and left home, and the more general desire of a culture no longer secure in a stable, gender-differentiated identity. As early as *Rear Window,* the plea had been there, buried in Jefferies's desperate though impersonalized declaration: "I just wanted to know what happened to the salesman's wife." In *Vertigo, Psycho, The Birds,* and *Marnie,* Hitchcock struggled to come to terms with the realization that the daughter—the knowable "other" and perfect complement to the father—was gone.

Spoto has written that "if one seeks a single word to describe the world of Hitchcock's films of this time it might indeed be 'loss.' "[16] Certainly, the tone of *Vertigo,* like that of *The Wrong Man,* is profoundly melancholy, and both end with dramatic scenes that are explicitly tragic. But *Vertigo* (unlike *The Wrong Man,* which carries the finality that we associate with a one-time "true" experience) is a film that spirals back upon itself, making it possible to return to it in a later context and see it from a new perspective. Consider, for example, how one scene that might be viewed as no more than a simple transitional moment can give rise to a line of thought totally at odds with the film's dominant tone. The scene I have in mind directly follows the famous vertiginous embrace, in which Scottie, having convinced Judy to transform herself physically, has had his fantasy realized. The scene in question shows Scottie chatting with Judy/Madeleine as she sits before the vanity, putting on her earrings. This is actually the first time in the film in which he seems relaxed and content. The fact that Judy's voice and manner inhabit Madeleine's image seems not to bother him at all. She too is represented as happy at this moment—so much so, in fact, that her frank references to her own constructedness ("Don't touch; I just put on my face") put a new spin on the idea of what it means to be one's own woman. Her assumption of the hybrid Judy/Madeleine persona and his williness to accept the mix seem a triumph for the accommodating potential of the couple.[17]

However, as Scottie fastens the necklace around Judy's neck and realizes that it belonged to Madeleine, he suddenly understands the plot by which he has been duped, and the moment of ease is destroyed. I assume that others have experienced what I did at this moment: a wave of irritation that that necklace gave it all away. Had the additional piece of knowledge not been presented (had Hitchcock not felt constrained to make his protagonist "see," or had Scottie let the hint go and not pushed to find the true meaning behind the illusion), everyone might have lived happily ever after. The desire aroused in us to let well enough alone has its source, I suspect, less in a desire to be deluded than in a postmodern recognition, one which the film itself teaches, that experience is, by definition, constructed and hence delusionary. The "true" Judy behind the role is only another facsimile of our own desire, cohabiting uneasily with what does not quite fit the mold of that desire. If the world is nothing but the constructions we place on it, then we would do well not to push too hard for additional meanings, which are likely to topple whatever structure we have put in place. This is a vision of meaning as bricolage rather than as psychological truth, and it is the guiding spirit of Hitchcock's last films.

8 The Emergence of Mother: *Psycho*

During the 1950s, Hitchcock cast Cary Grant and James Stewart in parts ostensibly designed for younger men. (In *North by Northwest*, for example, Grant is actually older than the actress who plays his mother.) The disparity in age between the male lead and the female in the 1950s was the logical extrapolation of the father-daughter dynamic. And Hitchcock's personal relationships to the actresses Vera Miles and Tippi Hedren in the late 1950s and early 1960s reflect a similar extrapolation: these women were the age of his daughter and were chosen as protégées to be molded by him into leading ladies, but, unlike earlier actresses in his films whom he seemed content to cultivate professionally (and hence to maintain a paternalistic distance from), these women were also made objects of intense sexual interest.[1]

Hitchcock's 1950s films expose the paradox not only at the heart of his own relationship with his daughter but also of his culture's gender ideology. On the one hand, in transforming the father-daughter relationship into a romantic ideal, these films reinforce the hierarchy of the couple. An older man is presumably more secure and a younger woman less able to threaten his authority. But the older man/younger woman alliance is also a precarious inequality, since advantages of health and sexual desirability tend to lie with the woman. Moreover, the woman's daughterly associations make her more capable of returning the man's look and hence qualifying his power (the dynamic I have termed the "daughter's effect"). Almost all the films directly before and after *Rear Window* use gender complementarity as an organizing structure but with various degrees of skepticism and strain. *Strangers on a Train* and *Dial M for Murder* represent their protagonists' marriages in an unflattering light (though both hold out the prospect of a new and better partner at the end). *The Trouble with Harry* and *To Catch a Thief* satirize the romantic plot. At the end of the latter, the reformed cat burglar faces the prospect of having the beautiful American heiress move into his villa with her mother—an event certainly complicated by the fact that the mother and the future husband are the same age. Even *Rear Window,* for all its ingenuity, avoids representing the life of the couple directly. If the film's final scene can be read as a triumph of old-style gender complementarity (Lisa now prepared to be the woman Jefferies wants her to be), it can also be read as a triumph of role reversal (Lisa become the keeper of the now domesticated Jefferies). The darkest films of this period, *The Wrong Man* and *Vertigo,* are about the shattering of relationship, and both *The Wrong Man* and *The Man Who Knew Too Much* are invocations of gender complementarity as the one structure of support in a brutal world. In *The Wrong Man,* that structure cannot hold up; in *The Man Who Knew Too Much,* husband and wife emerge in a triumphant alliance, although the film also points beyond itself to the disequilibrating mother-child structure that will dominate the 1960s films. Even *North by Northwest,* that supremely confident and cheerful film, must rely on the filmmaker's wit in editing to carry off a *deus ex machina* uniting hero and heroine in the last seconds.

Thus, while the 1950s films can be analyzed in terms of gender complementarity, they can also be seen as anticipating its breakdown and its replacement by a new configuration. In the three films of the early 1960s—*Psycho, The Birds,* and *Marnie*—that new configuration begins to emerge. The mother, or rather the idea of the mother in the imagination of the child, becomes central to the plot, a powerful obstacle to the union of hero and heroine.

Admittedly, the mother had been portrayed in unflattering terms throughout Hitchcock's career. (The exception is *The Man Who Knew Too Much,* where, as already noted, the mothering is directed at a child rather than at an adult.) Madame Sebastian manipulates her son in *Notorious,* and Roger Thornhill's mother treats him like an irresponsible little boy in *North by Northwest*. Lisa begins as a kind of badgering mother figure in *Rear Window*, a role played as well by the secondary character, Midge, in *Vertigo.* Young Charlie's mother in *Shadow of a Doubt,* Eve's in *Stage Fright,* and Bruno's in *Strangers on a Train* are all women radically bereft of common sense and oblivious to the nature of their children. Yet in all these cases, the representations are of marginal thematic importance and most are comically drawn, whereas in *Psycho, The Birds,* and *Marnie* the destructive potential of the mother is taken seriously and made central to the plot. The hostility toward the mother reflected in Hitchcock's films has been analyzed by critics in psychoanalytic terms, but these interpretations tend to treat the films in an undifferentiated way (in which certain themes and structures are simply repeated in different guises). They fail to note the shift in tone that occurs in the three films of the early 1960s and to address the question of why, at this juncture in his career, Hitchcock directs his venom at the mother so intensely.[2]

The reason, I would suggest, involves changes in the balance of Hitchcock's personal life as it dovetailed with a newly emerging cultural ethos. Following World War II, the cult of motherhood, which had been given circulation in America since the turn of the century, began to undergo mutation. Social experts drawn from a variety of fields began to depict the American mother as an emasculating influence, operating from within her domestic fortress to destroy the psyches of her children. *Momism* was the term coined by ego psychologist Erik Erikson to describe this overprotective and controlling maternal influence.[3] "It was suddenly discovered during this period [the late 1940s through the early 1960s]," wrote Betty Friedan, "that the mother could be blamed for almost anything. In every case history of the troubled child; alcoholic, suicidal, homosexual male; frigid, promiscuous female; ulcerous, asthmatic, and otherwise disturbed American, could be found a mother. A frustrated, repressed, never satisfied, unhappy woman."[4] According to Barbara Ehrenreich and Deirdre English, this "blame the mother" tendency had its roots in women's growing consumer power.[5] With the widespread introduction of first radio and then television as a conduit for messages into the home, the housewife gained obvious prestige with advertisers. Once limited in her influence to whatever she might be able to persuade her husband to do, she had now become part of an interest group with leverage in the marketplace. Jo McKenna's mobilization of her emotions to avert an assassination attempt in *The Man Who Knew Too Much* can be read, in this context, as a socially symbolic act. It dramatizes the increased pressure that the private sphere associated with women was beginning to exert on the public sphere.

But, in the culture of the 1950s, the emerging focus on the mother can also be understood with respect to the evolution of the nuclear family itself. It was during this period that psychotherapists and social workers defined a condition of family function that they termed *pseudo-mutuality*—where surface relationships within the family appear highly conventional but where no real investment exists in the system.[6] The pressure to conform to prescribed roles was especially powerful during the1950s, an issue that gets treated indirectly in *Rear Window* and in the remake of *The Man Who Knew Too Much,* and from another angle in *The Wrong Man*. Given this pressure to conform, a

"Donna Reed" family image often covered tensions and dissatisfactions that would eventually intrude in the form of alcoholism and psychosomatic illness, and would produce a steadily climbing divorce rate beginning in the 1960s. (The much-talked-about documentary about the Louds, a seemingly conventional California family that fell apart over the course of a year-long filming, illustrates the point dramatically.)[7] As the family member assigned the responsibility for family preservation, the mother in this context became the focus of resentment—by her children for enforcing a facade of unanimity and contentment, and by the culture for failing to maintain that facade.

These societal trends coincided with changes in Hitchcock's status during this period and were likely to have intensified feelings of resentment and vulnerability in him. His health had begun to decline seriously, and his wife began to wield increasing power in their relationship. From the late 1950s on, he also experienced increased competition from young American and foreign directors.[8] We might also extend Ehrenreich and English's observation about the leverage of the American mother in the marketplace to include her leverage in the movie theater and to speculate as to whether an intensification of Hitchcock's hostility toward the figure of the mother might not spring, in part, from a resentment of her influence on the box-office success of his films. (This is a replay of the influence that women were seen to have had on the content of novels during the nineteeth century.) Finally, it should be noted that his daughter had married and left home in 1952, and this marked an opening in the structure of his relationships. Donald Spoto notes that a "strained distance" characterized his attitude toward his daughter following her marriage.[9] If his daughter had served, both literally and symbolically, as a support and a check for his authority, her loss removed both. The results may be seen in his abusive dealings with actresses during this period and in a countervailing sense of increased vulnerability, of being open to attack on a variety of fronts.

The shift in focus that occurred in Hitchcock's work in the early 1960s can be described in structural terms if we examine the mock strangulation scene in *Strangers on a Train,* released in 1951. This scene has already been analyzed as coding the complex dynamic embedded in the father-daughter relationship. However, an analysis of this scene can be extended to elucidate the role of the mother as she lurks in the background of this relationship, to be brought into the foreground a decade later.

To the extent that the scene enacts Barbara's recognition of Bruno (symbolically, the mutual recognition of daughter and father), it also shows the act of violence being directed against the character who fails to recognize Bruno for who he is—the silly older woman whom Bruno charms and excites with his titillating talk about murder, a woman who physically and emotionally resembles his mother, introduced earlier in the film. The mother figure is there beneath his hands, structurally necessary to the scene but thematically negligible because the scene's center rests with Bruno's and Barbara's intense communion. Thus we have a substitution of one kind of relationship for another. The older woman, oblivious to what kind of man she is dealing with (just as Bruno's mother is oblivious to her son's true character), is being strangled as a surrogate for the younger woman who truly recognizes Bruno for what he is. The configuration, then, codes the way Hitchcock's films tended to eclipse the mother by the daughter during this period. It also graphically demonstrates a causal sequence embedded in the structure of the family. That is, when the father's relationship with the daughter breaks down, it is the mother who will have to pay. That would seem to explain the evolution of Hitchcock's perspective on the mother: a focused anger at the mother emerges in his 1960s films when a male-female complementarity has ceased to be viable. Or, to take this development from another angle, given the way that Hitchcock's films work during the 1940s and 1950s, the fit of father and daughter in mutual recognition could only happen over an oblivious "other." This third body must be there, like the mass audience itself—game, gullible, never entirely aware of what is going on. Yet as I have mentioned earlier, Hitchcock did not see the mass audience this way until the 1960s, when the loss of his daughter to marriage, the decline in his health, and his sense of more formidable competition within the cinematic marketplace combined to alter his perspective.

Psycho, released in 1960, is the first self-conscious attempt to fracture the powerful symmetries of the family nexus. It follows the fate of Marion Crane (Janet Leigh), a young woman involved in an affair with a recently divorced man, Sam Loomis (John Gavin), who claims to be too financially strapped to marry her. Frustrated by his argument and craving the respectability of marriage, she impulsively steals money from her employer and sets off on a long car trip to visit him. In the course of her journey, she stops at a motel run by Norman Bates (Anthony Perkins), the shy son of a presumably tyrannical mother. That evening as Marion takes a shower in her hotel room, she is stabbed to death by what looks like an old woman, whom we assume to be Mrs. Bates. The film proceeds to record the search for Marion by Sam, now in partnership with her sister, Lila (Vera Miles). We ultimately learn, through their efforts, that the murder was committed by Norman, who had assumed the personality (and the wardrobe) of his dead mother as part of a pathological personality disorder.

Significantly, this was Pat Hitchcock's last film for her father, as well as the first in which she was cast as the married woman she was (having married eight years earlier, following her appearance in *Strangers on a Train*). She plays Marion's fellow office-worker and appears only briefly at the beginning of the film. Her character, however, is not that of a wise-cracking girl, the role familiar to us from previous films, but of a catty, matronly woman. She is vulgar, manipulative, and nasty to Marion Crane, who is the unmarried, love-sick daughter figure at this point in the film. The character has no charm and reflects no paternal indulgence. Indeed, her mean-spiritedness sets the tone for the way the mother, Mrs. Bates, is supposed to be in the second half of the film.

In the same way that this minor character anticipates the major (but hidden) character of Mrs. Bates, the first half of the film can be said to anticipate in a muted or more routine way the family dysfunction that appears in monstrous, undiluted form in the second half.[10] The film delivers a continual series of relationships damaged or obstructed by the existence of a third party. Sam and Marion, meeting illicitly in a hotel room during her lunch hour, discuss whether they should marry. Issues raised include paying his dead father's debts and his ex-wife's alimony and conforming to her dead mother's notion of respectability (a painting of Marion's mother is referred to as hanging over her mantlepiece—a symbol of surveillance and judgment). Back at work, Marion is confronted by her office-mate, Caroline (played by Pat Hitchcock), whose constant talk about her mother's advice on her own marriage provides another glimpse of an unhealthy triangle. When the boss appears with his client, a Texas oil man named Cassidy (Frank Albertson), the discussion turns to the impending marriage of Cassidy's daughter and his determination to give her everything she wants. (His vulgar boasts, delivered in the presence of Hitchcock's real daughter, suggest an ironic commentary on their relationship, perhaps a self-critique of his willingness to cast her in the film.[11]) The conversation goads Marion into stealing Cassidy's $40,000—money she has been asked to deposit in the bank for him.

Although Cassidy boasts of his generosity regarding his own daughter, he is oblivious to Marion's status as a daughter in need of support. He is the first of three potential father figures who fail Marion. As she drives away from the office with the stolen money, she next sees her boss as he crosses the street. He registers no sympathetic recognition, only a vague disapproval—presumably because he suspects she has left work early on false pretenses. Last is her encounter with a policeman who notes her suspicious behavior and follows her. Here, perhaps, she has found a figure willing to attend to her, even if it means enforcing punishment. She seems to be consciously seeking that intervention when, despite his surveillance, she guiltily trades in her car for another and overpays in cash for the exchange. But instead of having his suspicions confirmed by this dubious transaction, the policeman unaccountably abandons pursuit. Critics have noted that the policeman's choice to give up his surveillance ironically engenders a sense of relief in us; had he remained, she would have escaped being murdered. But this sense of relief is connected less with his surveillance as such than with the quality of his gaze, masked by opaque sunglasses. That gaze is blank; it registers neither hostility nor protectiveness and reflects back the shallowness and gratuitousness of the world Marion inhabits.[12] The impression relayed is that she has been set adrift with no father to protect her, making her more vulnerable than Eve in *Stage Fright* and Barbara in *Strangers on a Train.*

When Marion finally arrives at the Bates Motel, Norman Bates reveals his enmeshment with a tyrannical, ailing mother—the last frontier, as it were, of emotional intensity and commitment. Interestingly, while Marion has been cast in a daughter's role up until this point, she now assumes a maternal role with Norman. When he confides in her and she responds, it is as if she is a benign, understanding counterpoint to the cruel, demanding woman he must live with. Her reasonable and calm response to his situation also contrasts her earlier more intense attitude in the hotel room with her boyfriend.

At the point of meeting Norman, then, the heroine's role can be said to change from that of an abandoned and beleaguered girl to that of a counseling woman: a change from daughter to mother. The movie too can be said to shift here from its apparent loyalty to old patterns based on father-daughter complementarity obstructed and drained of content, to a new pattern where a mother-son dynamic becomes the dominant structure within a landscape of loss and fragmentation.

The killing of Marion, occurring directly after her maternal conversation with Norman, carries no hostility toward her as a particularized identity. Indeed, the distinction between the real and the imagined mother is important here as in the two other mother-animus films of the 1960s. This distinction gives these films their peculiar pathos. Norman's mother is not guilty of anything as far as we can tell, despite what the pontificating psychiatrist at the end would have us believe. It is Norman's imagination of his mother, his projection of an idea onto her corpse, that constitutes Mrs. Bates in the film (as it is the projection of an idea onto the body under the shower that precipitates the stabbing of Marion Crane). So, too, it is not Mrs. Brenner in *The Birds* who is malevolent, but the way her son Mitch has responded to her neediness. The life-controlling mother has been fashioned out of what we see is only a vulnerable and lonely woman. Marnie's mother is another pathetic victim whom we see bears little relationship to the figure of Marnie's imagination. What the mother stands for, in these cases, is the imagination of a demanding but unresponsive figure, a figure who watches but cannot recognize the individual nature of her child.

This is also, significantly, the position assigned by Hitchcock to his audience at this juncture in his career. Unlike the films between *Strangers on a Train* and *Psycho* that depended upon investment in a particular daughter figure as she was fitted to the needs of the hero as surrogate for a father-like filmmaker (an investment that ultimately made the hero and the father's position less powerful through what we came to subjectively feel for and about the daughter), these later films have disrupted this complementarity and substituted a shallow and shifting relationship to character. The woman to whom Bruno offers to demonstrate his strangling technique in *Strangers on a Train* bears such a relationship to him. She is oblivious of his true nature and of the danger in which she has placed herself. Marion Crane is killed after placing herself in such a position with Norman Bates. Although her motives for involvement are more responsible, she is, like the woman who responds to Bruno's chatter, unaware of what she is dealing with. As William Rothman puts it, she "is totally unable to appreciate Norman's creations. His disdain for her, at one level, is that of an artist for a contemptible critic."[13] And her response is like the one we have been assigned in watching the film. We watch with a certain complacency, comfortable in our expectations and sympathies. We lend our attention to the movie, as Marion does to Norman's case, but, like her, we don't know with what we are dealing. The film then brutalizes us, as Norman does Marion, though without letting us know why or even what hit us (her). The mechanism of this film is therefore very different from previous films in which the rules of suspense provided us with more knowledge than the characters themselves or, barring that, at least gave us insight into character as a function of plot. In *Psycho,* and in a different way in *The Birds,* we are attacked with the same brutality as the characters. In *Marnie* we know more in some sense and less in another, because though we know that Marnie steals, we do not learn why until the end of the film. And even then we cannot know what Marnie feels for Mark, what drives Mark's desire for her, or what the future of such a relationship could possibly be. The relationship itself becomes the curiosity not because we can learn from it (as could be argued for the relationships in *Rear Window* and even *Vertigo*) but because of its incomprehensibility. Like the character of Norman Bates or the attacks of the birds, we are placed in the position of fascinated but uncomprehending observer.

The gaze that the film directs back at the audience in *Psycho* is, in Rothman's phrase, "murderous" precisely because it envisions the gaze of the spectator to be, like Norman Bates's mother, not capable of the right response—imaginatively, if not literally, dead. This being so, the film can only engage in acts of vengeance against the spectator, acts that it also attributes to the spectator as if seeking to animate it (Norman's strategy with his mother's corpse). Thus *Psycho* seeks both to animate us into an identification with the murderous Norman and to prove through doing so that we are morally empty in our ability to shift our investment from Marion to Norman and, finally, to accept meekly the posturing paternal verdict of the psychiatrist. The film works to ventriloquize our response, to animate it in order to kill it again. The "construction of a mental process" that Hitchcock had linked to the look in *Rear Window* has been replaced by its opposite, the dismantling or murder of the look. One critic has made a relevant observation with regard to the look in *Psycho*: "What is remarkable . . . is that most of the characters who stare at the public are dead when they do so."[14] Even the sophisticated montage technique in the *Pycho* shower scene is a model of its deconstructive method. The "cuts" that construct the narrative of the stabbing produce an illusion that is the exaggeration or literalization of what they, in fact, are: cuts in celluloid denote cuts in human flesh. If montage in its traditional usage conditioned us to see an integrated reality, montage in *Psych*o conditions us to see an unintegrated one—to expect the inexplicable and gratuitous.

What results from the murder of the look? If, as I have suggested, the look is the source of subjectivity in classical narrative cinema, the beginning of that process of narratization by which we come to acknowledge character as a unified and unique whole, then to murder the look is also to murder the idea of the subject. In the mother-animus films, this murder is bitterly ascribed to the "other,"—the engulfing female consciousness that is also equated with the uncomprehending, potentially abandoning audience. Yet the death of the look can also be understood in more affirmative terms. It can be connected with the triumph of cinematic representation over a literary idea of character.

The next chapter presents an overview of Hitchcock's films from the perspective of this cinematic evolution, showing how character is gradually disassociated from traditional notions of investment and identification. If, in the 1960s, Hitchcock represented the dismantling of character as a deeply structured, stable identity, in the 1970s, as a prelude to his own death, he pioneered the representation of character as a freewheeling, open-ended elaboration of surfaces.

Beyond the Family Nexus: *Topaz, Frenzy, Family Plot*

Hitchcock's last three films—*Topaz*, *Frenzy*, and *Family Plot,*—can be read as a return to the kind of flat characterizations and technical gimmickry that characterized his early films and prompted Selznick's comments about the need to curtail his "gags and bits." For many critics, this apparent slighting of character in favor of technique merely signaled the falling off of age, as if to say that, in his decline, Hitchcock took refuge in what he knew best. This seems to me both correct and incorrect. Insofar as a return to one's roots may well be a hallmark of age (suggesting that human life tends to follow the pattern of classical narrative film, in which the end answers the beginning), this does not mean that the return is a simple recapitulation of the beginning. The shot at the end of *Rear Window* both mimics the shot at the beginning and encodes a radical difference; the imaginative journey that the character has traveled is contained in the new context within which that shot is repeated. Similarly, we need to consider Hitchcock's last films as a return with a difference, carrying with them the cultural and personal legacy that brought him to this point. It becomes possible, in this light, to read the last films as both the repetition of old tricks and the logical extrapolation of a career.

In the last films, the notion of "depth," given substance and circulation by novels, is wholly replaced by the notion of "surface," given substance and circulation by cinema. I can begin an explanation of what this means by referring back to *Sabotage,* the film I singled out as the best example of Hitchcock's effort to define the cinematic early in his career. Of all the performances in that film, the one that seems most out of sync with the whole is not the supposedly weak performance of John Loder but the strong performance of Oscar Homolka. The jarring quality of Homolka's performance can be understood in two ways that clarify the distinction between depth and surface.

In one sense, Homolka's character suggests a psychological depth that the film is not interested in addressing. A literary narrative would make the motives and desires of this enigmatic figure available to us, precisely what Conrad does in the novel. But the film's drive has been to flatten and simplify the contradictions raised by the novel.

In another sense, however, Homolka's performance is too cinematic for the film. It calls for too many surface linkages that the film is not prepared to take up. If the literary narrative would focus on Homolka's psychology, digging down, as it were, into the hidden recesses of the self, a more fully cinematic exploitation of the character would explore the landscape of his relationships, finding a responding indeterminacy in his wife, in the detective, and in the other foreign agents who make up his world. But the film aggressively counters such indeterminacy in the other characters and delivers instead a simplified plot, a collection of caricatured villains, and a stereotypical romantic union at the end. When it does allow the wife to slide into indeterminacy during the stabbing scene (we are left in doubt as to what really precipitates the killing), this seems a function less of the characterization than of the demands of the plot that require that the heroine be left morally uncompromised so that she can go off with the wholesome detective at the end. On the other hand, when indetermancy is allowed to enter the film on the level of plot—in the sequence involving the death of the boy—the audience at the time refused to accept it, and Hitchcock retrospectively deemed it a mistake.

As Hitchcock's cinematic approach evolved in the course of his career, such effects, first confined to single characterizations and to idiosyncratic plotted moments, took over the landscape of his films. In *Rear Window,* this is achieved largely through the ingenuity of the set. The apartment complex that Jefferies's rear window overlooks serves to map the protagonist's subjective journey. It deserves comparison to an organizing image from Henry James's last novel, *The Golden Bowl,* in which the heroine is described as circling an exotic pagoda structure that is designated as her consciousness.[1] James's heroine attempts to gain access to this structure but finds no doors. The apartment building in *Rear Window* operates for Jefferies in much the same way. It is both a source of fascination, a cue to more knowledge, and an obstacle—a symbol of blindness and limitation. What distinguishes the cinematic image from the novelistic one is a function of the depth/surface distinction drawn above. Describing the interior of his heroine's mind, James is obliged to invent imagery. The structure of her consciousness is thus said to resemble an Oriental pagoda, a formation with no link to the external world his heroine inhabits. Indeed, the exoticism of the image as it jars with the landscape of her everyday life is precisely the point. Working in the medium of film, Hitchcock, by contrast, must conform to the requirements of visual realism. Thus the apartments into which Jefferies peers are presented to us as part of a recognizable external landscape. They are the literal backdrop against which the action of the film unfolds, as well as the site of his subjective development. Whereas the pagoda is the uniquely private image of the Jamesian heroine (it is the representation of her "deep" self that will gradually make itself felt in the course of the narrative), the apartment building that faces Jefferies, even though it is connected with his subjectivity, stands in some kind of relationship to all the characters in the film (both Lisa and Stella eventually become as involved in looking at it as Jefferies). It operates as a collective "optical unconscious" (to use Walter Benjamin's phrase) that happens, for the purposes of the narrative, to concentrate its effects on Jefferies.

The kind of surface subjectivity that begins to emerge as a by-product of Hitchcock's visual realism is more dramatically rendered in *Vertigo.* Unlike the contrived attempts to probe the individual past of the protagonist in *Spellbound, Vertigo* makes no pretense of wanting to understand the childhood triggers to Scottie's present behavior. His case has interest only as it exists in the present, as a starting point for a cultural diagnosis. A brilliant set piece denoting what the film is doing occurs when Scottie follows Madeleine down a back alley and through a door, only to find himself in a florist shop full of light and clatter. This is Freud's idea of the psyche turned inside out: not the world leading into the mysteries of the individual mind but the individual mind opening out into the chaos of the world. By the same token, the image of the woman, which had in prior films served to evoke psychological character, turns out to be only the simulacrum of mystery and complexity. Madeleine is "really" Judy, who is less a character in her own right than a vehicle for potential identities. Scottie is caught at the crossroads of a literary and a cinematic concept of character. He enacts a backward-looking glance to a novelistic conception of character as depth, but, in the process of nostalgically invoking this lost figure, he increasingly reveals to us (and eventually to himself) the constructed nature of that ideal and the futility of a search into the past or into the self for meaning.

Vertigo, despite its message of radical disillusionment, continues to depend upon conventional assumptions about the nature of character and relationship to make its point. Hitchcock's films of the 1960s are more transparent acts of deconstruction. They offer up worlds which fail to evoke more than a fleeting sense of the reality of individual character. *Marnie,* for example—the story of a female kleptomaniac (Tippi Hedren) romantically pursued by a wealthy entrepreneur(Sean Connery)—has moved very far from a psychological concept of character, despite its references to Freud and its ostensible concern for the childhood events behind Marnie's adult behavior. From its opening shot, focusing with crude insistence on the wrinkled yellow pocketbook under Marnie's arm as she strides away from her latest robbery, the film links everday objects not to individual character (we have not even seen Marnie's face at this point) but to a vocabulary about sex and death that can be manipulated to produce new effects. The film has been read as a reductionist attempt to impose Freudian symbolism, but Hitchcock appears to have used Freud in this film as little more than a resource for imagery and atmospheric effects. (It seems significant that now, when a Freudian methodology for elucidating character is generally derided but Freudian ideas and images have been enshrined in the realm of mythology and folklore, *Marnie* is more compelling to audiences.[2]) The sense of the constructedness of life gets expressed in the concentration on objects, colors, gestures, and patterns of behavior and relationship. The blatantly artificial back projection for the horseback riding scenes and the obviously pasteboard ship that looms up at the end of Marnie's mother's street (derided as amateurishly distracting by earlier critics) contribute to the effect of a constructed landscape. Female accoutrements like purses, jewelry, and hair continue to be focused on in this film, but they are no longer evocative of a literary narrative associated with femininity. Rather, they are positioned in opposition to such a text. Marnie's hair is dyed; her purse, the repository of stolen money; her jewels, the emblems of her captivity; and her desirable feminine appearance, the envelope for a passionless body. Hitchcock once explained his preference for Nordic-featured actresses as a function of the difference between an appearance of coldness and a potential for desire ("It's more interesting to discover sex in a woman than to have it thrown at you"[3])—another way of coding that disjunction between surface and depth that defines a psychological self. In Marnie's case, however, there is no desire to be sparked; the surface coldness speaks the truth. The effect is reinforced by the way Hitchcock orchestrates Hedren's voice in the film. The lines are delivered without particular emphasis or intensity, distilled into a kind of vocal effect, an extension of her physical effect.[4] Even the male character, the site of traditional authority, is reduced to such an effect. Mark Rutland, who, like Scottie in *Vertigo,* has been driven by a desire to plumb Marnie's depths (both to activate passion in her and to discover her past), becomes less a detective (a surrogate for a controlling filmmaker and spectator) than another version of Marnie—a collection of peculiar desires and behaviors. Perhaps it is more correct to say that, in the character of Rutland, control and authority have themselves devolved into idiosyncracy—as evidenced by his collection of animal artifacts and his inclination for predatory metaphors. Marnie herself gives voice to this idea, turning the tables on his attempt to analyze her by questioning his desire for a woman who cannot respond to him. Indeed, it is Mark, not Marnie, whose peculiarity Hitchcock initially focused on in his discussion with Truffaut: "A man wants to go to bed with a thief because she is a thief."[5] The character's function in the film, one might conclude, is not to cure Marnie at all, but rather to generate behavior patterns complementary to Marnie's, to elaborate an exotic behavioral landscape based on their mutual pathology. In the end, the unearthing of Marnie's childhood trauma seems strangely irrelevant to her adult persona which, in its very oddness and its ability to entangle others within it, becomes it own justification for being.

The last three films of Hitchcock's career are the culmination of this vision. In the films of the 1960s, Hitchcock registered the loss of gender complementarity and of a novelistic idea of character. They situated the spectator in a position of misrecognition that confirmed the filmmaker's sense of loss and reflected his bitterness at that loss. In the films of the 1970s (and here I include *Topaz,* released in 1969), Hitchcock attempted to create a new lexicon that no longer relied on a nostalgia for gender complementarity or even on psychological symbolism as a structural or atmospheric resource. Very different from each other in theme and imagery, each of these films can be viewed as a variation on a postmodern idea.

Topaz, based on a sprawling Leon Uris novel by the same name, superficially looks like an attempt at a big international thriller on the order of Otto Preminger's *Exodus* (a huge hit, which may account for Hitchcock's decision to use its star, Paul Newman, in *Torn Curtain,* made three years earlier). *Topaz* concerns the mission of a French embassy official, André Devereaux (Frederick Stafford), to unmask a Communist spy operating at the highest levels of French security. Set during the Cuban missile crisis, the film opens in Copenhagen and then moves from Washington, to New York, to Cuba, back to Washington, and finally to Paris. A number of amorous relationships transpire against this political backdrop: André is having an affair with Juanita (Karen Dor), a member of the Cuban Resistance, whose other lover, Rico (John Vernon), is a high-level official under Castro. André's wife (Dany Robin) is involved with another agent in France, who turns out to be the Communist spy her husband is after. Other couples figure fleetingly at each of the geographical sites and further complicate the story.

Topaz marks a departure from the tight plotting and deft characterization of the 1960s films (although *Torn Curtain,* with its lackluster characterizations, has points of resemblance). It is very hard to tell the good guys from the bad ones or even to establish the hero until well into the film. Many of the characters look alike and appear for only short intervals. The shifting locales and the assortment of international performers, some of them dubbed, add to the confusion.

Exasperating as all this is, however, it is also strangely compelling (at least to a spectator who has followed Hitchcock's career closely and tried to generalize about the effects of his films). In *Topaz,* confusion seems to have been elevated to the level of method. Indeed, it is not so much confusion as profusion that characterizes the film—a seeming determination "to charge the screen with emotion" and "fill the whole tapestry"[6] (as Hitchcock termed his cinematic drive) in a more literal way than ever before by refusing to subordinate characters, images, and thematic lines to each other. The title refers to the code name used for the group of Communist spies buried in French security, hence the suggestion of a secret entangled within the secrecy of top-level intelligence. In a treatment of the theme during the 1940s or 1950s, Hitchcock would no doubt have concentrated on the notion of levels of secrecy, paring down the number of characters to focus on a single relationship in which the duplicity could be dramatized as a function of character. This is the approach taken in *Notorious,* in which the hero and heroine's real feelings are shown to exist undercover of a misleading facade. But in *Topaz* it is not secret plots or hidden feelings so much as the patterns produced in the wake of secrecy that become the subject. We have designs enmeshed, as it were, with other designs. The topaz, a form of quartz that is principally yellow but that also occurs as red and pink, appears to have supplied Hitchcock with a key visual motif for expressing this idea of enmeshed patterns. Yellow furnishings, flowers, and clothing are used to designate French characters. Red accessorizes yellow for those Communist characters who happen also to be French. Pink and lavender are used to designate emotional relationships as these overlay both national and political loyalties. Thus Juanita first wears red when we see her in Cuba, changes to yellow when she greets Devereaux, and, finally, in the scene of her death, wears lavender. The color coding here is not a matter of separating characters but of trying to chart a complex blending and divergence. This seems the goal as well in the peculiar mixing of accents, the accumulation of characters often with physical resemblances to each other, and the use of settings in diverse locales that echo each other (bathrooms, hotel rooms, political meetings rooms, clandestine back rooms). Truffaut commented that *Topaz* "involved too many locations, too many conversations, and too many characters," and Robin Wood called it "one of the most uneven films in the history of cinema."[7] But perhaps because of its clutter and unevenness, the film relays, more than any other in the Hitchcock repertory, an impression of immanence—a sense that a supremely intricate and subtle design pulses beneath its murky surface.

One scene in particular seems to operate as an analogue for this larger design. It occurs when Juanita is stabbed by her Cuban lover after he discovers that she has betrayed their cause. As Juanita falls to the ground, Hitchcock shoots the fall with a high overhead shot of the kind he favors to encode the complex authority of the filmmaker with respect to his character. A similar perspective is employed in the library scene in *Shadow of a Doubt,* discussed in chapter 4. Here, however, the emphasis is on pattern, not on character. The shot records Juanita's dress billowing out around her with the graceful symmetry of a giant flower, at once rare and monstrous (the motif of "arranged" flowers figures throughout the film, suggesting the artifice and the fragility of relationships, both personal and political). The aerial perspective from which we see Juanita's dress removes us to a place which, were we to remain there, would give us access to the film's larger design. Of course, this perspective is not sustainable. The need to render the particulars of the story and to conform to the requirements of realistic representation obscures the pattern that the film produces in its wake. As Spoto notes of the use of color in the film, "all this would be mere coincidence were there not production files indicating Hitchcock's specific directions and his meticulous work with production designer Henry Bumstead."[8] Only, in other words, when we are given background information or are set up to "see" (as Hitchcock is able to do at intervals through dramatic camera work such as in Juanita's death) can we leave the story and the characters and see the design. The film's failure might be better ascertained by comparing it to a film that more successfully highlights an aesthetic design and links it to a social context (Robert Altman's *Nashville,* for example). But it is also possible to see *Topaz* as a film pushing against the limitations that narrative film poses in its allegiance to representational realism, and as pointing toward other genres that deal more effectively in abstractions: either abstract design, that allows the visual to take over (as in abstract art or certain strands of avant-garde film) or the abstraction of ideas, where the specificity of visual representation is left behind (as in philosophy and critical theory).

In *Frenzy,* released three years later, narrative patterning is more effectively combined with visual patterning because it returns to familiar locales and themes: the vegetable markets and pubs of Hitchcock's London childhood, and the machinery of domestic violence and suspense that had fueled his most successful films. *Frenzy* focuses on Richard Blaney (Jon Finch), who is pursued by police for a series of rapes and murders. Blaney is a former RAF pilot who has been unable to hold down a job or a marriage. Disreputable though he is, however, he is innocent of the crimes of which he is accused. These were actually committed by his friend, Bob Rusk (Barry Foster), a seemingly genial wholesale grocer. After Rusk sets his friend up for arrest, Blaney realizes the truth and plans an escape from prison in order to exact revenge. The police follow him and find irrefutable proof of Rusk's guilt: a woman's dead body in his bed.

The film is organized around two motifs—marriage and murder—each represented as parodic of their traditional manifestation. Blaney's ex-wife, Brenda (Barbara Leigh-Hunt), who will become Rusk's most graphic victim, owns a marriage agency. A confident and successful professional (in contrast to the down-and-out Blaney), Brenda's work consists in "constructing" relationships—forming, based on what she has at hand, new combinations. One example, presented in an early vignette, satirizes the implications of a reconfigured gender complementarity: a woman descending the stairs of Brenda's agency with her soon-to-be husband is heard instructing him on the innumerable domestic chores she expects him to perform once they're married. Brenda herself is another variation on this role reversal: she pays for her ex-husband's meal and slips some extra cash into his pocket when he isn't looking. Yet if Brenda Blaney is meant to satirize new relational and role possibilities, the serial murderer Rusk, who strangles her, is a chilling parody of the reactionary position. He seeks exaggeratedly submissive women: women who like to be hurt (Brenda has already presumably sent him away when he consulted her agency before the film begins). One could argue, of course, that the murderer is meant to be the scourge of the new order, brought on by its excesses. But the world of the film does not support such a polemic. Brenda is, by far, the most attractive person in the film. Moreover, her creativity in casting relationships and her air of professionalism make her seem the character most akin to the filmmaker.

Hitchcock does not seem to be interested in resurrecting an old-style gender complementarity in this film. His goal appears to be the more disinterested one of recording his society's reshufflings and resistances. Rusk's mother, referred to in passing and shown for only a moment at a window, recalls the traumatizing role played by the mother in earlier Hitchcock films, but her presence here seems no more than a fleeting allusion to a time when individual relationships still served an explanatory function. Although viewers may try to press the mother into service as the reason for the killer's pathology, the film makes no effort to fill out this hypothesis. The mother exists only as another part of the kaleidoscopic picture within which Rusk happens to figure as a destructive element. Indeed, what makes the rape and strangulation of Brenda Blaney so particularly horrific is its unmediated presentation. It lacks the kind of narrative meaning attached to deaths in earlier films. Even *Psycho,* which relied for its effect on the gratuitousness of Marion Crane's murder, made that death serve the rage of Norman Bates and of the filmmaker toward the sins of some imagined mother/audience. In *Frenzy,* the filmmaker seems to have lost interest in ascribing blame. To blame is still to sustain an interest in individual character. Instead, murder simply happens, often behind the blandest facades—as the camera dramatically reminds us as it moves back from the closed door behind which Rusk is committing another atrocity. It is, as it were, a *statistical* reality and could happen to any of us—and not just getting murdered, but being a murderer, as Blaney's final act illustrates (he clubs the corpse that was Rusk's latest victim, thinking it is Rusk). We cannot take refuge in the assumption that the film has set up these deaths to promote its own aesthetic or moral interests. Death, as presented here amid the tawdry gridwork of London's shops, pubs, markets, and rented rooms, is part of the design of life.

In *Family Plot,* Hitchcock's last film, released in 1976, the loss of gender complementarity and the embrace of relational pattern at the expense of individual character and linear plot seem to be articulated in another register. There is an ease and humor here that suggests that the filmmaker is taking genuine pleasure in his new perspective. The title of the film takes on a special irony when we consider that it marks the full dissolution of the idea of family that had structured Hitchcock's films for most of his career.

The mother figure in this film is an old lady named Julia Rainbird (Cathleen Nesbitt), who is searching for her heir—her sister's illegitimate son, given up at birth for adoption at her insistence. She has retained Blanche (Barbara Harris), an alleged psychic, to help. Blanche and her boyfriend, Lumley (Bruce Dern), are bumbling con artists, determined to find the lost Rainbird in order to collect a reward. As they embark on their search, we meet the missing nephew (William Devane) in a parallel plot. He is the antithesis of what we would expect to find in this kind of rags-to-riches story. Having murdered his adopted parents years earlier, he has assumed the name Arthur Adamson. He now operates a successful jewelry business, which he stocks by exchanging kidnapped dignitaries for precious gems. He is helped in these transactions by his girlfriend Fran (Karen Black). As Blanche and Lumley close in on the lost heir, Adamson believes they are after him for his crimes. He captures Blanche, but Lumley rescues her. Then, Blanche and Lumley manage to trap Adamson and Fran in their own house and find the diamond hidden on the premises.

The film proceeds by fits and starts, discarding provocative plot lines as it goes. We never learn about the circumstances surrounding Adamson's birth or why he would have been driven to murder his adoptive parents. The auto mechanic who helped him kill his adoptive family is introduced, complete with a wife who grieves at his death, but no attempt is made to fill in his story. The mother-surrogate, Julia Rainbird, who sets the plot in motion, also dwindles to insignificance soon after her appearance and fails to reappear at the end (thus breaking the symmetry we expect from classical narrative film). In short, the film is strewn with loose ends, as if creating curiosity in the viewer about possible plots and characterizations that it perversely fails to gratify.

The impression is one of perpetual motion. Automobiles dominate the landscape: Lumley drives a taxi, and almost everything of importance happens in cars or garages.[9] Truffaut described the film as "the passage from one geometric figure to another" and, indeed, passages *between* places are emphasized over destinations. Each voyage out, beginning with Blanche's mock psychic journey at the beginning of the film, leads to a destination that proves to be only a temporary stopover, the launching place for a new journey. Even as the two sets of characters conjoin and the plot ostensibly closes, no real sense of closure is relayed. There is only a sudden, highly contrived termination punctuated by Blanche's winking directly at the camera in the final shot.

The character of Blanche embodies the film's method. She is a free-associative artist—out for herself, but not manipulative or possessive in anything but the most temporary and superficial way. She whines rather than emotes, is cute not beautiful, wears jeans and sneakers and not glamorous gowns. Even her name is the epitome of anti-glamour. We are a far cry from the self-immolation for country and for love of Ingrid Bergman in *Notorious*. Fran, on the other hand, superficially resembles traditional Hitchcock women (she even wears a blond wig during the kidnapping transactions), but she is their self-consciously artificial derivative, a woman who explicitly fulfills what has been the implicit ideological function of woman in film throughout the classical period: to serve masculine perogatives and plot-driven ends. This function had always been countered to some extent in Hitchcock's films by a narrative of subjectivity, the legacy of the nineteenth-century novel, that the female image continued to evoke despite the effort of film to quell it. Fran marks the exhaustion of this narrative. She is the shell of the psychologically resonant heroine far more profoundly than Marnie, whose trauma at least marked the place where an old-style subjectivity might have been. Fran no longer evokes such a narrative; she simply assumes a disguise as a practical cover for criminal activity.

The difference between Blanche and Fran is less a matter of morality versus immorality as it is a matter of freedom versus constraint. Blanche is free from having to do anything or serve anyone, and she need not compromise herself in order to live. Her counterpart is not Fran but Adamson, whose freedom is also absolute. Blanche prevails over Adamson, I would be tempted to say, because Hitchcock is viewing female freedom, broken loose from the constraints of patriarchy, as intrinsically more creative, more likely to win, than male freedom, which continues to define itself at others' expense and, hence, gets sidetracked by assumptions relating to power and personal pride (as when Adamson insists that Fran be complicitous in murder as proof of her loyalty to him).

The feminist implications of such a reading are certainly the logical derivative of the postmodern point of view that I associate with the last Hitchcock films, but one cannot push such a reading too far. For one thing, there is too much whimsy in *Family Plot* to support doctrine. For another, the relationship between Blanche and Lumley still manages to conform to an old-style gender complementarity, albeit reduced to low-intensity interactions: she nags him for attention and commitment, and he complains of being henpecked. By the same token, it is the very laconic and basically good-humored style in which Blanche and Lumley carry on their gender-stereotyped bickering that makes it conform to a new model for the couple (recalling the easy banter of Scottie and Judy/Madeleine in those brief moments before his discovery of the ruse). The viability of Blanche and Lumley's partnership is evidenced by the fact that she tracks down their man, he rescues her, and they both go off with the reward money. This recalls the division of labor in the remake of *The Man Who Knew Too Much,* but it is extrapolated into a more gender-diffuse, morally relativistic terrain.[10]

Family Plot was Hitchcock's last film, made four years before his death. Critics have labeled it optimistic, but even this seems too categorical a way to describe it. It is simply a film made in a good mood. Moods not philosophies (or even attitudes) are more appropriate ways of gauging the state of mind of people approaching death. Moods are also the catalysts by which the most unpredictable designs come into being.[11]

In the last three films of his career, Hitchcock, like Blanche, was exercising a freedom that knew few constraints, that did not keep to the priorities of plot, character, or moral code that had anchored his films in the past, and that diffused his signature into effects rather than meanings. Even the steady working out of irony and the need to manipulate an audience that had driven films such as *Psycho* and *The Birds* have disappeared. In the last films, the structuring formula is playful and free associative: the mixing of accents and nationalities in the creation on screen of a global village in *Topaz*; the linking of food, marriage, and murder in *Frenzy*; the flux of a car culture—of going from here to there with destination always inconsequential or mistaken—in *Family Plot.*

The spirit of these last films seems to me to be embodied by the two scenes in *Family Plot* that have often been singled out by critics as highly orchestrated Hitchcockian moments. The first is the excruciatingly self-indulgent scene in which Blanche struggles with Lumley to control the steering wheel of their out-of-control car (sabotaged at Adamson's directive). The scene is too long to be comic. It becomes a metaphor for lack of control, for a crazy, screwball ride without brakes. Blanche's panic-stricken contortions are the equivalent of vaudevillian pratfalls inserted into a context where they seem puzzlingly out of place. The counterpoint to the scene in the car is the scene in the mazelike cemetery, where Lumley meets the widow of the man who tried to kill them but whom they fortuitously caused to steer off the road to his death. The cemetery scene uses the aerial shot that Hitchcock employed throughout his career to assert perspective and provide transition.

Storyboards for the two scenes are included in Spoto's *Art of Alfred Hitchcock,* but the sketches fail to relay what makes the scenes so oddly memorable.[12] In the first case (Blanche and Lumley careening down a cliff in a car without brakes), the storyboards do not record Blanche's contortions during the ride. In the second (Lumley's encounter in the cemetery with the widow of the man who tried to kill them), they do not relay the degree to which the scene concentrates on formal blocking (the length of time that the high shot tracking the walking figures is sustained, and the way in which the interaction between Lumley and the widow becomes a staged symmetry through the use of a prolonged floating two-shot). What we have in these two scenes are intervals of extraordinary visual interest that have been drained of meaning with respect to both plot and character. One gives us plot run amok; the other, character reduced to pure figuration. The out-of-control car ride and the cemetery maze exist as limit points in the film which also happen to describe the two extremes of postmodern culture: chaos and temporary order within chaos—both framed by references to death, the only ultimate source of closure.

The last films also represent a significant departure from a lexicon of images that had served Hitchcock in the past. All but gone is the familiar vertical symbolism—what William Rothman refers to as the //// sign—often obtained by filming a character behind the bars of a staircase or gate, or simply by superimposing a vertical arrangement of light and shadow. Rothman claims this to be Hitchcock's highly personal code for the cinematic screen—that which separates the viewer from what is being represented and that also asserts the filmmaker's mastery.[13] It is also, of course, the symbol of imprisonment and carries with it the opposing idea of freedom or liberation. Although Hitchcock may have begun to grow skeptical about this duality in *The Wrong Man* and *Vertigo,* he continued to evoke it, if only as a metaphor for alienation and loss of meaning in the 1960s films: "I think we're all in our private traps," says Norman Bates to Marion Crane; Mark Rutland refers to Marnie as a trapped animal. In the 1970s films, this imagery diminishes and appears only for ironic or purely aesthetic purposes. Notions of detachment, investment, and control—the bulwarks of psychological character and gender complementarity—have ceased to be meaningful. The idea is dramatized in *Family Plot* when Adamson's latest kidnap victim is shown enjoying a meal in the underground room in which his captors have placed him, obviously taking his imprisonment very lightly indeed.

Hitchcock's last three films also lack "stars." Or, to put this more accurately, they resist our putting much emphasis on who was in them. Truffaut remarked upon the unavailability of the actors and actresses who had served the filmmaker in the past, suggesting that the more diffuse effect of the later films may be due to the absence of Cary Grant, James Stewart, and Grace Kelly. But it seems clear that Hitchcock's last three films are intent on eschewing the idea of character to which the star system conforms and on avoiding the mistake of *Torn Curtain,* where the stars hung like dead weights on the production (and were expensive to boot). Not only are there no star personae in the last films, there are no parts that would have lent themselves to these personae. Siegfried Kracauer, in his *Theory of Film,* might have been diagnosing the problem with *Torn Curtain* and describing the performances of Hitchcock's last three films when he stipulated that film actors "must breath a certain casualness marking them as fragments of an inexhaustible texture."[14] It would be hard to find a better description of Bruce Dern's laconic acting style in *Family Plot.*

In an interview during the filming of *Topaz,* Hitchcock told Truffaut that he had originally intended to end with a duel between Devereaux and the exposed spy Granville (Michel Piccoli), who had been having an affair with Devereaux's wife. When he filmed the scene, however, spectators on the set snickered, and he decided not to use the footage. He explained to Truffaut that "young Americans had become too cynical and materialistic to accept the concept of chivalrous behavior."[15] Yet the attitude of "young Amercans" was at least partially due to the kind of lessons that Hitchcock's 1960s films had taught about the need to distrust an attachment to character. The shower scene in *Psycho* is often referred to as the moment when an entire generation of moviegoers lost their innocence. Pauline Kael has noted that it was not only the killing of the heroine midway through the film that was so shocking but the killing of the marquee star.[16] It destroyed at a sweep everything that had come to be believed about the meshing of plot and character. With that killing, the resurrection of the star as someone in whom it was worthwhile investing would become increasingly difficult. Hitchcock referred to the characters in the second part of *Psycho* as "merely figures"[17]—as if to say that the consequence of Marion Crane's death was the death of three-dimensional, "deep" character. It is perhaps easier to comprehend, in this context, why Hitchcock's last films, although they continue to reflect his desire for commercial success, nonetheless exhibit a certain indifference to audience response.[18] There is neither a sense of kinship with his audience (as in the 1930s films), nor of complementarity with them (as in the 1940s and 1950s), nor even of bitterness toward them (as in the 1960s films). It is as though by abandoning a literary notion of character inside the films, Hitchcock no longer needed to consider the audience outside them as anything more than "figures"—or, more crassly, pocketbooks.

In describing how he sought to define the character of Adamson in *Family Plot,* William Devane explained that he wanted to keep it light and decided "to play the clothes."[19] "The clothes," that had once pointed to what lay beneath them, had now become the emblem of a surface self, linking characters, audience, and filmmaker in an intricate but airy game.

10 After Hitchcock

Hitchcock's foray into television in 1955 with *Alfred Hitchcock Presents* was a step as important in its way as any in his cinematic development. Its importance had little to do with his involvement in production. He actually directed only a small fraction of the programs in the series, and the time constraints placed severe limitations on what could be done creatively. Instead, what seems to have distinguished the series in the public imagination were Hitchcock's brief appearances on it, particularly his materialization out of line and shadow during the opening credits. Robert Kapsis has noted that the appearance evoked "the idea of Hitchcock as a creative and almost supernatural force behind the program."[1] But more than the idea of the man was the idea of the Hitchcockian experience, a composite of elements associated with his films, the thriller genre, and cinema itself.

Up until the late 1960s, Hitchcock's films could be situated with respect to a novelistic tradition—they either opposed such a tradition, attempted to retrieve it, or mourned its loss. His last films severed that connection, making not literature but film, and the Hitchcock film in particular, their precursors. Hitchcock's introduction to his television series laid the groundwork for these last films, drawing attention to the conventions of his genre through his extravagant tongue-in-cheek delivery. The last films contain the structural equivalent of such a narrator in the way they appropriate themes, images, and camera techniques known to us from previous films but make no attempt to recreate the "feel" of the original contexts. Thus the silent blond at the beginning of *Family Plot* recalls the type of the Hitchcock heroine, only here the appearance is a temporary disguise assumed by the character for the purpose of conducting a crime. Likewise, the image of a hand closed tight over an incriminating object in *Frenzy* recalls a similar image in *Notorious,* only here the fist is closed not out of love or loyalty but due to the physiological fact of rigor mortis. And, as a final example, the camera rotating around Juanita and her Cuban lover in *Topaz* recalls the scene in *Vertigo* of Scottie's ecstatic embrace of Judy made over into Madeleine, only here the camera maneuver relays no intense emotion; it merely draws attention to itself and sets us up for a subsequent visual effect.

Why is this trend in late Hitchcock culturally significant? Hitchcock's last films stand in the same relation to his previous career that all images have come to stand in relation to the cinematic tradition. The referents for images are now other images, where once they were written words. Film and television have developed their own intertextuality and literary texts have been relegated to the periphery as blueprints for visuals or starting blocks for improvisation. This shift has entailed a wholly new concept of character. Novels had introduced a concept of character based on a narrative of subjectivity. This narrative had consisted of two components: a notion of the self as unique and replete with transcendent hidden meaning (that correlated to descriptive elements in the literary text) and a notion of the self as mutable, in process and unboundaried (that correlated with plotted elements). Film, lacking a descriptive dimension, had accommodated these two notions of the self through an action/spectacle separation along gender lines: change was associated with male action and character depth with female spectacle. However, once the female image ceased to evoke depth, having lost its association with novelistic narrative, both gender difference and a stable meaning for the self lost their anchorage. In *Vertigo,* Madeleine first evokes a transcendent notion of identity (the legacy of a literary past) and then proves it to be an illusion. Janus-like, she looks both backward and forward with respect to the representation of character.

Judy is Madeleine's forward-looking aspect, and her case helps delineate the two sides of the debate about whether or not postmodernism is good for women. One side sees Judy as an affirmative model. Thus Holly Body, a Judy derivative in Brian de Palma's Hitchcock-derived *Body Double,* becomes, according to a critic in this school, a woman who "remains in control of her body as a commodity, never susceptible to making the exchange an emotional one"—her character relaying "a strength and charisma that make for a feminist moment in the film."[2] The opposing view, however, asks what such strength and charisma serve if an emotional exchange is no longer possible. According to this view, we have arrived at a "processed feminism"—an elaborate form of enslavement to consumerist habits and desires.[3]

Such sliding between the idea of enlarged freedom and more elaborate constraint is, in fact, built into the postmodern method, with its reliance on a signifier that continually shifts from one meaning to the next. Ultimately, an image-conditioned reality leaves things open, favoring us with the possibilities of infinite interpretation rather than belief or feeling. Frederic Jameson notes that in a postmodern experience a "waning of affect" accompanies a proliferation of theoretical discourse.[4] Blanche's wink at the end of *Family Plot* is a postmodern gesture in this mode; it throws us into the realm of play. We could theorize forever on what that wink means, and its function seems precisely to provoke us to interpretation. The effect is very different from Ingrid Bergman's smile which requires no interpretation and simply announces that we have reached the end of the story. Television is the medium of the wink, supplying us with images that seem designed to thwart closure not only because there are always more of them but also because of the ways in which they are narratized. The soap opera and the news broadcast are both predicated on the notion that they will not end. Styles of watching TV—channel surfing, for example—further militate against the possibility that the image will have closure or yield a definitive meaning. Even in televised court cases, which would seem to depend on the idea of empirical truth, the audience soon ceases to be concerned about what "really" happened and views the proceedings as a stream of images whose interpretation depends on individual political agendas, ethnic and class loyalties, and personal tastes.

The layering of the image that this postmodern notion of meaning assumes doubles back to make words no longer the vestigial remnants of a literary tradition but themselves the reflections of images. Books get written less to be read than to be optioned as movies. Some theorists have taken this a step further: "If we can speak now of power and TV," they write, "this just might mean . . . that the disappearing locus of power has probably already slipped away from TV as the real world, and taken up residence now in that digital paradise, that perfectly postmodern world, of the computer."[5] Indeed, the image may have begun to fade as we move into a realm that detaches meaning even from the material play of surfaces and lets it spin into pure sensation on the one hand and pure abstraction on the other. Both can be said to be anticipated by Hitchcock in the two contrasting scenes in *Family Plot* discussed in the last chapter: in the out-of-control car and in the cemetery maze. The former rides the moment in all its disorderly rush; the latter assumes an arbitrary perspective by which to relay a temporary illusion of meaning and order. One might be correlated with the frenetic, nonnarratized images of MTV, the other with the elaborate but highly provisional structures of critical discourse.

As far back as *Rear Window,* Hitchcock teased us with the possibility that the murder might have been called into being by the protagonist's imagination. We may reach back further and see the germs of this perspective in *Young and Innocent,* in which the murderer is revealed by the camera's tracking to the drummer and holding its gaze there as if willing the revealing twitch of the eyes to happen. Is the film telling us that the camera brings the plot into being and fingers the villain as an analogue for the way we construct the plots of our lives and people them with heroes and villains? But if it is telling us this, it is only in hindsight, in the context of our postmodern understanding. For only when the conventions of representation that separated movie plots from life plots had dissolved could such an idea be seriously entertained. Only after having the image naturalized for us could the cable that had linked the image to the word finally be cut. I have tried to demonstrate how Hitchcock's career was a long, slow development toward this point, how his films helped condition us into a new way not only of seeing but of being.

Hitchcock's films charted an evolution from the Victorian to the postmodern that corresponded to his own personal evolution from youth to old age. One could cite quite a number of nineteenth-century novelists whose work had the same ability to both chronicle a life and illuminate a stretch of cultural history. What makes Hitchcock's achievement unique is that it happened during this century in the medium of film. Film has never been solicitous of the individual—indeed, it has been my argument that early film sought above all to level and conventionalize an idea of individual character that novels had elaborated. Moreover, as the film industry has matured, stylistic distinctiveness has been increasingly curtailed as well—the filmmaker's signature diffused or cancelled by supplementary or competing interests. Yet Hitchcock, entering film in its infancy and mastering its technical side, was for a time able to force this most modern and communal medium into the service of a traditional concept of the individual. His films reclaimed something akin to literary character, and they articulated a distinct and coherent Hitchcockian vision. At the same time, they also helped to erode the idea of individual character as it had been elaborated through a literary tradition. When Hitchcock died in 1980 at the age of 81, the literal fact of his death seemed to coincide with the death of the auteur as a cultural idea, a death that, through the evolution of his films, he had helped to engineer.

Notes

Introduction

1. The auteur theory approach to Hitchcock was pioneered in the 1950s by the French critics attached to the journal *Cahiers du Cinema.* Eric Rohmer and Claude Chabrol's 1957 study, *Hitchcock* (Paris: Editions Universitaires), opened the way for a series of auteur treatments by Jean Douchet, André Bazin, and François Truffaut in France, and by Andrew Sarris and Robin Wood in America. By the late 1970s, film criticism had taken a different turn and had begun to rely heavily on Lacanian psychoanalysis and Derridean deconstruction. Most recent studies of Hitchcock are strongly influenced by these methodologies, the most noteworthy perhaps being several essays by Raymond Bellour in *Camera Obscura: A Journal of Feminism and Film Theory.* Tania Modleski and Robin Wood have also helped bring a feminist leavening to this perspective.

Some recent books on Hitchcock take rather amusing pains to differentiate the man from the ideological matrix (sometimes resorting to the use of quotation marks whenever his name is used with respect to a film). What the trend suggests conforms to the thesis of this book: Hitchcock was part of a cultural evolution toward a new concept of the subject. But it is only toward such a concept that his films tend; indeed, along the way, they reflect a strenuous attempt to recoup the psychological subject for film. It seems to me impossible to talk of figures still bound to an individualistic ideology in the terms of an advance guard. Hitchcock existed as an individual behind his films because he lived in an age that conceived of him as capable of existing there and that, as a result, made room for him to exist there—gave him the resources, the authority, and the billing that would support this conception. We may be moving toward a time when this kind of individual delineation will cease to occur. Then, I suspect, we will no longer have to try so hard to erase authorship, since we will no longer have at our disposal the names of single directors whose relationship to films we will have to deny.

2. François Truffaut, *Hitchcock,* rev. ed. (New York: Touchstone, 1985), 347. Filmmaker David Plaut (in personal conversation) has noted that Hitchcock's lack of

athletic prowess may account for his having needed to achieve "impossible" shots—pushing his cameramen and technicians, and indeed the camera itself, to perform acts to which he could lay claim. This became a means both of symbolically getting back at those who laughed at him (making others exert themselves on his behalf) and of compensating, through fantasy feats, for his own physical incapacity.

3. Truffaut, *Hitchcock,* 43.

4. Ibid., *Hitchcock*, 49.

5. In *The Art of the Novel* (New York: Charles Scribner's Sons, 1934), Henry James describes many of the factual "germs" behind his plots.

6. Interview, "Hitchcock and the Dying Art," *Film* (London) (summer 1966).

7. Truffaut, *Hitchcock,* 111.

8. Siegfried Kracauer, *Theory of Film: The Redemption of Physical Reality* (New York: Oxford, 1960), 96. Hitchcock compared actors to cattle a number of times. On one occasion, before the Cambridge Film Society, he facetiously pointed out an important distinction: "I was once asked 'Is it true that you said actors are cattle?' I said, 'It's a confounded lie. All I said was that they should be *treated* like cattle.' " James Stewart also recalled Hitchcock's making this distinction at the 1979 American Film Institute Life Achievement Award ceremony honoring Hitchcock.

9. Hitchcock recounted the story in his 1979 acceptance of the Life Achievement Award from the American Film Institute. He seems to have told many versions of the story over the years, laying stress on different variables, depending upon the point he wished to make.

10. See Lawrence Stone, *The Family, Sex and Marriage in England, 1500–1800* (London: Weidenfeld and Nicolson, 1977), for the most definitive study of these changes in the family in Western culture.

11. Paula Marantz Cohen, *The Daughter's Dilemma: Family Process and the Nineteenth-Century Domestic Novel* (Ann Arbor: Univ. of Michigan Press, 1991).

1. The Rise of Narrative Film

1. Laura Mulvey, "Visual Pleasure and Narrative Cinema," rpt. in *Visual and Other Pleasures* (Bloomington: Indiana Univ. Press, 1989); originally published in 1975.

2. See, for example, Dana Polan, *Power and Paranoia: History, Narrative and the American Cinema, 1940–50* (New York: Columbia Univ. Press, 1986). Michel Foucault's work on the way resistance operates within ideology has influenced this line of thinking.

3. This is Robin Wood's alleged objective in his revised edition of *Hitchcock's Films: Hitchcock's Films Revisited* (New York: Columbia Univ. Press, 1989), 371.

4. Teresa de Lauretis, *Alice Doesn't: Feminism, Semiotics, Cinema* (Bloomington: Indiana Univ. Press, 1984). De Lauretis does not take up the self-reflexive implications of her own critique of film theory: "[Film theorists] fail to envisage a materially, historically, and experientially constituted subject, a subject engendered, we might say, precisely by the process of its engagement in the narrative genres" (106).

5. Among the first modern critics to explore the link between women and the novel was Queenie Leavis, *Fiction and the Reading Public* (London: Chatto and Windus, 1932). Also see Ian Watt, *The Rise of the Novel: Studies in Defoe, Richardson and Fielding* (Berkeley: Univ. of California Press, 1957); Richard D. Altick, *The English Common Reader: A Social History of the Mass Reading Public, 1800–1900* (Chicago: Univ. of Chicago Press, 1957); and Kate Flint, *The Woman Reader, 1837–1914* (Oxford: Clarendon Press, 1993).

6. Watt, *The Rise of the Novel,* 47. Watt also cites Mrs. Thrale's statement that her husband's order that she not "think of the kitchen" drove her to "literature as [her] sole resource" (44).

7. Jane Austen, *Persuasion,* rpt. (New York: Penguin, 1965), 236; originally published in 1818.

8. George Eliot, *The Mill on the Floss,* rpt. (New York: Penguin, 1979), 405; originally published in 1860.

9. Watt, *The Rise of the Novel,* 162.

10. James, *The Art of the Novel,* 49, 51.

11. Elaine Showalter, *A Literature of Their Own: British Women Novelists from Brontë to Lessing* (Princeton: Princeton Univ. Press, 1977), 181.

12. See Flint, *The Woman Reader,* for a discussion of the controversial figure of the Victorian woman reader.

13. Quoted in Showalter, *A Literature of Their Own,* 96–97, 39.

14. Lydia Ginzburg, *On Psychological Prose,* trans. Judson Rosengrant (Princeton: Princeton Univ. Press, 1991), 15.

15. See Mrs. Oliphant, "Modern Novelists—Great and Small," rpt. in *The Brontës: The Critical Heritage,* ed. Miriam Allott (Boston: Routledge and Kegan Paul, 1974).

16. Ann Douglas, *The Feminization of American Culture* (New York: Alfred A. Knopf, 1977). Although Douglas focuses on American culture, her thesis can be applied to Western culture in general. Also see Sandra M. Gilbert and Susan Gubar, *No Man's Land: The Place of the Woman Writer in the Twentieth Century,* vol. I, *The War of the Words* (New Haven: Yale Univ. Press, 1988), for a discussion of the escalation of feminist activity in the nineteenth century and what, by the end of the century, came to be termed "the woman problem."

17. Gaye Tuchman and Nina Fortin, in their study of social pressures on nineteenth-century female novelists, *Edging Women Out: Victorian Novelists, Publishers, and Social Change* (New Haven: Yale Univ. Press, 1989), have noted that before 1840 novels were mostly written by women; men began to enter the field as it became more lucrative. Although women novelists continued to compete with men throughout the nineteenth century, by the end of the century, critical criteria had been developed to exclude them. Between 1901 and 1917 women had been successfully edged out and men's hold on the novel became institutionalized. Also see Paul Lauter, *Canons and Contexts* (New York: Oxford Univ. Press, 1991), on the canonization of American literature as a means of excluding less "serious," feminine work.

18. The notion of film repeating and superseding novelistic narrative has been

noted by both Siegfried Kracauer and Christian Metz, but the gender relationship of the two forms has hardly been considered. An exception is Margaret Morse, "Paradoxes of Realism," in *Explorations in Film Theory: Selected Essays from Cine-Tracts*, ed. Ron Burnett (Bloomington: Indiana Univ. Press, 1991), 158: "If the novel is a female-sympathetic model, as [Ian] Watt implicitly claims, it may be possible to show how and why film is a male-sympathetic model." Unfortunately, Morse's strict Marxist orientation narrows the kind of conclusions she can reach about these gender linkages.

19. F.W. Murnau's The *Last Laugh* had no intertitles and was generally regarded as a model of cinematic art. See Roy Huss and Norman Silverstein, *The Film Experience: Elements of Motion Picture Art* (New York: Delta, 1968), 75; and Christian Metz, *Film Language: A Semiotics of the Cinema* (New York: Oxford Univ. Press, 1974), 49–50, on silent film's "attack" on speech.

20. Huss and Silverstein, *The Film Experience,* 15–16. Also see Emmanuelle Toulet, "Cinema at the Universal Exposition, Paris, 1900," *Persistence of Vision* 9 (1991): 23, who argues that, in 1900, film "molded itself to older forms of spectacle."

21. Annette Kuhn, *Women's Pictures: Feminism and Cinema* (New York: Routledge and Kegan Paul, 1982), 22, stresses the multiple economic and ideological factors influencing the development of narrative film.

22. Molly Haskell made this point twenty years ago in *From Reverence to Rape: The Treatment of Women in the Movies* (Chicago: Univ. of Chicago Press, 1974).

23. De Lauretis, *Alice Doesn't,* 27.

24. Showalter, *A Literature of Their Own,* chap. 6.

25. Mary Ann Doane, "Film and Masquerade: Theorizing a Female Space," *Screen* 23, no. 3–4 (Sept.–Oct., 1982): 79.

26. Jeanine Basinger, *A Woman's View: How Hollywood Spoke to Women, 1930–1960* (New York: Alfred A. Knopf, 1993), 5–6.

27. Compare feminist film criticism with feminist novel criticism. In the latter, critics identify freely and proudly with fictional characters (Rachel M. Brownstein's *Becoming a Heroine: Thinking about Women in Novels* [New York: Viking, 1982] is one of the finest examples of this tendency). Investment in movies, by contrast, seems to have centered on the "stars"—and certainly, we find more feminist apology for Marilyn Monroe than for the characters she played. It is as if women, failing to find adequate imaginative fodder in the cinematic roles, sought for it in the real lives of the actresses who inhabited those roles.

28. Judith Mayne, *Private Novels, Public Films* (Athens: Univ. of Georgia Press, 1988), has addressed this separation of spheres with respect to both novels and films. Novels, she argues, helped to delineate a private space of personal desire in the nineteenth century; films, a public space of consumerism in the twentieth. Mayne's argument does not, however, connect the two genres systemically or explore the way gender operates in supporting and subverting the separation of private and public spheres.

29. Metz, *Film Language,* 44.

30. See Nancy Armstrong, *Desire and Domestic Fiction: A Political History of the Novel* (New York: Oxford Univ. Press, 1987); and Cohen, *The Daughter's Dilemma.*

31. Critics often note Freud's novelistic tendencies. See, for example, Steven Marcus, "Freud and Dora: Story, History, Case History," in *Representations: Essays on Literature and Society* (New York: Random House, 1975).

32. Robert Scholes, *Fabulation and Metafiction* (Urbana: Univ. of Illinois Press, 1979); and Stephen Heath, *Questions of Cinema* (London: Macmillan, 1981).

33. Sergei Eisenstein, "Dickens, Griffith and the Film Today," rpt. in *Film Form,* ed. and trans. Jay Leyda (Cleveland: World Publishing Co., 1957), 206; originally published in 1944. Also see André Gaudreault, "Singular Narrative, Iterative Narrative: Au Bagne (Pathé, 1905)," *Persistence of Vision,* no. 9 (1991): 66–74, on the relationship between narrative and character in primitive film.

34. The most obvious place to look for interesting shifts in the balance of male and female character conceptions is screwball comedy, and a number of books have explored the genre for its subversive possibilities, most notably Elizabeth Kendall, *The Runaway Bride: Hollywood Romantic Comedy of the 1930s* (New York: Alfred A. Knopf, 1990); and Stanley Cavell, *Pursuits of Happiness: The Hollywood Comedy of Remarriage* (Cambridge, Mass.: Harvard Univ. Press, 1981). The problem with screwball comedy is that it blaringly announces its wackiness. Gender reversals and deviations become gaglike and predictable and get rigidly tied to star personae in the roles.

35. Wendy Lesser, *His Other Half: Men Looking at Women Through Art* (Cambridge, Mass.: Harvard Univ. Press, 1991), 121.

36. Wendy Steiner, *Pictures of Romance: Form Against Context in Painting and Literature* (Chicago: Univ. of Chicago Press, 1988), 2.

37. See Judith Mayne, "Feminist Film Theory and Criticism," *Signs* 11, no. 1 (Autumn 1985); and Mulvey, "Notes on Sirk and Melodrama," rpt. in *Visual and Other Pleasures* (originally published in 1977).

38. The notion that, as he developed, Hitchcock went about changing the rules by which his films worked is the guiding principle of Thomas M. Leitch's study, *Find the Director and Other Hitchcock Games* (Athens: Univ. of Georgia Press, 1991). Leitch sees Hitchcock's development in terms of an evolving "pleasure contract" between filmmaker and audience: the films are games at which both play, whose rules change at important junctures.

39. Steiner, *Pictures of Romance,* 2, 6.

2. Novel into Film: *Sabotage*

1. Truffaut, *Hitchcock,* 71. It should be noted thatt Conrad had done his own stage adaptation of *The Secret Agent* in the early 1920s, which Hitchcock had seen and which may have sparked an interest in adaptation that he might otherwise not have had.

2. Joseph Conrad, "Author's Note," *The Secret Agent: A Simple Tale* (Garden City, N.Y.: Anchor Books, 1953), 10.

3. Conrad, *The Secret Agent,* 85. See James Goodwin, "Conrad and Hitchcock: Secret Sharers," in *The English Novel and the Movies* (New York: Frederick Ungar, 1981), 226, for further discussion of their shared interest in this theme.

4. Truffaut, *Hitchcock,* 71. It should be noted that Hitchcock was not, as this quote might suggest, wholly dismissive of literature. According to Spoto (*The Dark Side of Genius,* chap. 2), he was exposed to Shakespeare, Dante, and a range of novelistic fiction while at school and continued to read following graduation. Indeed, Hitchcock alluded frequently in interviews to nineteenth-century novels and liked to say that his favorite character was Emma Bovary. However, in an interview with Truffaut toward the end of his life (*Hitchcock,* 316), he claimed to be impatient with literary description and said he avoided reading novels because he couldn't help wondering as he read whether they'd make good movies.

5. Conrad, *The Secret Agent,* 11, 127.

6. Ibid., 25.

7. Ibid., 66.

8. Ibid., 65.

9. See Michael A. Anderegg, "Conrad and Hitchcock: *The Secret Agent* Inspires *Sabotage*," *Literature/Film Quarterly* 3, no. 3 (Summer 1975): 218, for more examples of borrowings from the novel.

10. Frederick Karl, *Joseph Conrad: The Three Lives* (New York: Farrar, Straus and Giroux, 1979).

11. See Gilbert and Gubar, *No Man's Land,* vol. 1, who persuasively argue that women—or rather the threat of a burgeoning female power—"caused modernism." See also Bonnie Kime Scott, ed., *The Gender of Modernism: A Critical Anthology,* (Bloomington: Indiana Univ. Press, 1990).

12. Conrad scholars with whom I've spoken have criticized the film severely, but the accusation of treason was actually used more qualifiedly by Rohmer and Chabrol, *Hitchcock,* 53, who argue that the novel was adapted "faithfully enough to prevent a cry of treason but with enough license to make clear that it is his" (my translation).

13. Conrad, *The Secret Agent,* 77.

14. See Maurice Yacowar, *Hitchcock's British Films* (Hamden, Conn.: Archon Books, 1977), 211, for his indirect support of this contention in his statement that Hitchcock, in *Sabotage,* "plays the family for its sentimental values" and (in a misreading that tells us something about the expectations the film sets up) that "Verloc is a warm and attentive head of the family." Truffaut, *Hitchcock,* 109, also notes an avuncular quality to Verloc that makes the idea of a flirtation between Mrs. Verloc and Ted early in the film distasteful to the viewer.

15. *Blackmail* seems to fall somewhere between *The Lodger* and *Sabotage* in its view of the policeman's action. Tania Modleski, *The Women Who Knew Too Much: Hitchcock and Feminist Theory* (New York: Methuen, 1988), chap. 1, places the policeman on the side of an oppressive patriarchy, but this fails to take into account the degree to which the film supports the woman's right to kill her potential rapist by having the policeman refuse to turn her in.

16. Ralph W. Rader, "*Lord Jim* and the Formal Development of the English Novel," in *Reading Narrative: Form, Ethics, Ideology,* ed. James Phelan (Columbus: Ohio State Univ. Press, 1989), positions Conrad with respect to the late Victorian novel on the one hand and to the classic modern novel on the other, supporting many of my own comments about Conrad and other protomodernists' transitional loyalties.

17. Conrad, *The Secret Agent,* 216, 143.

18. See Hitchcock's remarks to Truffaut about this scene: "We had to make the viewer feel like killing a man" (*Hitchcock,* 110).

19. Truffaut and Spoto note Hitchcock's preference for the sidelines during his early years. See my discussion of this idea in chapter 7 as it relates to *The Wrong Man.*

20. Charles Dickens, *Litte Dorrit* (New York: Penguin, 1967), 895.

21. Truffaut, *Hitchcock,* 109.

22. Wood, *Hitchcock's Films Revisited,* 207.

23. Hitchcock, whose recollection of the film in his interview with Truffaut appears to be shakey, notes that the hero's killing of the wrong man was bad "from the public's point of view" (*Hitchcock,* 105). He was no doubt extrapolating from the public's outraged response to Stevie's death in *Sabotage,* released the same year.

24. See Robert E. Kapsis, *Hitchcock: The Making of a Reputation* (Chicago: Univ. of Chicago Press, 1992), 60, on audience response to *Psycho.* According to Kapsis, the film appealed to a younger audience, which was culturally prepared to accept it, having already been tutored by Hitchcock's "macabre little teleplays."

25. Modleski, *The Women Who Knew Too Much,* 113.

3. Psychoanalysis versus Surrealism: *Spellbound*

1. Selznick used the same logic with *Spellbound,* according to Leonard J. Leff, *Hitchcock and Selznick: The Rich and Strange Collaboration of Alfred Hitchcock and David O. Selznick in Hollywood* (New York: Weidenfeld and Nicolson, 1987), 161: "Hitchcock's name would guarantee the film its 'masculine appeal.' Changing *Edwards* [the working title for the film had been *The House of Dr. Edwards*] to *Spellbound* vexed Hitchcock, yet boosted the marquee value of the picture [by appealing to women]."

2. Truffaut, *Hitchcock,* 129.

3. See Bradford K. Mudge, "The Man with Two Brains: Gothic Novels, Popular Culture, Literary History," *PMLA* 107, no. 1 (January 1992), 92–104, for a discussion of women's association with the gothic and the resulting denigration of the genre dating from the eighteenth century.

4. See Modleski, *The Women Who Knew Too Much,* chap. 3.

5. In his detailed correspondence with Hitchcock during the filming, Selznick makes a point of suggesting additional close-ups of Joan Fontaine. See, for example, his instructions about filming de Winter's marriage proposal, in *Memo from David O. Selznick,* ed. Rudy Behlmer (New York: Viking, 1972), 291.

6. Some twenty-five years later, in *Marnie,* Hitchcock was able to create a more sympathetic characterization of a husband driven by enigmatic motives. Ironically, he would fault the later film for its casting: someone like Olivier (rather than Sean

Connery) in the male role would have "heightened the fetishistic concept" by emphasizing the difference in class and age between the male and female protagonists, he explained to Truffaut (*Hitchcock,* 306). However, in *Rebecca,* Olivier was arguably too young for the role. The comment suggests that a remake of *Rebecca* with not only an older Olivier but a more independent and mature Hitchcock would have resulted in a better film than *Marnie*.

7. Some confusion surrounds Hitchcock's view of the ending of *Suspicion.* Hitchcock claimed to Truffaut that he "had something else in mind" (*Hitchcock,* 142) (presumably that Cary Grant's character would be shown to intend to kill his wife) but that the studio didn't want to cast Grant as a killer. However, Spoto, in *The Art of Alfred Hitchcock: Fifty Years of His Motion Pictures,* 2d and rev. ed. (New York: Anchor Books, 1992), 101, argues that the film represents Hitchcock's original intention—that he wanted to represent a neurotic female imagination. If this is true, it reflects a self-initiated continuation of the concern for female psychology that had been inaugurated, against his will, with *Rebecca.*

8. Leff, *Hitchcock and Selznick,* 117.

9. Quoted in ibid., 117.

10. The question of how successful she was seems to be a matter of historical perspective. When the film appeared, it was taken to be a relatively sophisticated treatment of psychoanalysis. When Hitchcock was "discovered" by critics in the 1960s, however, *Spellbound* was judged to be among his weakest Hollywood films, with criticism centering on what was then seen as a reductive, commercial exploitation of Freudian ideas. Now the tables seem to have turned yet again, and the film has been rehabilitated to some extent. This may be because psychoanalysis has entered the realm of metaphor and folklore, and the use of psychoanalytic imagery is taken less literally.

11. Truffaut, *Hitchcock,* 194.

12. Samuel Russell Taylor, *Hitch: The Life and Times of Alfred Hitchcock* (New York: Pantheon,1978), 194, also notes that Hitchcock "longed, loath though he was to admit it, for the sounding-board of David O. Selznick."

13. Selznick granted the credit with mixed grace. A memo from him reads: "I have voluntarily . . . given to Hitchcock a double credit, calling my new picture Alfred Hitchcock's *Spellbound*, using 'Hitchcock' half the size of the title, solely and simply because I think he is entitled to it. . . . Despite the fact that I produced the picture and that I worked for many months on both the script and editing . . . Hitchcock secured such remarkable quality with such prompt efficiency" (*Memo from David O. Selznick,* 367).

14. Quoted in Leff, *Hitchcock and Selznick,* 120; and Truffaut, *Hitchcock,* 165.

15. George Eliot, *The Mill on the Floss,* 611–12.

16. See Robert Stam, "Hitchcock and Buñuel: Authority, Desire and the Absurd," in *Hitchcock's Rereleased Films: From* Rope *to* Vertigo (Detroit: Wayne State Univ. Press, 1991), for a discussion of surrealist and absurdist influences on Hitchcock's work (he cites *The Trouble with Harry* as an example of "domesticated surrealism" whose form resembles that of the surrealist games). For an interesting

take on the relationship between cinema and surrealism, see J. Hoberman's essay "Bad Movies," in *Vulgar Modernism: Writing on Movies and Other Media* (Philadelphia: Temple Univ. Press, 1991), in which he discusses the surrealists' argument for the "sublimity" of bad movies.

17. André Bazin, *What Is Cinema?* vol. 1, trans. Hugh Gray (Berkeley: Univ. of California Press, 1967), 15.

18. In its purging of the demarcations associated with the subject, surrealism can be said to presage a movement away from gender distinctions and to have points in common with postmodernist "free play." Virginia Woolf's concept of androgeny also reflects a kinship with this current of surrealism.

19. Leff, *Hitchcock and Selznick,* 82.

20. There is a certain irony attached to Hitchcock's choice of Dali to create a surrealist sequence for his film. By this time, Dali had become estranged from the ideological goals of surrealism and was scorned by the few artists still connected with the movement. Of course, it was precisely Dali's yen for self-promotion and for money that made him open to this kind of project in the first place.

21. Leff, *Hitchcock and Selznick,* 82.

22. Roberta E. Pearson and William Uricchio, "How to be a Stage Napoleon: Vitagraph's Vision of History," *Persistence of Vision,* no. 9 (1991): 75–76.

23. Leff, *Hitchcock and Selznick,* 124, explains the logic of a female psychoanalyst in more popular terms: "Linking the practice of psychiatry to a woman's nurturing instincts—a masterstroke—would make a scientific, thus foreign and cold, subject more palatable to motion picture audiences." This kind of statement testifies, uncritically, to the associations I have discussed as culturally "built in" to the female image.

24. Wood, *Hitchcock's Films Revisited,* 316.

25. See Leff, *Hitchcock and Selznick,* 161.

26. Truffaut, *Hitchcock,* 167.

4. The Father-Daughter Plot: *Shadow of a Doubt, Stage Fright, Strangers on a Train*

1. See Lesley Brill, *The Hitchcock Romance: Love and Irony in Hitchcock's Films* (Princeton: Princeton Univ. Press, 1988); William Rothman, *Hitchcock—The Murderous Gaze* (Cambridge, Mass.: Harvard Univ. Press, 1982); and Modleski, *The Women Who Knew Too Much.* Leitch's *Find the Director and Other Hitchcock Games* is unique among recent theoretical studies of Hitchcock because it takes an explicitly developmental approach. He traces the evolution of Hitchcock's games, both thematically inside the films and cinematically with his audience.

2. Truffaut, *Hitchcock,* 314.

3. Virginia Woolf, "Mr. Bennett and Mrs. Brown," in *Collected Essays* (New York, 1967), 1, 320; originally published in 1924.

4. Neal Gabler, *An Empire of Their Own: How the Jews Invented Hollywood* (New York: Anchor Books, 1989), has argued a related point with respect to the way Jewish immigrants, who dominated the American film industry in the 1920s, 1930s

and 1940s, went about constructing a fantasy of small-town America. Their insecurity as outsiders caused them to create an image of American life as a network of small, supportive communities. As with these moguls, whose American fantasy was eventually sold to America and became part of the country's imagination of itself, so Hitchcock's fantasy of Victorianism came to seem representative of the values of his audience.

5. Quoted in Spoto, *The Dark Side of Genius,* 128.

6. Spoto, *The Dark Side of Genius,* 163, recounts how on the first day of the filming of *The 39 Steps,* Hitchcock introduced Robert Donat and Madeleine Carroll and snapped a pair of handcuffs on their wrists, then vanished with the key until late afternoon. Spoto also recounts an earlier, more vicious practical joke of Hitchcock's in which he dared a technician to remain chained to a camera overnight and then secretly laced the man's drink with a strong laxative (p. 124).

7. One visitor recalls that Pat Hitchcock was expected to behave like a proper Victorian daughter: she sat at her own little table in the kitchen and curtsied to visitors (Spoto, *The Dark Side of Genius,* 147).

8. In a provocative essay, "All in the Family: Alfred Hitchcock's *Shadow of a Doubt,*" in *The Hitchcock Reader*, ed. Marshall Deutelbaum and Leland Poague (Ames: Iowa State Univ. Press, 1986), James McLaughlin argues that young Charlie's real desire is to be like the widows her uncle murders: women with the means to be on their own. Yet this misses the degree to which young Charlie defines herself in relationship. Her desire is not to be free but to have a "miracle" happen to her—to enter into a new kind of relationship—that is realized with Uncle Charlie's appearance on the scene.

9. See Stefan Sharff, *Alfred Hitchcock's High Vernacular: Theory and Practice* (New York: Columbia Univ. Press, 1991), 98, for a discussion of Hitchcock's use of high shots.

10. Spoto, *The Dark Side of Genius,* 169, refers to Hitchcock's "contradictory treatment of Madeleine Carroll—devoted at one moment, almost cruel the next," as the beginning of a "schizoid pattern" that would escalate in relationships with actresses during the 1950s. At the same time, Hitchcock was known to have treated his "girl" actresses, Nova Pilbeam and Teresa Wright, with a great deal of gentleness.

11. Truffaut, *Hitchcock,* 191, 190.

12. Molly Haskell, *From Reverence to Rape,* 353, also addresses the way Hitchcock's daughter is cast in his films: "Perhaps he is punishing his daughter as an extension of himself. . . . And so he lays it on—the spectacles, the beady eyes—a little too thick. Not as thick as the usual Hollywood idea of ugly (and hence their superiority as examples of plain women) but just enough so that they are more appalling than appealing as sexual beings." By the same token, his representation of his daughter may also relate to his disgust with the artificial vanity associated with actors and actresses. Spoto, *The Dark Side of Genius,* 317–18, quotes a 1947 outburst on the subject: "Think of it: little bits of powder, little bits of paint on the face of adult men and women so they can pay the rent. My own daughter Patricia made her Broadway debut recently. I sometimes shudder when I think of a daughter of mine doing that."

13. Modleski, *The Women Who Knew Too Much,* 115–118.

14. Modleski, *The Women Who Knew Too Much,* 13, notes that young Charlie is typical of Hitchcock heroines in seeming "to possess special, incriminating knowledge about men"—precisely what Barbara, in a sudden moment of revelation, appears to possess about Bruno. Also see Linda Williams, "When the Woman Looks," *Film Theory and Criticism: Introductory Readings,* 4th ed., ed. Gerald Mast, Marshall Cohen, Leo Braudy (New York: Oxford, 1992), 563, who argues that only the screen vamp tends to return the male look, and she is generally punished for it. Miriam's look seems to bring on her fate with a vengeance, but Barbara's look is different; it responds to the male look and triumphs.

15. Patricia Highsmith, *Strangers on a Train,* rpt. (New York: Penguin, 1974), 239, 240; originally published in 1950.

16. Spoto, *The Art of Alfred Hitchcock,* 1st (unrevised) ed. (New York: Doubleday), 218.

17. Spoto, *The Dark Side of Genius,* 346–47. Pat Hitchcock, unsurprisingly, never confirmed this story (though she never denied it). In an interview following the release of the Spoto biography, she claimed not to have read the book but to have "heard several quotes from it. So far I haven't heard one quote that it true" (Stephen M. Silverman, "People Yearn for Hitchcock Movies, Says His Daughter," *New York Post,* 5 March 1984).

18. Spoto, *The Dark Side of Genius,* 353.

19. Truffaut, *Hitchcock,* 195.

5. Digression: *Rope, I Confess*

1. De Lauretis, *Alice Doesn't,* 15.

2. Claude Lévi-Strauss, *The Elementary Structures of Kinship,* trans. J.H. Bell, J.R. von Sturmer, and R. Needham (Boston: Beacon Press, 1969).

3. See Jean E. Kennard, *Victims of Convention* (Hamden, Conn.: Archon, 1978), for her discussion of this thematic, which she calls "the two-suitor convention," in the novel.

4. Eve Kosofsky Sedgwick, *Between Men: English Literature and Male Homosocial Desire* (New York: Columbia Univ. Press, 1985).

5. Modleski, *The Women Who Knew Too Much,* 21, says the scene "foregrounds the problems of woman's speaking," despite what she refers to as other critics' concentration on the "manipulations of sound without discussing its narrative function." Yet these other critics' perspective reflects, it seems to me, the film's true loyalties. The "woman's speaking" is not foregrounded at all.

6. See, for example, E. Ann Kaplan, ed., *Women in Film Noir* (London: British Film Institute, 1978).

7. Truffaut, *Hitchcock,* 179.

8. See Sedgwick's discussion in *Between Men* about how men become conditioned into masculinity through imitation. Also see Renée Girard, *Deceit, Desire and the Novel,* trans. Yvonne Freccero (Baltimore: Johns Hopkins Univ. Press, 1965), on

"triangular desire," in which male desire is predicated on an imitation of another man's desire for the same object.

9. Truffaut, *Hitchcock,* 184. Rothman, *The Murderous Gaze,* 247, says that "*Rope* presents what is usually taken for granted in a film, continuity, as its signal achievement."

10. "The really important thing being rehearsed here is the camera, not the actors!" James Stewart is quoted as saying during the filming (Spoto, *The Dark Side of Genius,* 324).

11. Wood, *Hitchcock's Films Revisited,* 364–65.

12. Thomas M. Bauso, "*Rope*: Hitchcock's Unkindest Cut," in *Hitchcock's Rereleased Films,* 234.

13. See Elaine Showalter, *Sexual Anarchy*: *Gender and Culture in the Fin de Siècle* (New York: Viking, 1990)

14. Stanley Cavell, "What Becomes of Things on Film?" in *Themes Out of School* (San Francisco: Northpoint Press, 1984), 179.

15. See Wood, *Hitchcock's Films Revisited,* 349–57; and D.A. Miller, "Anal *Rope*," *Representations* 32 (Fall 1990): 113–133. Different as they are in style, both pieces are energetic attempts to "fill in" through personal experience and critical brilliance what the film leaves unaddressed.

16. Truffaut, *Hitchcock,* 202, praised Clift as "truly remarkable" in the role, although Hitchcock was more reticent. He elsewhere admitted not liking Method actors, of which Clift was a supreme example. Interestingly, he had originally wanted Clift to play the role of Brandon in *Rope.* Clift refused, Spoto implies in *The Dark Side of Genius,* 323, because he didn't want to run the risk early in his career of publicizing his homosexuality.

17. Truffaut, *Hitchcock,* 203.

18. See Wood, *Hitchcock's Films Revisited,* 63, who critiques Rohmer and Chabrol's insistence upon a Catholic reading of Hitchcock.

19. See Christine van Boheemen's discussion of this idea in *The Novel as Family Romance* (Ithaca: Cornell Univ. Press, 1987), 11.

6. The Daughter's Effect: *Rear Window, The Man Who Knew Too Much*

1. Heidi Schlupmann, "The Subject of Survival: On Kracauer's *Theory of Film*," *New German Critique* 54 (Fall 1991): 121.

2. Truffaut, *Hitchcock,* 71.

3. Mulvey, "Visual Pleasure and Narrative Cinema," in *Visual and Other Pleasures,* 19.

4. Hitchcock makes the comparison in structural terms: "On one side of the yard you have the Stewart-Kelly couple, with him immobilized by his leg in a cast, while she can move about freely. And on the other side there is a sick woman who's confined to her bed, while the husband comes and goes" (Truffaut, *Hitchcock,* 216).

5. Mulvey introduced this reading in "Visual Pleasure and Narrative Cinema." Modleski, *The Women Who Knew Too Much,* 82, although she differs in her analysis

of Lisa's role, nonetheless argues similarly that Jefferies is driven to "repudiate the feminine identification the film originally sets up."

6. See John Kucich, *Repression in Victorian Fiction: Charlotte Brontë, George Eliot, and Charles Dickens* (Berkeley: Univ. of California Press, 1987).

7. Metz, *Film Language,* 70. See also Seymour Chatman, "What Novels Can Do That Films Can't (And Vice Versa)," in *On Narrative,* ed. W.J.T. Mitchell (Chicago: Univ. of Chicago Press, 198), on film's inability to offer descriptive narrative—to "freeze us" in time and space—the way novels can: "Pressure from the narrative component is too great. Events move too fast" (p. 122).

8. A comparison suggests itself between Jefferies and Ralph Touchett in Henry James's *Portrait of a Lady* (New York: Penguin,1982). James describes the paradoxical kind of freedom that Touchett's condition of being an invalid afforded him: His "[ill] health had seemed not a limitation, but a kind of intellectual advantage; it absolved him from all professional emotion and left him the luxury of being simply personal" (p. 154). Like Hitchcock, James can also be compared to his character in suffering a physical ailment—in his case, a back problem—that exempted him from military service in the Civil War.

9. Quoted in Spoto, *The Art of Alfred Hitchcock,* 224.

10. The notion of "suture" was introduced by Jean-Pierre Oudart in a series of *Cahiers du Cinema* articles in the late 1960s.

11. See Barbara Stafford, "Voyeur or Observer? Enlightenment Thoughts on the Dilemmas of Display," *Configurations: A Journal of Literature, Science and Technology* 1, no. 1 (Winter 1993): 95–128.

12. "Fragment of an Analysis of a Case of Hysteria," *The Standard Edition of the Complete Psychological Works of Sigmund Freud,* vol. 7, trans. James Strachey (London: The Hogarth Press, 1953), 9.

13. This reverses the resolution of Jane Austen's late eighteenth-century novel, *Northanger Abbey.* In that novel, the heroine believes, like Jefferies, that a murder has been commited and proceeds to amass a body of evidence to support her hypothesis. She is, however, proven wrong at the end by the sensible hero. It seems that having read too many novels, her imagination lacks restraint, and the author wishes to chasten the tendency among women to find elaborate mysteries and plots in every cupboard. In *Rear Window,* one could argue, the hero's outlandish hypothesis is confirmed rather than denied because men need to cultivate subjective narratives.

14. Peter Middleton, *The Inward Gaze: Masculinity and Subjectivity in Modern Culture* (New York: Routledge, 1992), 3.

15. Thomas M. Leitch, "Self and World at Paramount," in *Hitchcock's Rereleased Films,* 40.

16. Spoto, *The Art of Alfred Hitchcock,* 222.

17. Middleton, *The Inward Gaze,* 10.

18. Jean Douchet, "Hitch and his Public," *Cahiers du Cinema* 19, no. 3 (November 1960):7–15.

19. Proof of my point is the wild divergence in interpretation of this last scene. Many feminist critics have read Lisa's positioning and garb to denote her capitulation

to the rule of the father. More traditional, "humanist" critics have concentrated on the idea that Jefferies has finally committed himself to relationship with Lisa. While either interpretation might have been affixed to the final image of Lisa in jeans and sneakers reading beside a sleeping Jefferies, the addition of the maneuver with the magazine upsets whatever interpretation has been settled upon. This opens the ending, asserting the idea of an undefined future and preparing the way for *The Man Who Knew Too Much,* which examines the life of a couple.

20. Carolyn G. Heilbrun, "Marriage Perceived: English Literature 1873–1941," in *What Manner of Woman: Essays on English and American Life and Literature,* ed. Marlene Springer (New York: New York Univ. Press, 1977), 164, 168.

21. See Kapsis, *The Making of a Reputation,* for a comparison of critical reaction to the two versions of *The Man Who Knew Too Much* at the time the second version was first released (pp. 43–45), and on the shift in critical response when it was rereleased in the mid-1980s (pp. 150–54).

22. Robin Wood, *Hitchcock's Films Revisited,* chap. 17, has also discussed the film in terms of a gender division involving female emotion and male reason, but has oriented his discussion toward the frustration of Jo's career aspirations, that is, the repression of her conventionally male side as opposed to the mobilization and expansion of her conventionally female side.

23. See Ina Rae Hark, "Revalidating Patriarchy: Why Hitchcock Remade *The Man Who Knew Too Much,*" in *Hitchcock's Rereleased Films,* 209–225.

24. Truffaut, *Hitchcock,* 89.

25. In depicting the life of the couple in the remake of *The Man Who Knew Too Much,* Hitchcock seems to have been after an effect closer to TV renditions of family life. Typical 1950s sitcoms like *Father Knows Best,* for all their apparent support of an authority structure where father had the definitive answer and last word, seemed to produce a greater tolerance for contention as part of everyday life than could be had from film (this tolerance, I might add, continues in our expectations of the genre to this day: marital discord within the good marriage remains the most enduring formula of situation comedy). Hitchcock addressed the difference between TV and film rather flippantly when he explained that viewers "are grown-up, you see, when they are getting something for free in their own homes. They become children again when they have to pay. . . . After all, why should they pay their good money just to be made miserable?" (quoted in Kapsis, *The Making of a Reputation,* 38). His point is well taken. The difference between the way television and movies treated family life seems a function of the way material was packaged for consumption by the two media. A film dealing with the mundane workings of a marriage found itself hard-pressed not to bring into service a plot-line involving infidelity, espionage, or eccentric comedy without losing its spectators to boredom or to a subversive anatomy of its subject. Television, from its origin, could remain formulaic and trivial because the time span of the show did not permit the elaboration of anything more than the mere skeleton of relationships and situations. At the same time, it could treat friction between family members without undue reaction from its audience because viewers were willing to believe that the family unit, programmed to appear again at

the same hour the next day or week, would survive. In the case of *The Man Who Knew Too Much,* Hitchcock manipulated the conventions of his genre even more radically than he had in *Rear Window,* where he made the action plot serve as a metaphor for the domestic plot. While still keeping the action plot in *The Man Who Knew Too Much* (and hence remaining within the conventions of his genre), he nonetheless subverted—or rather co-opted—its function as the site of primary interest by making it operate as an extension of the life of the couple. The action plot became the practical testing ground for the marriage and the means by which the relative priority of the couple's roles could be reassessed in the most literal way possible.

26. Wood, *Hitchcock's Films Revisited,* 364–65.

27. McLaughlin, "All in the Family," in *The Hitchcock Reader*, 150, addresses this kind of iconography in Hitchcock's films: "The world of the bed attempts to subvert the world of the upright—horizontal vs. vertical." But he goes on, in the fashion of many feminist critics, to oversimplify Hitchcock's loyalties: "The world of the bed is also the world of sick sexuality, the world of female sexuality, whose fiendish energy (so perceived by Hitchcock) breaks the bounds, breaks apart and levels the law of the Father, the order of Law and Time." This statement is too extreme, and simply does not apply to *Rear Window* and *The Man Who Knew Too Much,* which seem, on the contrary, to tip toward "the horizontal" in their loyalties. Wendy Lesser, *His Other Half,* 138, notes that where the 1934 version "gradually shifts from the wife to the husband . . . the 1956 version focuses increasingly on the wife and her relationship to her kidnapped son."

28. Lesser, *His Other Half,* 138–40, also stresses the way in which Hitchcock purposefully employs her "Doris Day-ness" and makes singing of central importance to the film.

7. Transition: *The Wrong Man*, *Vertigo*

1. Truffaut, *Hitchcock,* 237.

2. See Marshall Deutelbaum, "Finding the Right Man in *The Wrong Man,*" in *The Hitchcock Reader,* for a fuller discussion of how Hitchcock's film deviated from the facts of the case.

3. Quoted in Deutelbaum, "Finding the Right Man," 214.

4. Truffaut, *Hitchcock,* 242. Although the studio system was breaking down during this period, Warner Brothers had expanded into television and was apparently doing well.

5. Critics tend to compare Manny's situation to that of Joseph K. in Franz Kafka's *The Trial.* Kafka, however, manages to entwine a social critique with a critique of individual consciousness. Since we are brought into contact with the character's thoughts, his self-delusion and paranoia seem to play a part in his condition. By contrast, the film's wholly external orientation works to deny the very idea of consciousness for its character and hence to produce a far more complete picture of human passivity.

6. Truffaut, *Hitchcock,* 243.

7. Hitchcock includes a sequence in which the detectives come to Manny's

home to make the arrest and assume, based on their knowledge of his full name (Christopher Emmanuel Balestrero), that his nickname is Chris. They call out "Chris," which not only anticipates the string of mistaken identifications to follow but also acts subliminally to highlight our association of Manny's name with his character. For another angle on the name, see Robert Stam, "Hitchcock and Buñuel," in *Hitchcock's Rereleased Films,* 125.

8. See David Sterritt, *The Films of Alfred Hitchcock* (Cambridge: Cambridge Univ. Press, 1993), chap. 4, for a discussion of the relationship of *The Wrong Man* to 1950s conformism (and to the conventions of *film noir*).

9. Ironically, Hitchcock's appearance at the beginning of the film may be considered its most documentary aspect insofar as it introduces an element of self-reflexivity that conforms with contemporary documentary practice. It encourages us to see the ensuing film as the filmmaker's construction. See Jeanne Allen, "Self-Reflexivity in Documentary," in *Explorations in Film Theory,* 2.

10. Katie Trumpener, in her postmodern reading of *Vertigo,* "Fragments of the Mirror: Self-Reference, Mise-en-Abime, *Vertigo,*" in *Hitchcock's Rereleased Films,* addresses this confusion as part of the film's larger project of deconstruction: "The distinctions between levels of vision collapse in *Vertigo* along with all our other distinctions, our accustomed hierarchy of actor and audience, fiction and reality; as we lose our illusions, we simultaneously lose our bearings, our depth perception, our ability to tell apart the two-dimensional and the three" (p. 183).

11. Sterritt, *The Films of Alfred Hitchcock,* 84, notes that the spiral emerging from the eye in the opening credits "evokes the notion of birth, connoting all kinds of creation—among them synthesis, fabrication, performance—and linking them intimately with the act of seeing."

12. Spoto, *The Art of Alfred Hitchcock,* 279.

13. Truffaut, *Hitchcock,* 244.

14. Modleski, *The Women Who Knew Too Much,* 91, also notes that the early scene in which Midge shows Scottie a brassiere designed by an engineer is playing on the notion of femininity as the product of a male design.

15. Truffaut noted that Novak was not Hitchcock's original choice, but suggested that the film "was even more intriguing in light of the fact that the director had compelled a substitute to imitate the actress he had initially chosen for the role" (*Hitchcock,* 325). For a related discussion of character and performance, see Wendy Lesser, *His Other Half,* 132–44. For an interesting counterargument to mine, see Marian E. Keane, "A Closer Look at Scopophilia: Mulvey, Hitchcock, and *Vertigo,*" in *A Hitchcock Reader,* 231-248, who sees Novak's "metaphysical integrity" pushing through the role and asserting itself as a corporeal reality when the character looks directly at the camera before falling (jumping?) from the tower. I would also like to thank Rosemary Abbate for her observations on Novak's bad acting.

16. Spoto, *The Art of Alfred Hitchcock,* 280.

17. Molly Haskell, *From Reverence to Rape,* 352, argues that both Madeleine and Judy are unreal extremes and calls for a more realistic " 'fusion' woman." I posit

the existence of such a woman not as a more natural hybrid but as a compromise construction in the Madeleine/Judy composite.

8. The Emergence of Mother: *Psycho*

1. Spoto, *The Dark Side of Genius,* chap. 13, goes into considerable detail regarding Hitchcock's behavior toward these women, particularly his harassment of Hedren and it is largely on the basis of this episode that the book gained its undeserved reputation as a muckraking exposé.

2. See, for example, Sterritt, *The Films of Alfred Hitchcock,* chap. 6, for a discussion of anal-compulsive imagery in *Psycho* that fails to place this preoccupation in a historical context. Rothman, *The Murderous Gaze,* recognizes a progressive aspect to the films but tends to understand this in purely systemic and aesthetic terms.

3. Erikson discusses this concept in *Childhood and Society* (New York: W.W. Norton, 1950). Similar ideas about the mother were espoused by such important figures as Margaret Mead and R.D. Laing. Even in the more progressive family, we can see how the mother would become the focus of blame. The anthropologist Mary Douglas, *Natural Symbols: Explorations in Cosmology* (New York: Pantheon, 1970), 27, has described what seems to be an imagined ideal for the modern family: "No meals [would be] taken in common and no hierarchy recognised, but . . . the mother would attempt to meet the unique needs of each child by creating an entirely individual environment and time-table and services around each of her brood." But like the worst-case scenario, this vision of freedom requires the mother to administer it. As the individual upon whom other members are dependent, she becomes the final obstacle to their freedom, positioned once again to be blamed. This is the point made in psychoanalytic terms by Nancy Chodorow in *The Reproduction of Mothering* (Berkeley: Univ. of California Press, 1978).

4. Quoted in Barbara Ehrenreich and Deirdre English, *For Her Own Good: 150 Years of the Experts' Advice to Women* (Garden City, N.Y.: Anchor Books, 1979), 235.

5. Ibid., 236.

6. Lynn Hoffman, *Foundations of Family Therapy* (New York: Basic Books, 1981), 35.

7. For a discussion of the American family during the 1960s and 1970s, complete with statistics, see Sar A. Levitan and Richard S. Belous, *What's Happening to the American Family?* (Baltimore: Johns Hopkins Univ. Press, 1981). The Loud family documentary was entitled *An American Family* and was shown on PBS in 1973.

8. See Kapsis, *The Making of a Reputation,* 74, on Hitchcock's sense of being threatened by the new wave of American and foreign filmmakers and his desire to be taken seriously as an artist during the last fifteen years of his life.

9. Spoto, *The Dark Side of Genius,* 356.

10. Raymond Bellour, "Psychosis, Neurosis, Perversion," rpt. in *The Hitchcock Reader,* pioneered a structural psychoanalytic reading that interprets the film as divided into complementary parts, the first dealing with female neurosis, the second

with male psychosis. My more sociological, systemic approach to the film's two-part structure is not incompatible with his reading.

11. Stephen Rebello, *Alfred Hitchcock and the Making of* Psycho (New York: HarperPerennial, 1990), 66, reports that Hitchcock joked that "after ten years I thought it was time I gave her a job."

12. Screenwriter Joseph Stefano reports in Rebello, *Alfred Hitchcock and the Making of* Psycho, 44, that he had suggested that the police officer be handsome and flirt with Marion but that Hitchcock decided to change the characterization into something more menacing.

13. Rothman, *The Murderous Gaze,* 335.

14. W. Hesling, "Classical Cinema and the Spectator," *Literature/Film Quarterly* 15, no. 3 (1987): 186.

9. Beyond the Family Nexus: *Topaz, Frenzy, Family Plot*

1. The passage from Henry James's *The Golden Bowl* (New York: Penguin, 1966), 301, reads: "This situation had been occupying, for months and months, the very centre of the garden of her life, but it had reared itself there like some strange, tall tower of ivory, or perhaps rather some wonderful, beautiful, but outlandish pagoda. . . . She had walked round and round it . . . looking up, all the while, at the fair structure that spread itself so amply and rose so high, but never quite making out, as yet, where she might have entered had she wished."

2. Kapsis, *The Making of a Reputation,* 122–39, gives a detailed summary of shifts in critical response to *Marnie.*

3. Spoto, *The Dark Side of Genius,* 162.

4. This supports de Lauretis's observation in *Alice Doesn't,* 46: "As cinema becomes more conspicuously imaged, visually and aurally constructed—language becomes more and more incidental, as music used to be in silent cinema, often simply redundant or vaguely evocative, allusive, mythical." The orchestration of Hedren's voice can also be viewed as a component in what Stefan Sharff, *Alfred Hitchcock's High Vernacular,* 105, has referred to as "a whole network of specific continuity. The repetitions are not there to seal the items in the memory of the viewer but in order to create a linguistic continuum, a phrasing, a satisfactory cinematic sentence!"

5. Truffaut, *Hitchcock,* 301.

6. Ibid. 314.

7. Ibid., 330; Wood, *Hitchcock's Films Revisited,* 222.

8. Spoto, *The Art of Alfred Hitchcock,* 364–65.

9. Truffaut, *Hitchcock,* 341. I would like to thank Frank Nesko for pointing out the "car culture" of *Family Plot.*

10. Wood, *Hitchcock's Films Revisited,* 126, feels that both couples in *Family Plot* have relationships based on power, declaring that Blanche "manipulates" Lumley. I would say rather that Blanche plays at manipulating Lumley, and even if she does manipulate him, the impression is not one of a power dynamic but of a mode of negotiation, carrying its share of irritants but certainly more benign than a conventional, power-based relationship.

11. Wood, in his discussion of *Family Plot* in the revised portion of *Hitchcock's Films Revisited,* 226, reveals how much he remains tied to his earlier humanist psychological perspective despite claims to the contrary. The film, he asserts, is an exercise in "formal patterns, . . . deliberately avoiding those aspects of the original material [Victor Canning's thriller *The Rainbird Pattern*] that might have engaged *deeper* levels of [Hitchcock's] creative personality" (emphasis added).

12. Spoto, *The Art of Alfred Hitchcock,* 463–99. Scharff, *Alfred Hitchcock's High Vernacular,* does a shot-by-shot analysis of *Family Plot,* but his technical emphasis prevents him from sufficiently noting the emotional dissonance of these scenes.

13. Rothman, *The Murderous Gaze,* 33.

14. Kracauer, *The Theory of Film,* 95.

15. Truffaut, *Hitchcock,* 331. I had a similar experience recently when showing *The Birds* to a class of undergraduates. They snickered not only at the outmoded special effects but also at the representation of Lydia's emotion when she finds the body of her neighbor. Clearly, these students have learned to distrust the idea of strong, authentic emotion, especially in a horror film.

16. Pauline Kael, "Trash, Art and the Movies," in *Going Steady* (Boston: Little Brown, 1970), 88.

17. Quoted in Rebello, *The Making of Psycho,* 91.

18. Kapsis, *The Making of a Reputation,* 68, notes that by 1969 Hitchcock became relatively indifferent to mass-audience response and ceased trying to explicate his films for fans. Leitch, *Find the Director,* 223, agrees that the last films reduced characters "to relatively inexpressive game pieces," but insists that Hitchcock was still intensely involved with his audience.

19. Quoted in Spoto, *The Art of Alfred Hitchcock,* 388.

10. After Hitchcock

1. Kapsis, *The Making of a Reputation,* 31.

2. Ann Cvetkovich, "Postmodern *Vertigo:* The Sexual Politics of Allusion in De Palma's *Body Double,*" in *Hitchcock's Rereleased Films,* 159. Even pornography, in this context, can be seen to reflect what Teresa de Lauretis, in *Alice Doesn't,* 157, associates with "the most exciting work in cinema and in feminism today" since it is "narrative and oedipal with a vengeance."

3. Arthur Kroker and David Cook, *The Postmodern Scene: Excremental Culture and Hyper-Aesthetics* (New York: St. Martin's Press, 1986), 22.

4. Frederic Jameson, "Postmodernism and Consumer Society," in *Postmodernism and its Discontents: Theories and Practics,* ed. E. Ann Kaplan (London: Verso, 1988),15.

5. Kroker and Cook, *The Postmodern Scene,* 268.

Index